Doing Well *And* Good

The Human Face of the New Capitalism

A volume in
Ethics and Practice

Series Editors:
Robert Giacalone, *Fox School of Business, Temple University*
Carole L. Jurkiewicz, *Louisiana State University*

Ethics and Practice

Robert Giacalone and Carole L. Jurkiewicz, Series Editors

Doing Well And Good: The Human Face of the New Capitalism (2009)
edited by Julian Friedland

Advancing Business Ethics Education (2008)
edited by Diane L. Swanson and Dann G. Fisher

Critical Theory Ethics for Business and Public Administration (2008)
edited by David M. Boje

Human Resource Management Ethics (2006)
edited by John R. Deckop

*Positive Psychology in Business Ethics and
Corporate Responsibility* (2006)
edited by Robert A. Giacalone and Carole L. Jurkiewicz

Doing Well *And* Good

The Human Face of the New Capitalism

edited by

Julian Friedland
Fordham University

Information Age Publishing, Inc.
Charlotte, North Carolina • www.infoagepub.com

Library of Congress Cataloging-in-Publication Data

Doing well and good : the human face of the new capitalism / edited by
Julian Friedland.
p. cm. -- (Ethics in practice)
Includes bibliographical references.
ISBN 978-1-59311-787-0 (pbk.) -- ISBN 978-1-59311-788-7 (hbk.) 1.
Social responsibility of business. 2. Business ethics. 3.
Capitalism--Moral and ethical aspects. I. Friedland, Julian.
HD60.D65 2009 658.4'08--dc22
                          2009019533

ISBN: PB 978-1-59311-787-0
       HC 978-1-59311-788-7

Printed in the United States of America

CONTENTS

PART III: MAKING THE CHANGE HAPPEN: VOLUNTARY AND REGULATORY EXAMPLES

INTRODUCTION

Ushering-in the New Capitalism

Julian Friedland

It's a big and complicated globalized business world out there. So it's difficult to make any accurate sweeping generalizations about it. We can say for instance that companies are paying much more attention to corporate social responsibility than ever before. And we can point to myriad examples of how, by and by, that has helped to make them more successful. And that's of course what this book is all about. But on the other hand, rarely has corruption been so prevalent—at least in recent memory going back to the mid-twentieth century. The current U.S. economic recession (if not depression) has brought most of the rest of the global economy down with it. And the principle reason why this happened was what might be called over-deregulation of the marketplace, particularly in high finance. The lesson-learned is that the prevailing culture of investment banking has exploited this environment and become corrupted by the lure of short-term schemes. Thus, this collapse stands starkly before us as the great market failure of our time.

It's of course not the first time this has happened. The last time was in 1929, after banks were allowed by a careless so-called "conservative" federal government to become over-burdened with debt. Tragically, the bankers and legislators of today did not learn from history, nor did they listen to the myriad top economists who predicted a repeat, namely,

Hyman Minsky, Paul Volcker, Paul Krugman, Noriel Roubini, Stephen Roach, David Mick, Robert Shiller, and too many more to mention. So long as everyone is making money, too few will listen to inconvenient truths offered by dismal science, history, or reason. This problem puts us in a very difficult and precarious position culturally, politically, economically, and indeed environmentally. It's a textbook case of the Tragedy of the Commons.[1] That is to say, when it benefits no individual to take responsibility in business for the sustainable use a natural resource, no one (or too few) will, unless the government steps in to force everyone to do so. In this case, the natural resources include the environment (global warming) and economic productivity fueled by access to financial credit. Both of these resources have now been exploited to disastrous effect. As a result, governments are scrambling to pick up the pieces and set up strong regulatory systems to keep the phenomenon from causing widespread economic and environmental cataclysms in the near and long terms.

Unfortunately, history seems to teach us that even if such positive change occurs and the global economy stabilizes at a sustainable rate of activity, blind greed will once more rear its ugly head after a few generations come to pass. History will repeat itself. This is deeply frustrating to all those who, like me, dedicate their professional lives to seeking and exposing the truth and wisdom that may deliver us from ignorance. Is this ultimately a futile pursuit? Only time will tell. But part of the answer lies in the essential theme of this volume, namely, its emphasis on transforming the very culture of capitalism. For the only way long-term lessons are learned is when they become deeply embedded in the culture. For that to happen, we cannot simply rely on government regulation, corporate leadership, or consumers. None of these forces alone can exercise sufficient force to sustain genuine and lasting transformation. Recent events have shown that we cannot expect sufficient corporate leadership in ethics to arise from the marketplace. But then if the private sector relies entirely on regulation to dictate its mandates for corporate social responsibility, it will become inefficient. And if we rely only on consumers to shop responsibly, we are setting up a precarious system at the mercy of another tragedy of the commons in which it's often cheaper to shop less responsibly. So all three of these socioeconomic forces must play a role. And until businesses start to see themselves as an integral part of this change, the culture of modern capitalism has no chance of evolving to a level of perpetually sustained equilibrium.

So what does this new and enlightened ethic of corporate identity consist of? Every chapter of this book helps define it. Essentially, it is this:

Ethical Business Creates Social Value

Any business that sees itself this way will never look at profit as its sole ethos. It will consider first and foremost what good it is providing to the world by its very existence. Interestingly, Jim Collins, in his bestselling *Built to Last*,[2] shows an astounding amount of evidence that companies that see themselves this way tend to outlast ones that aim entirely at generating profit. Why is this? Basically, because they are primarily focused on providing what people really need and want, and less focused on concocting complicated competitive maneuvers to eek out greater short-term gains. Rather, they continually retain and reinforce their commitment to a practical reason for existence, and thereby turn out better value than their competition. This is the heart of corporate social responsibility and what unites all the leading and farsighted companies helping to usher-in a new kind of capitalism.

That said, certain companies are more socially responsible than others. Some companies look too narrowly at what social value they are creating, while at the very same time turning a blind eye to great harm they are causing in other areas. And others are too idealistic about making a difference everywhere and thus can falter fiscally from lack of focus. This volume does not seek to rate and rank different companies against each other. Rather, it seeks to show the need for greater ethical vision at the very core of business, map what that vision looks like, and bring well-reasoned and time-tested means of achieving it to the fore.

As I said at the outset, there has never been a greater need for this kind of change in recent memory. While numerous companies are already part of it, evidence suggests they are still but a conspicuous minority. The latest National Business Ethics Survey (NBES) from 2007—a poll conducted bi-yearly via random interviews of nearly 2000 private sector employees—provides a fairly accurate time-slice image of how workers tend to perceive the level and efficacy of ethics standards both inside their own companies and across corporate America more generally.[3] It also provides data on what kinds of characteristics comprise an effective ethical culture—at least from an employee's point of view.

First the Bad News

- Ethical misconduct in general is very high and back to pre-Enron levels—during the past year, more than half of employees saw ethical misconduct of some kind.

- Many employees do not report what they observe—they are fearful about retaliation and skeptical that their reporting will make a difference. In fact, one in eight employees experiences some form of retaliation for reporting misconduct.

- The number of companies that are successful in incorporating a strong enterprise-wide ethical culture into their business has declined since 2005. Only 9% of companies have strong ethical cultures.

If we look at these findings together, it's no surprise that we witnessed massive corruption scandals throughout 2008—primarily in finance. But the findings suggest that many more scandals may still be brewing in other industries. If employees are not reporting misconduct as a result of a sense of futility and fear, management may not be aware (or remain in denial) and thus have little or no warning of an impending meltdown.

Now the Good News

- The number of formal ethics and compliance programs is on the rise. Furthermore, in companies with well-implemented programs, there is increased reporting, reducing ethics risk.
- The 2007 NBES has been able to show definitively that companies that move beyond a singular commitment to complying with laws and regulations and adopt an enterprise-wide ethical culture dramatically reduce misconduct.
- The 2007 NBES has identified the characteristics that comprise an effective ethical culture, providing a blueprint for individuals within companies responsible for corporate governance and compliance.

The NBES found that only 25% of companies had a well-implemented ethics and compliance program. That's because the other 75% focus primarily on telling employees what not to do. Hence, these companies tend to suffer from lack of proactive employee reporting of misconduct. Essentially, they harbor a myopic view of what business ethics consists of. They see it as mere rule-following, that is, compliance with corporate policy and government regulation. This is a grave misconception. The data clearly show that such environments which only focus on the bare moral minimum are ripe for abuse. An important aspect of psychological reality is that many ethical dilemmas don't necessarily appear to everyone as dilemmas at first blush. Institutional habit, social pressure, and lack of ethical vision regularly allow myriad ethical transgressions to go unnoticed by the very persons committing them. Ethical and legal rules may become stretched to the breaking point via loopholes for years until they begin to act like a cancer that eats away at the bottom line. And at that point it's often too late to avoid a major crisis.

First and foremost, these data show that companies must foster an atmosphere in which employees are given a clear and genuine sense of ethical corporate mission so they may feel positively about their company. And this includes providing them with the means for obtaining advice about ethical questions that may arise. Once the attitude of reflection and inquisitiveness becomes embedded as a core value, employees are much more likely to report (and to resolve) everything from moral hazards, such as potential conflicts of interests, to more clear-cut regulatory breaches. And once employees take the risk of behaving proactively in this manner, that behavior must be rewarded. For example, one way of fostering this kind of atmosphere is by instituting 360 degree reviewing. So that employees get to review their superiors. This encourages and empowers them to protect the company in tangible long-term ways. It makes for a highly gratifying and loyal corporate culture. But it also works to break down excessive hubris in the executive class that can lead many in that group to ignore or brush aside unwelcome news from below. Mathew Hayward discusses this phenomenon a length in his excellent book *Ego Check*.[4]

Another way to check and to hone the vision and performance of the executive class is to consider capping compensation, specifically the over-reliance on stock options. Traditionally, stock options are heavily used for executive compensation, for two basic reasons: They're cheap, and they're meant to tie the interests of the executive with that of ordinary shareholders. The problem is that when most of the CEO's income is derived from stock options, this can provide a great incentive to take risks such as cutbacks and mergers that can payoff handsomely in the short term, but eventually leave the company worse off in the longer term.[5] Another problem is that recent research across several industries has shown that windfall profits can be distracting to the CEO, leading to decreased performance. For example, if the money is used to buy an estate, mansion, or prominent vacation home, those kinds of purchases can take a lot of time to set up, thus taking the CEO's attention away from running the company.

The Wall Street Journal points to several studies including one co-authored by David Yermack, Professor of Finance at New York University, finding that on average, the stocks of companies run by leaders who buy or build megamansions sharply underperform the market. The researchers don't claim to know why. But they theorize that some of these executives might be more focused on enjoying their wealth than on working hard. One CEO included in the study was Trevor Fetter of Tenet

Healthcare Corp., who bought a 10,057-square-foot mansion in 2005. Since then, Tenet's stock is down more than 60%, while the broader market has risen. A spokesman for the hospital chain said it was aware of the study but had no comment.[6]

Capping executive compensation in general can also boost employee morale. The NBES and other studies have shown that nationally, workplace loyalty has plummeted. One of the principle reasons for this decline many argue is an increasingly winner-take-all attitude within corporate American culture. What angers many employees is knowing their CEO can retire after a single good year, while they're struggling with higher costs of health care, education, food, and other expenses. As a result, many employees feel they're barely treading water.[7]

Even upper management executives can feel frustration toward CEO compensation. As Rakesh Khurana, Associate Professor at Harvard Business School observes "when executives talk about talent shortage in their ranks, they're really talking about commitment shortage," which stems partly from pay inequality. As General Electric CEO Jeffrey Immelt said in recent interviews,

> the key relationship is the one between the CEO and the top 25 managers of the company, because that's the key team. Should the CEO make five times, three times, or twice what this group makes? That's debatable, but 20 times is lunacy.[8]

Generally speaking, Khurana says, "the greater the inequality, the less willing employees are to learn specific ways of doing things that aren't going to be useful to their next employer." As a result, ambitious employees figure their best chance to close the pay gap is to keep zigzagging between companies or even entire industries. Day to day, employee frustrations at inequality can lead to increased expenses from greater turnover, absenteeism, theft, worsening customer service. In short, everything that comes from low morale. To inhibit such negative trends, many successful companies only grant 100% bonuses to top executives and senior managers if the company achieves 110% of its growth targets. "The higher up you go, the more your compensation is at risk," says Analytical Graphics CEO Paul Graziani.[9]

Another way to inhibit these trends is to institute a policy, now present at several Fortune 500 companies including Costco and Whole Foods, whereby no executive salary exceeds 14 times the average employee's. This sends a strong message that executives are not there for purely materialistic reasons. Research by Robert Giacalone, shows that as people's basic material needs are met, they gradually shift their attention to what he calls "postmaterialistic" values, that is, ones that concern community connectedness, interpersonal relationships, quality of life, and family. Polls have shown that in 1970, for every four materialists, there was only one postmaterialist. But by the mid-1990s, the ratio was four to three. And these values are becoming even more prominent today. In sum, this trend has created an atmosphere in which workers are increasingly apt to seek out socially responsible companies that uphold these postmaterialistic values.[10] And those are of course exactly the kinds of ethically-minded workers corporations should seek to attract. Furthermore, saving money on executive salaries can help fund various programs, which might lower costs in the longer term, such as converting to sustainable energy sources and other green practices. When corporations announce such changes, using the millions saved yearly to fund corporate social responsibility programs and increase the quality of work-life and/or salaries of employees, that can be a great morale-booster. And high morale is key to achieving any successful ethics and compliance program.

These are but a few general examples of management approaches that take business ethics seriously in the positive and proactive sense. The following chapters provide many more. Some offer generalized theories. Others present empirical data in specific context. But before you press on, dear reader, to those meatier morsels, let me draw your attention to the following self-assessment tool.

A good place to start evaluating your own company's ethical culture is by taking this relatively brief eInsight Ethics survey online: http://www.einsight.org/index1.cfm made available by the Hill Center For Ethical Business Leadership.

It's a shorter version of the excellent SAIP (Self-Assessment & Improvement Process) executive and board survey, created my Kenneth Goodpaster and Dean Maines of the University of St. Thomas' Opus College of Business. This longer version is published in Goodpaster's *Conscience and Corporate Culture*. It can also be obtained through the colleges' SAIP Institute: http://www.stthomas.edu/business/centers/saip.

Finally, one last word about why business ethics is needed now more than ever. Our globalized world makes it impossible for corporations to hide from the public spotlight. All it takes is for one intrepid observer with a webcam to tarnish an institution's reputation literally overnight. And entire websites are devoted to doing precisely that. Perhaps the best of these reporting on corporate malfeasance is corpwatch.org. But all anyone needs nowadays to expose a nefarious corporate practice—and start an international boycott—is access to youtube.com. Craig Smith of INSEAD, provides a perfect example:

> In August of 2006, the Reuters news agency published a photo showing massive billows of smoke over the city of Beirut after a strike by the Israeli

Air Force. Within hours, online bloggers began to question the picture's authenticity, suggesting the photographer had electronically added more smoke to the image to make the attack look worse than it was. Reuters—a company with integrity at the heart of its reputation—quickly responded by pulling the photo, confirming that it had been altered, and ending its relationship with the freelance photographer who had taken the image.

Globalization and instant communication are here to stay, and business must learn to deal with this new reality where any news and any actions can be made public within a matter of minutes. That means business schools must work within that same reality—and prepare their students to do so as well.[11]

Clearly, an important and inescapable aspect about this new marketplace is transparency. Successful businesses will either embrace that or ignore it at their peril. This, by the way, is something the Obama administration seems to understand. It's best to avoid trying to control information leaks. Letting information leak out instills trust at all levels of the chain of communication, and acts as the best shield from competitors seeking to undermine one's credibility. And one only has to look so far as what happened at Hewlett Packard—once a model of business ethics—to see how the desire to control information can lead to a toxic obsession, clouding one's moral compass, and eventually destroying one's reputation and career. Here is the abridged story as recounted by Wikipedia.org:

On September 5, 2006 *Newsweek* published a story revealing that the chairwoman of HP, Patricia Dunn, had hired a team of independent electronic-security experts that later spied on HP board members and several journalists, to determine the source of a leak of confidential details regarding HP's long-term strategy in January, 2006. The independent, third party company used a technique known as pretexting to obtain call records of HP board members and nine journalists, including reporters for CNET, the *New York Times* and the *Wall Street Journal*. Dunn has claimed she did not know the methods the investigators used to determine the source of the leak. Board member George Keyworth was ultimately outed as the source.

On September 12, 2006 Keyworth resigned from the board and HP announced that Mark Hurd, the current CEO and president, would replace Dunn as Chairman after the HP board meeting on January 18, 2007.

On September 22, 2006 Hurd announced at a special press briefing that Dunn had resigned effective immediately from both the Chairmanship role and as a director of the Board;

On September 28, 2006, Ann Baskins, HP's general counsel (head attorney) resigned hours before she was to appear as a witness at which she would later invoke the Fifth Amendment to "not be held to answer for a capital, or otherwise infamous crime."[12]

How does one establish an ethical business culture in which such transgressions are unlikely to happen? That's one of the questions to which this book provides proven time-tested answers. Ultimately, I hope it succeeds in launching a wide discussion of what exactly we should expect the moral duty of business to be.

Julian Friedland
April 21, 2009
Boulder, Colorado

NOTES

1. Hardin, G. (1968). Tragedy of the commons. *Science, 162*, 1243–1248.
2. Collins, J., & Porras, J. (1997). *Built to last: Successful habits of visionary companies*. New York: HarperCollins.
3. National Business Ethics Survey. (2007). Web site: http://www.ethics.org/research/NBESOffers.asp
4. Hayward, M. (2007). *Ego check: Why executive hubris is wrecking companies and careers and how to avoid the trap*. New York: Kaplan Business.
5. Andresky Fraser, G. (2002). *White-collar sweatshop: The deterioration of work and its rewards in corporate America*. New York: W. W. Norton & Company.
6. Maremont, M. (2007, Sept.). Scholars link success of firms to lives of CEOs. *Wall Street Journal*, p. A1.
7. Hymowitz, C. (2008, April). Pay gap fuels worker woes. *Wall Street Journal*, p. 28.
8. Hymowitz.
9. Hymowitz.
10. Giacalone, R. A. (2008). On ethics and social responsibility: The impact of materialism, postmaterialism, and hope. *Human Relations, 61*(4), 483–514.
11. Smith, N. C. (2008. May–June). On ethics and social responsibility. *BizEd*, 28–29.
12. Smith.

PART I

THE ROLE OF CORPORATE CULTURE

CHAPTER 1

GETTING BUSINESS OFF STEROIDS

Maximilian B. Torres

Culture is to organization as character is to person. Each serves to guide the activity of the entity that possesses it; the organization on one hand or a person on the other, as if by default. Nevertheless, each can be altered: the default for organizational action as well as personal action is dynamic rather than fixed. This chapter argues that organizational culture and personal character are symbiotic phenomena. Culture depends primordially on character, as any aggregate depends upon the individual entities comprising it. In turn, personal character depends upon exercises of freedom in the choice of means employed to attain preselected ends. These exercises of freedom are nonetheless instructed, and thus partly shaped by culture. Ultimately, action is ordered to one end or another: excellence or victory. The choice is momentous for culture as well as for persons, as illustrated by relatively recent events in distinct yet analogous "playing fields": big business and Major League Baseball in the United States. The former has been vexed by fraud, the latter by steroids; each a species of opportunism—that is, choice ordered to victory irrespective of excellence—rooted in character. I provide a decision-making tool for individuals in organizations to help get business off steroids—as it were—and baseball off fraud.

Doing Well And Good: The Human Face of the New Capitalism, pp. 3–29
Copyright © 2009 by Information Age Publishing
All rights of reproduction in any form reserved.

INTRODUCTION

The present tome heralds a "new capitalism" with a "human face." The "old" has lavished society with wealth and prosperity beyond the wildest dreams of a Smith or a Marx, but at a cost many fear is not sustainably affordable.[1] This chapter proposes a simple *decision-making tool* in the form of *three questions* upon which to construct a political economy grounded in the nobler part of a human person—beyond fear and greed, while cognizant of them. This task is crucial for ultimately it is the activity of persons (i.e., *personal action*) taken collectively which engenders, bolsters, and foments sustainable prosperity on the one hand or social calamity on the other. It analogizes problems in business to problems in sport, specifically the use of performance-enhancing drugs in Major League Baseball, and argues that corrupt human behavior in every activity is rooted in (1) a *personal* selection of inapposite *ends*, (2) the consequent misidentification of *values* and (3) the embrace of misidentified values resulting in (4) potentially destructive, personal *character* habits.

It is important to study social phenomena from the perspective of what occurs within an individual person because, as the scholastics following the classics taught, *agere sequitur esse*: "doing follows being," or what you *do* comes from what you *are*. Problematic actions such as cooking the books, shredding documents in anticipation of litigation or taking steroids proceed from bad habits (vicious character) in otherwise normal people. Recent problems in business and sport—*personal* first, *social* derivatively—are manifested as "cheating" and "fraud," which are grounded in a pursuit of *victory* and the choice of values (or *goods*) proper to it to the neglect of *excellence* and its goods. "Steroids" are simply the preferred mode of cheating in contemporary sports and serve as a metaphor for problems in the world of business.

THE RECENT PAST

Is there a more infamous chieftain in the pantheon of fallen idols than Ken Lay of Enron? Lay transformed a sleepy natural gas pipeline company, El Paso Natural Gas, into a cutting-edge energy trader and "new economy" miracle: "the world's leading integrated electricity and natural gas company." He eventually handed over the reins of Enron to Harvard MBA Jeff Skilling, the man behind the "crooked E's" mark-to-market (read, "hypothetical") accounting, a key ingredient of Enron's "success," however illusory.[2] Lay, Skilling and chief lieutenant CFO Andy Fastow were hailed as visionaries for unleashing creativity and innovation in ways heretofore unknown in the energy business, or nearly any business for that matter.[3] Each man scaled the pinnacles of success and enjoyed media accolades, lavish compensation and the power of a pulpit reserved for *winners* and *leaders* of companies whose common stock beguiles Wall Street. In 2001 the company, then the seventh largest firm in the United States,[4] dissolved in a mist of fraudulent accounting and obfuscatory transactions utilizing special purpose entities (SPE's). Once Enron's true financial position came to light, Fastow, the architect of the fraud, was convicted under the securities laws and sentenced to 5 years in a federal penitentiary,[5] a lenient sentence granted in return for his cooperation with the prosecutions of Lay and Skilling. Both men were convicted in May of 2006.[6,7] Juror Wendy Vaughan commenting afterwards said "I wanted very badly to believe what they were saying…. There were places in the testimony I felt their character was questionable."[8] Skilling is presently seeking to overturn his 24-year sentence on appeal.[9] Poignantly, Ken Lay died of an apparent heart attack in July of 2006 while on an Aspen, Colorado respite before filing an appeal.[10] He was 64 years old.

Enron's collapse was followed shortly by the discovery of an $11 billion accounting fraud at telecom giant WorldCom involving rank violations of generally accepted accounting principles (GAAP).[11] The company inflated earnings by capitalizing line costs (an operating expense) thereby illicitly spreading costs into future periods and minimizing their impact on current results. Its bankruptcy in 2002 surpassed Enron's as the largest evisceration of shareholder wealth in history up to that time.[12] Enron and WorldCom's auditor, the legendary accounting firm of Arthur Andersen, collapsed shortly thereafter under the weight of a criminal indictment by the U.S. Department of Justice (DOJ) and the avalanche of client defections that followed. Its partner in charge of the Enron audit, David Duncan, had ordered and supervised the destruction of audit papers and sensitive documents in response to subtle hints by Nancy Temple, an in-house Andersen lawyer.[13] At trial, Duncan was described by fellow partner Ben Neuhausen as an auditor who stretched accounting rules "to excess."[14] Nevertheless, he had ascended to the position of Andersen's lead auditor for the firm's fifth largest client. In the years preceding its untimely demise, Andersen had been fined by the Securities and Exchange Commission (SEC) for accounting irregularities at clients Sunbeam and Waste Management, and was implicated in lawsuits involving yet other clients including Qwest Communications and Global Crossing.[15] Apparently, in its rush to replace consulting business lost in a messy divorce with Andersen Consulting (now Accenture), and to embrace a practice labeled "billing our brains out" by Andersen ethicist Barbara Ley Toffler,[16] the firm achieved "results" at the expense of its reputation, integrity and, ultimately, existence.

In December of that same year, 10 of the world's leading investment banks including Goldman Sachs and Morgan Stanley—as of this writing, the only large, independent American banks left standing, though in the altered form of federally-regulated holding companies—were forced to settle with then New York State Attorney General Elliot Spitzer, the SEC and a host of other regulators for producing dishonestly flattering research in exchange for lucrative underwriting business and fees from issuers.[17] Four hundred million of the unprecedented $1.4 billion settlement was borne by the firm of Salomon Smith Barney whose star Telecom analyst, Jack Grubman, was referred to as the Pied Piper of Wall Street. In his heyday, Grubman was cautioned about his friendly relationships with CEOs of the companies he researched, but responded that "what used to be a conflict is now a synergy."[18] He even boasted of his friendship with WorldCom Executive Chairman Bernie Ebbers and bragged about attending Ebbers' wedding in March 1999.[19] For his part in the scandal Grubman was barred from the securities industry for life. As a postscript to the affair, in November 2004 a federal court approved a $2.58 billion settlement between Citigroup (Salomon's parent company) and plaintiffs who alleged, *inter alia*, that Grubman inflated the value of WorldCom stock by knowingly producing inaccurate research.[20]

In retrospect, the Dotcom crash of 2000–2002[21] revealed the great bull market of the "90s" soft underbelly of misstated financials, compromised research, valueless IPO's and over-inflated stock prices. It also ushered in a period of financial turmoil, cathartic reform and harsh recriminations over an era of fraud, pump-and-dump schemes and discredited leaders. Society, the economy and business (writ large) have labored mightily these past few years to put the debacle behind us.[22] In the end, the scandal eviscerated billions of dollars in market capitalization, shattered countless illusions, threw tens of thousands of employees out of work while menacing their retirements, and imposed punitive legislation on all commercial enterprise in the guise of Sarbanes-Oxley,[23] an Act widely credited with leading the United States' decline from preeminence in global capital markets.[24] Quite evidently a repeat of recent events is something that business, the economy and society can ill afford to experience, and should desperately seek to avoid.

The purpose here is not to indict business—the engine of advancement in humanity's quest for material prosperity and self-determination—or to single out any companies or "players" for derision. Rather it is to learn from history lest we be condemned to repeat it, and to underscore a point. In the search for analyst-pleasing, short-term financial performance, riches, glory, fame and the kind of adulation that dominance in business confers, too many market actors cut too many corners in the pursuit of achievements that would ensure receipt of these prizes. In the process they endangered all of us by putting the cart before the horse through valuing the *goods* of financial success above and beyond their regard for *professional excellence*. The mass phenomenon of cheating and fraud among executives and market professionals in turn suggests that in the search for magazine covers, option compensation, levitating stock prices and market supremacy—in a word, "success"—"America, Inc." turned a blind eye to its protagonists' skewed values. In the process, it succumbed to a culture of fraud and financial restatements. The result is that its most worthwhile accomplishments—producing wealth, generating employment, expanding the circle of productivity and exchange, lifting standards of living—go overlooked, underappreciated and unremarked, to the point that its integrity (as opposed to its appeal) as a human activity is impugned.

PARALLEL HISTORY

Something similar happened in the world of American sport that sheds light on this phenomenon in business, namely the crisis besetting Major League Baseball regarding steroid use among players.[25] The recently released Mitchell report—issued pursuant to baseball commissioner Bud Selig's request for an investigation in 2006, and authored by former U.S. Senator George Mitchell of Maine—named 89 professional baseball players for their use of performance enhancing drugs including some of the sport's greatest.[26] Most notorious among those implicated was baseball's newly crowned *home run* king, Barry Bonds. He pursued the career record under a cloud of suspicion after experiencing an eyebrow-raising growth spurt and age-defying power surge relatively late in an already glorious career.[27] In 2007, Bonds claimed baseball's preeminent statistic by breaking the *career record* of 755 home runs held by Hall of Fame outfielder, Hank Aaron.[28] In 2001, Bonds broke Mark McGwire's *single-season record* of 70 home runs, which stood for only 3 years.[29] McGwire's 1998 chase of Roger Maris's record 61 home runs (set in 1961) with Sammy Sosa in hot pursuit captivated the nation's attention[30] and resuscitated fan interest in baseball, which had drowned in a sea of resentment after a player's strike cancelled the 1994 season.[31] The adulation that both men received, culminating in their joint naming as Sports Illustrated magazine's "Sportsman of the Year" in the "easiest selection in our history,[32] is credited with provoking the luminescent yet overshadowed Bonds to *begin* using steroids.[33]

A reporter covering 1998's chase of history noticed a bottle of Androstenedione ("Andro"), a performance enhancing drug, in McGwire's locker.[34] This unsettling revelation focused attention on modern ballplayers' unusual size and power, and raised the uncomfortable suspicion that their accomplishments in this most statistics-conscious of sports might lack integrity. The worst fears were "confirmed" by the salacious memoirs of one-time superstar and self-confessed "juicer," Jose Canseco, the first player in history to hit 40 home runs and steal 40 bases in a single season.[35] Steroids, he said, were "as prevalent in ... the late 1980s and 1990s as a cup of coffee."[36] The controversy surrounding his unrepentant confession and tawdry allegations, coupled with the surfeit of home runs orbiting Major League stadiums, spurred Congress to convoke hearings on steroid use in baseball. It subpoenaed McGwire and Sosa, both implicated in Canseco's tell-all, to testify in 2005 before the House Government Reform Committee.[37] The hearing, titled "Restoring Faith In America's Pastime: Evaluating Major League Baseball's Efforts to Eradicate Steroid Use," was marked by culpable evasions (McGwire: "I'm not here to discuss the past ... I'm here to be positive about this subject") and crafty denials (Sosa: [I have not] "broken the laws of the United States or the laws of the Dominican Republic").[38] In consequence, McGwire, a player with Hall of Fame credentials, has already been denied entry into that august body in his first 2 years of eligibility.[39] In 2003, Barry Bonds was called to appear before a federal grand jury impaneled to investigate activities at the Bay Area Laboratory Co-operative (BALCO), a veritable steroids dispensary, where he testified under oath to never *knowingly* having taken performance-enhancing drugs.[40]

A subsequent exposé of BALCO and its clientele focused on Bonds' alleged use of human growth hormone (a substance not banned by baseball at the time) and cast serious doubts on the veracity of his testimony.[41] Victor Conte, the laboratory's founder and president who ultimately served four months in prison and four under house arrest for his role in the scandal was fond of articulating what might be considered the catch-phrase of the steroids era: "Cheat or lose."[42] Bonds, arguably the greatest ballplayer of all time, currently faces perjury charges relating to his grand jury testimony.[43] His contract with his long-time team, the San Francisco Giants, expired after the 2007 season and was not renewed. No other team picked him up for the 2008 season though he expressed a strong desire to continue playing and appeared capable of doing so at a very high level.[44] Adding insult to injury, Marc Ecko, the owner of the record-breaking home run ball (#756) had it branded with a laser-cut asterisk before donating it to the Baseball Hall of Fame in Cooperstown, New York for display.[45] Congress punctuated the "steroids era" of the game with an exclamation point by referring the 2008 testimony of superstar Roger Clemens before the House Committee on Oversight and Government Reform to the FBI for investigation.[46] It is exploring whether sufficient evidence exists that the most dominant pitcher of his era—and a player with Hall-of-Fame credentials to rival Bonds'—committed perjury by denying (emphatically) and disputing (vigorously) charges leveled against him in the Mitchell Report.

Again, the purpose here is not to indict baseball or single out specific athletes, teams or sports,[47] but to learn from history lest we be condemned to repeat it, and to underscore a point so as to shed light on problems in business by analogy. In the search for records, riches, and glory, something went wrong. Too many players and teams cut too many corners in the pursuit of accomplishments that would ensure receipt of these prizes. Those that engaged in cheating put the cart before the horse by *valuing*, in actions, the *goods* of victory over those of spirited athletic competition and the personal excellence necessary to ensure competitiveness in the longer term. The alleged mass phenomenon of steroids use among ballplayers suggests in turn that Major League Baseball (incidentally, a very large business) was itself complicit in the deceit. In the quest to achieve fan interest, gate receipts, advertising revenue, consumer fealty, and network deals, "America's Pastime, Inc." turned a blind eye to the embrace of skewed values by its players. In the process, it succumbed to a culture of steroids, cheating, and fraud. The result is that its most hallowed records stand tarnished, indeed branded, its greatest players stand accused and face a potential loss of liberty, and the very integrity (as opposed to appeal) of the game is questioned.

THE PROBLEM:
AIMING AT THE "FENCES" RATHER THAN AT "MAKING CONTACT"

Every child that has played baseball knows that swinging at the ball with an aim to reaching the home run barrier (i.e., the fence) is a certain recipe for "striking out," that is for achieving the ultimate failure in an at bat rather than its most perfect outcome. Hitting a moving baseball with a bat is harder than it looks, and to hit it far, one must first hit it. Consequently, children are coached to aim at solidly meeting the ball with the bat, at *making contact*, the regular achievement of which is the sign of an accomplished hitter. A person with moderate power will reach the fences on occasion by habitually making solid contact with the ball. Ironically, then, the means to accomplishing the ultimate success in an at bat (i.e., a home run) is to not aim for that ultimate success, but rather to aim at that which brings it about.[48] Something similar happens in all endeavors including the practice of business.

Professional baseball is "big business," and thus corrupt competition in the sport is a species of business ethics gone awry. But the importance of the analogy lies elsewhere. Summarizing what has preceded thus far, in the case of both business and baseball, too many "players" were inclined to grasp at prizes (by hook or crook) that are intended to honor and reward honest achievement. That is, they valued honor, glory, riches, fame and the like, which they could only attain through professional excellence or by cheating, and proved willing to cheat rather than restrain their desires or reorient their values. The result has been scandal, taint, downfall and social disturbance. It would be irrational for companies or teams to encourage the development of such unhealthy and self-defeating tendencies. Yet that is precisely what they incentivize via extravagant compensation for executives and players alike. The 1980s came to be known as the "Decade of Greed" for illicit trafficking in, and profiting from, privileged information by investment bankers, arbitrageurs and sundry financial professionals personified by Dennis Levine, Ivan Boesky, and Michael Milkin.[49] This past decade has compounded treachery with deceit and constitutes (in its worst light) an "Era of Fraud" for the pump-and-dump schemes of corporate chieftains, hoodwinked auditors and starry-eyed analysts personified by Ken Lay, David Duncan and Jack Grubman.[50]

Former Chairman of the SEC, Arthur Levitt, warned in 1998 of the dangerous "game of nods and winks" in which erstwhile market fiduciaries conspired to satisfy consensus earnings estimates by fraud-light, thereby placing "integrity in financial reporting ... under stress."[51] In baseball, the universally decried use of performance enhancing drugs is merely the *external*, empirical manifestation of an *interior* predilection rooted in deformed *character*. Embedded within the unchecked wills and passions of both business practitioners and athletes alike, the problem is "cheating," which in the first instance is a personal inclination or disposition to win by any means necessary, and at any eventual cost including that of excellence, honesty, sociability[52] (i.e., fitness for social relations)[53] and the like. Cheating and fraud signify competition gone awry by way of personal defects in competitors. Only after the problem manifests itself in restated financials and deflated stock prices, or inflated home run totals and tarnished records does the resulting outcry provoke structural change and the imposition of external controls such as law, regulation or compliance regimes, for example, mandatory drug testing. Fear of getting caught is powerful motivator, but not a lasting one. To be truly effective in getting business off steroids (or baseball off fraud), correctives must address the interior, hidden problem in addition to the secondary and contingent, observable ones. A lens through which to view the problem from the perspective of interior personal development is needed.

In *Whose Justice? Which Rationality?*[54] Aristotelian virtue ethicist Alasdair MacIntyre proposes an interpretive device that can be of great service to this project. In it he suggests that *citizens* of a *polis*—think "employees of a company," "players on a team," "market participants within a capitalist political economy," "professional athletes" or even "members of a global village"—might alternatively be directed (and historically have been) toward one of two ends, that ultimately explain human activity: *victory* on one hand, or *excellence* on the other.[55] In the final analysis, either victory or excellence might serve to answer questions regarding the *rationality* of human action such as why a person acts as he does, or regarding the *morality* of human action such as why she ought to act in this way or that.[56] The rationality and morality of human acts are necessarily anchored in one end or the other. The steroids controversy in Major League Baseball merely dramatizes in a popular and accessible forum the consequences of prioritizing victory (swinging for the fences) over excellence (making contact with the ball). It renders the problem transparent to all, and less threatening to consider than does the collapse of a world-class business such as Enron or Andersen. At bottom, contemporary crises in business and baseball are cut from the same cloth: cheating, an interior disorder, which begins in the personal misidentification of ends. To solve the problem, practitioners must be encouraged—perhaps coached, as are children learning to hit a baseball—to focus on the end of excellence.

To posit the ends of victory and excellence as alternatives to one another is not to suggest that they are mutually exclusive. As we know, victory is often the just reward for excellence, and excellence often brings victory. Mediocrity is rarely rewarded with victory in a competitive setting, and the excellent are rarely drubbed in competition. But to win does not always mean to be excellent, and vice-versa. The ends conflict when the excellent professional nevertheless loses due to bad luck, an official's error, political chicanery, deceit, treachery or a host of reasons including the greater excellence of another. When Enron's Andy Fastow created and managed SPEs effectively to keep the company's debt off its balance sheet and deceive capital markets, regulators, investors, lenders, analysts, and reporters as to its true financial condition, the ends of victory and excellence collided. He appeared to achieve victory as a CFO, but in retrospect only jimmy-rigged a short cut to its trappings, for example, wealth, fame, glory, prestige— prizes reserved for those who achieve excellence. In reality, he excelled at cooking the books and duping gullible investment bankers into funding his "Raptors." Thus, Enron, his *polis*, is to be faulted for incentivizing him toward the end of victory to the neglect of excellence.

Orientation toward either end (or purpose) directs professionals to the appreciation and choice of *values*, or *goods* proper to it. As stated, a company effects this attraction by offering incentives to which the hearts and minds of employees adhere. These are what employees and officers, players and coaches learn to desire, strive for and love. They motivate the choice of an action, which serves as a *means* to the end. A person aiming at victory will choose action geared towards what MacIntyre calls "*goods of cooperative effectiveness*" such as wealth and riches, power, status and honor, prestige and glory. And a *polis* ordered toward victory and conquest will motivate citizens toward these values. A person aiming at excellence will rather choose action geared toward "*goods of excellence*" such as knowledge for its own sake, life and health, aesthetic appreciation, friendship and sociability. And a company or team driven toward excellence will motivate its employees' or players' actions toward such values. In the case of either victory or excellence, the intelligibility of an action chosen is conferred by the end aimed at and the goods valued. Note that a polis will not achieve excellence by motivating citizens toward goods of cooperative effectiveness such as stock options, lavish bonuses or incentive clauses written into contracts because by highlighting and incentivizing these goods of cooperative effectiveness, the polis will orient citizens towards the end of victory rather than that of excellence.

Repeated motivation toward values and action aimed at victory or excellence builds habits, or *virtues* in the person so choosing. These personal qualities (habitual dispositions or cultivated inclinations) dispose a person's choices to the attainment of goods through action. The end selected, goods chosen and actions taken as means toward the end consequentially develop corresponding virtues in a person, analogous to the way in which water pulled downstream by gravity carves a canal, or the sun and its rays orient a sunflower.[57] In some cases the virtue required and developed to guide action toward victory or excellence will coincide, as in the case of resoluteness, or resolve, that is, determination, purposefulness. That virtue is necessary to achieve either end by guiding action toward the attainment of either's proper goods when those goods are elusive or difficult to attain. Separately, the end of excellence can only be sustained in a *polis*, which cannot subsist without wealth, power and other goods of cooperative effectiveness. That is to say, "the goods of excellence can only be sustained by being provided with institutionalized settings [whose maintenance] always requires the acquisition and retention of some degree of power and some degree of wealth."[58] Consequently, a polis or person aiming for excellence cannot achieve it without cultivating some modicum of virtue in "citizens" disposed toward victory and the goods of cooperative effectiveness. The challenging implication of this need for a company, which cannot survive without some level of profitability, is that its pursuit of excellence will oblige some orientation of human action toward victory. Its people must value wealth, status, power and prestige to some extent,[59] but not too much lest they, and it, fall prey to the ravages of cheating. Regardless, the qualities or virtues necessary to achieve excellence will not always coincide with those necessary to achieve victory. And a quality constituting a virtue in the light of one end may not be a virtue in light of the other.

For example, action directed toward either victory or excellence will engender some inclination towards justice. But justice for the person aiming at excellence is a habitual disposition to act in a way that gives each person his or her due. External rules are fair to the extent that they make it possible to reward those who merit it. The actual virtue of justice, however, has value independent of the rules and is their measure. Alternatively, justice for the person aiming at victory will consist of no more than a fixed disposition to abide by agreed-upon rules which reflect only the outcome of negotiation, and not any intrinsic value. In this view, rules are arbitrary and simply convenient to the party with superior bargaining power. That negotiated rules will vary according to the relative strength of the ones bargaining and hence reflect the will of the powerful is of no significant concern to such a person. The implicit conclusion for one aiming at victory, therefore, is "might makes right," as was explicitly (and unsuccessfully) argued by Thrasymachus against Socrates in Plato's *Republic*: "I proclaim that justice is nothing else than the interest of the stronger."[60] For the one aiming at excellence, just rules always bind because to violate them is to commit injustice, which first and foremost harms the violator. Hence Socrates' argument against Polus in Plato's *Gorgias*: "The greatest of all misfortunes is to do wrong…. If I had to choose one or the other I would rather suffer wrong than do wrong."[61] We need not fear such a person's falsifying a financial statement or research report, or enhancing performance with steroids because she will police herself. She would personally lose her orientation towards excellence by cheating, develop bad habits[62] inclining her away from that end and forfeit the goods of knowledge, friendship, sociability, and the like that she prizes. Being showered with goods of cooperative effectiveness such as bonus compensation or fame for tainted achievements would afford scant recompense.

Not so for one aiming at victory, who is bound by rules only to the extent that he fears getting caught breaching them. Such a person will engage in *strategic compliance* and conduct a probability-weighted cost-benefit analysis to determine whether or not to abide by the rules[63] and, moreover, consider himself rational (in an economic sense) in the bargain. As long as one is not caught breaching the rules, to be unjust harms only cheated competitors. One does not lose one's way and set oneself against desired goods by cheating; to the contrary, doing so brings one closer to their possession. For such a person, to have these goods is the proof of deserving them. Unfortunately, we all need to fear such a person because she will not police herself and is likely to behave opportunistically if not controlled externally by law, rules, testing regimes, etc. As economists explain, opportunism drives up agency costs.[64] Yet, agency costs are not inevitable; nor need they continually escalate in response to ever more sophisticated forms of opportunism. MacIntyre's theory—and Aristotelian virtue ethics generally—fleshes out the interior dynamic of opportunism: action pursuant to the guidance of justice in one whose end is victory, who pursues goods of cooperative effectiveness without concern for merit or just deserts. Virtue in one pursuing excellence is a truly rational control system: personal, interior control, which reduces agency costs to society. Conversely, virtue in one aimed solely at victory increases such costs. Consider the case of much-heralded Bernie Ebbers, who led World-Com to a position of preeminence in the Telecom industry through a series of mergers and acquisitions. No less than 85% of his net worth consisted of company stock—ironically, much of it granted as compensation intended to align his values with shareholders'—which he used to collateralize $400 million in loans. Had he aimed primarily at excellence, he might have thought twice before leveraging himself into such a position, or liquidated stock and other assets to reduce personal debt when a sharp downturn hit the industry (and stock price in consequence). In brief, he would have suffered the downturn and acted to ameliorate its effects on the company, cautioning and protecting shareholders as fiduciary duties required of him. Rather, he acted to retain the goods of wealth, power and fame by insisting that CFO Scott Sullivan "hit our numbers" in impossible conditions, a command the CFO interpreted as a mandate to cook the books. Sullivan's alleged pleas to quit lying to Wall Street were rebuffed with comments such as "We can't lower our guidance. We just announced new guidance.... Now you get to work on it."[65] Such is the posture of one aiming at mere victory, not genuine excellence. Constituents expecting justice from company executives in the form of honest reporting in accordance with GAAP hoped in vain.

Other virtues such as self-control (temperance) and courage (fortitude) are also necessary to guide action toward the goods germane to either end. For instance, to one aiming at excellence self-control requires the transformation of desires, aversions and dispositions so that one may better judge and move toward the goods of excellence. "Thus temperateness is a virtue which transforms both what I judge to be a good and what I am moved by as a good."[66] For instance, a Jack Grubman in possession of temperateness respecting goods of excellence would come to view the production of honest research at the expense of Bernie Ebbers' ire as preferable to an invitation to Ebbers' wedding at the expense of research integrity. By contrast, to one aiming solely at victory self-control "is a virtue only because and insofar as it enables me to achieve more efficiently goods antecedently recognized as such and desired." Self-control in this light would lead a David Duncan to avidly golf and play tennis at the tony Houston Racquet Club, not to stay fit for performing better risk assessments and audits, but to better "make rain" by consorting there with Ken Lay and other Houston luminaries.[67] Courage for the person aiming at either excellence or victory will include *endurance* and the ability to *confront harms and dangers*. But, the person exclusively seeking victory will risk danger only for the sake of power, honor or glory. Conversely, the seeker of excellence will risk danger for the sake of another person, group, institution or practice aside from personal benefit simply because that entity is the bearer of some great good.

The case of Cynthia Cooper, Vice President of internal auditing at WorldCom, is instructive in this regard. Though primarily an operational auditor who monitored performance of WorldCom units and ensured proper spending controls, she turned her attention to financial auditing when a subordinate stumbled onto $500 million of undocumented expenses.[68] Within a month, her team's surreptitious investigation had discovered $3.8 billion in misallocated operating expenses and fraudulent entries. She'd earlier raised the issue of improper reserve transfers with external auditors from Arthur Andersen who'd brushed her off. She was warned off her sleuthing activities by none other than Scott Sullivan, her boss, who she nevertheless defied at great peril to herself. Eventually, she successfully confronted Sullivan before the board's audit committee, which asked him for an explanation and then his resignation. The highly-praised Sullivan risked danger for the sake of maintaining power, wealth and glory whereas Cooper risked it for the integrity of the company's financial reporting. Sullivan controlled his employees, ordering them to make questionable transfers of reserves and false entries in the books in order to carry out the fraud,[69] whereas Cooper controlled her fears and overcame her aversion to bringing the fraud to light, which would expose her company and its thousands of innocent employees to danger.[70] She doggedly adhered to a greater good than expedience. Were it not for her courage, perseverance and self-control, the accounting misdeeds at WorldCom might have remained hidden, buried in goodwill at the next consolidated merger. One might even say with justice that the "human face" of the "new capitalism" is hers.

GETTING BUSINESS OFF "STEROIDS"

This analysis suggests that no amount of law, regulation, or controls—even those signed off on by executives and attested to by outside auditors, as required by the much-dreaded and—bewailed Section 404 of Sarbanes Oxley—will rid the marketplace of cheating unless and until business practitioners develop interior control, or good character. To acknowledge this truth is not to advocate abandoning external and internal controls. It is rather to point the direction towards a freer marketplace in which fewer constraints would be needed and fewer agency costs would be expended.

The ultimate solution for problems in business, or sport, is for people to control themselves. This is the domain of *ethics*. WorldCom will inexorably be followed into the abyss by a Lehman Brothers and whoever is next for want of prudent judgment, justice, courage, and self-control.[71] As argued, the problem lies fundamentally in the widespread orientation of business practitioners (and ballplayers) towards the end of victory irrespective of excellence, despite much palaver to the contrary. In the Aristotelian tradition, every decision-maker chooses goods (values in today's parlance) which become motives for action towards an end. Agents need to, and do, develop corresponding virtues through the interior "act" of freely choosing goods in order to attain ends. These virtues become dispositions, inclinations to action—a sort of canal for the flowing water of human behavior—directed toward the end. Through virtuous action, each and every person inclines toward sustainable prosperity (Socratic excellence) on the one hand, or social turmoil (Thrasymachan conquest) on the other. Thus, the place to address the problems discussed in this chapter is at the level of virtue formation in the person, by influencing her to elect excellence as the end of personal action. In accord with Herbert Simon's theory of administrative behavior,[72] it is a matter of addressing the choice that precedes human action and informing it as to the preeminent value of goods of excellence: for example, knowledge for its own sake, life and health, aesthetic appreciation, friendship, and sociability. People who value these goods first and foremost are less likely to cheat and precipitate social calamity. And, because a company (and every *polis*) needs profit to survive, the cultivation of a moderate appreciation for goods of cooperative effectiveness is also required: for example, wealth, power, status, honor, prestige, and glory. Nevertheless, notice is served by recent events in the worlds of business and sport that an excessive preoccupation with these latter goods underlies the problem of cheating and its social manifestations.

Following Perez-Lopez[73] I propose three questions for routine consideration by decision-makers (i.e., by everyone) in order that each might inform his own freedom with respect to the broad spectrum of goods available in each and every choice. The questions are ordered in a manner conducive to sustainable prosperity by first addressing the necessary modicum for survival of goods of cooperative effectiveness, and then addressing goods of excellence.[74]

1. If I act in the following way,[75] will this "action plan" accomplish my immediate objective?

Note that this question directs the decision maker to consider some "bottom line" respecting the decision being made, which is commonly referred to as "getting results," though it is actually only one of three separate and distinct results—each addressed by a separate question—attained through action. Accomplishing immediate objectives is a necessary but insufficient condition for achieving excellence, though it might lead to (Pyrrhic) victory. Through the artful solution of immediate problems one is directed to solvency if not wealth, and advancement if not glory. Through the accomplishment of successive objectives one moves toward the goods of cooperative effectiveness. Note that at this stage of analysis, taking steroids would be an acceptable action plan for a ballplayer desirous of hitting home runs, just as cooking the books would be one for a CFO desirous of meeting Wall Street's expectations. Andy Fastow, Scott Sullivan and their respective bosses tended to this question with great solicitude. Their failures were in not following it up, and checking the answer, by asking the following two questions.

2.   Will accomplishing my immediate objective this way make me (and by extension, make my organization) more knowledgeable and adept at accomplishing objectives of this type in the future (in a word, more competent)?

Professionalism and competence are their own rewards, though possessing these traits also goes a long way toward ensuring the achievement of goods of cooperative effectiveness. Nevertheless, the development of expertise moves a problem-solver toward goods of excellence such as knowledge for its own sake and the appreciation of work well done. Note that with each fraudulent entry, Sullivan gained no additional expertise in his function with which to honestly solve WorldCom's future problems. He'd solved the immediate ones (hitting the numbers), but in a way that did not prepare him or the company to address its true needs, namely, making the changes and adjustments necessary to hit the numbers indefinitely into the future. Such a solution would have included giving Wall Street realistic guidance, rather than simply telling it what it, and the CEO, wanted to hear. The result of his decision making was illicitly transferred reserves and five consecutive quarters of fraudulent entries in the capital accounts. Sullivan was enough of a craftsman to defend the booking of leased telephone line costs as "prepaid capacity" in a "White Paper" for the board's audit committee. But, smoke and mirrors are neither necessary nor sufficient tools for the long term; thus, it is better to avoid recourse to them in the short term, all things considered. By neglecting to ask whether the path he'd embarked on would habituate him to cheating rather than to capably solving tomorrow's problems, he continued on a path that led to his and others' destruction,[76] as well as his company's.

3.   Will accomplishing my immediate objective this way increase coop-
     eration around me (and by extension, in my organization) and
     likely lead to increased trust?

The example of Scott Sullivan indicates how dangerous a modicum of
competence can be in a person lacking a corresponding solicitude for
trust, the glue that binds all social actors. Bear Stearns discovered this the
hard way when its store of trust within the banking community evaporated
in March 2008, precipitating its overnight collapse and government-
aided absorption into JPMorgan Chase. Barry Bonds learned the same
lesson when baseball passed him over in 2008 despite his oft-verbalized
wish, and evident ability, to continue playing. Tending to one's own trustworthiness habituates a person to a consideration of others, such as the
fans who cheer athletic feats, or the investors who rely on honest research
and financial statements. A person so habituated develops virtues that
guide action toward excellence and its goods, for example, friendship and
sociability. A person that acts so as to be trustworthy (or professionally
competent) is not apt to behave opportunistically. Decisions (choices)
based routinely on the concerns expressed in all three questions—(1)
achieving the immediate objective while building (2) competence and (3)
trustworthiness—cultivate a person's *motivational structure*, that is, her
capacity to be motivated at multiple levels of value, or good, and act
accordingly. She builds virtues to guide her action toward the ends of
excellence primarily, and victory to the extent necessary for vitality. A
person so structured is certain to relish her fair share of victory—no more,
or less. The implication is that given the possibility of a decision-makers
self-induced interior change, truly rational choice is a three-dimensional
act, which shapes virtues in three ways: (1) those necessary for achievement now, (2) those necessary for achievement tomorrow through crafts-
manship in one's field (roughly, *arte*, or *techne* in Aristotelian terms) and
(3) those necessary for sustainable, meaningful relationships with others
(roughly, *moral virtue* in Aristotelian terms).
    This chapter has reviewed a number of recent scandals in business,
analogized them to the steroids controversy in Major League Baseball,
and assigned the blame for both to an exclusive, mistaken and ultimately
self-defeating orientation of key decision-makers toward the end of victory. In consequence, protagonists were habituated to values that lured
them to defeat despite their seeming achievement of victory. Ironically,
the actors highlighted were all once praised for their professional virtuos-
ity and lionized as exemplars worthy of emulating. Today their stories
serve as cautionary, rather than exemplary, tales. The three questions proposed herein constitute a self-administered device with which to address
and rectify the problems identified, and orient decision-makers toward

flourishing lives of excellence, and perhaps even victory. This way is ultimately society's only sure path to sustainable prosperity. In conclusion, these questions are proposed as decision rules for businessmen and -women, as well as practitioners of the "national pastime" in the belief their use will help clear the field of "steroids," reduce the intrusion of umpires into the game, and let the players play ball.

NOTES

1. Though this chapter will not directly address the crisis that engulfed Wall Street, the financial sector and, indeed, the world's credit and capital markets in Fall '08, the analysis, descriptions and prescriptions contained herein apply equally to it. At bottom, the credit crisis of '08 which threatens to plunge the global economy into a prolonged, severe recession and perhaps depression is the result of an ethical problem, imprudence, manifest by the reckless leveraging of home mortgages by house purchasers who couldn't afford them, lending institutions that issued them without performing due diligence, regulators that coerced lenders into making them, investment bankers that tranched, packaged and sold them without ascertaining their true risk or even value, and investors who jumped into securities backed by them without researching what they were buying.

    Separately, perennial concerns regarding unfairness and economic inequality continue to resonate as evidenced by the award of 2008's Nobel Prize in Economic Sciences to Princeton economist, Paul Krugman. While ostensibly awarded the Nobel for scholarly research on international trade and economic geography, the ideas concerning political economy for which he is popularly known are diffused regularly through the editorial page of the New York Times and in bestselling books. In his recent manifesto he offers an argument for redistributive programs, and a trenchant critique of free market economics and conservative politics. *See*, PAUL KRUGMAN, *THE CONSCIENCE OF A LIBERAL*, (W. W. Norton) (2007).

2. MCLEAN, BETHANY & PETER ELKIND, *SMARTEST GUYS IN THE ROOM: THE AMAZING RISE AND SCANDALOUS FALL OF ENRON*, (Penguin Group) (2003).

3. Marianne Levelle & Matthew Benjamin, THE BIGGEST BUST, *U.S. NEWS & WORLD REP.*, Dec. 10, 2001, at 34.

4. Id

5. *U.S. v. Fastow*, No. H-02-0665 (S.D. Tex. 2004), available at http:/fl1.findlaw.com/news.findlaw.com/hdocs/docs/enron/usafastow11404plea.pdf

6. *U.S. v. Skilling*, No. H-04-25, 2006 WL 1444909 (S.D. Tex. May 26, 2006).

7. *U.S. v. Lay*, No. H-04-25, 2006 WL 1444908 (S.D. Tex. May 25, 2006).

8. John Emshwiller, *Enron's Kenneth Lay is Dead at 64*, WALL ST. J., July 5, 2006.

9. His appeal was argued in April 2008.

10. Kurt Eichenwald, *An Enron Chapter Closes: The Overview; Enron Founder, Awaiting Prison, Dies in Colorado*, N.Y. TIMES, July 6, 2006, at A1.

11. Ken Belson & Jennifer Bayot, *Ebbers Sentencing to Proceed as Judge Denies Plea for Retrial*, N.Y. TIMES, July 13, 2005, at C2.

12. In September 2008, WorldCom's bankruptcy was dwarfed by investment bank Lehman Brothers' declaration. That institution, begun in 1844, bet heavily and recklessly in the subprime mortgage market. It also acquired excessively leveraged properties for its own portfolio, which totaled $88 billion as compared to shareholder equity of $22.5 billion. *See*, Bill Jamieson, *How the Masters of the Universe Ran Amok and Cost us the Earth*, THE SCOTSMAN, September 16, 2008, at 1. At minimum, the leaders at Lehman can be faulted for losing their heads and making extremely imprudent bets that they couldn't afford to lose. The day following Lehman's bankruptcy, the government stepped in to prevent an even larger one, that of insurance giant and Dow Jones 30 Industrial component AIG, which compounded those same faults with others.

On September 25th, the government siezed the nation's largest thrift institution, Washington Mutual. With its $307 billion in assets, WaMu's failure eclipsed Continental Illinois' 1984 collapse ($40 billion in assets) as the largest banking bust in history. *See*, Robin Sidel, David Enrich & Dan Fitzpatrick, *WaMu is Seized, Sold Off to J.P. Morgan In Largest Failure in U.S. Banking History*, WALL ST. J., September 26, 2008.

13. *Arthur Andersen LLP v. U.S.*, 544 U.S. 696 (2005).

14. David Teather, *Partner says Duncan stretched rules to excess*, GUARDIAN UNLIMITED, May 10, 2002.

15. MIKE BREWSTER, UNACCOUNTABLE: HOW THE ACCOUNTING PROFESSION FORFEITED A PUBLIC TRUST, (Wiley) (2003).

16. BARBARA LEY TOFFLER, FINAL ACCOUNTING: AMBITION, GREED AND THE FALL OF ARTHUR ANDERSEN, (Broadway Books) (2003).

17. Alex Berenson & Andrew Ross Sorkin, *How Wall Street was Tamed*, N.Y. TIMES, Dec. 22, 2002 at 31

18. Editor, *How Not to Conduct Business*, BUSINESS WEEK, August 5, 2002.

19. Randall Smith & Deborah Solomon, *Ebbers's Exit Hurts WorldCom's Biggest Fan*, WALL ST. J., May 3, 2002, at C1. Ebbers was convicted of conspiracy and securities fraud in March 2005 and sentenced to 25 years in prison. He was 63 years old. The conviction and sentence were upheld in July 2006. The Supreme Court turned down Ebber's appeal without comment in May 2007. CFO Scott Sullivan, the architect of the WorldCom fraud pled guilty in 2004 to manipulating earnings, and received a lenient five year sentence for cooperating with federal prosecutors in the Ebbers trial.

20. Mitchell Pacelle, *Citigroup's WorldCom Payment Is Finalized at $2.58 Billion*, WALL ST. J., Nov. 8, 2004, at C5.

21. Between March 11, 2000 and October 9, 2002 the Nasdaq Composite Index dropped from 5046.86 to 1114.11, a collapse of 78%.

22. To little or no avail, as the events between March and September 2008— the period between Bear Stearns and Washington Mutual's meltdowns— indicate.

23.   Sarbanes-Oxley of 2002, Pub.L. 107-204, 116 Stat. 745 (2002).

24.   In November 2006, the independent Committee on Capital Markets
      Regulation, a "bipartisan and diverse group of 22 experts from the investor
      community, business, finance, law, accounting and academia" found
      significant erosion in the U.S.'s traditionally dominant position in global
      capital markets, and that regulation and litigation are keeping foreign
      issuers and investors out of the public market. The Committee
      recommended a number of correctives, specifically an adjustment in the
      implementation of Section 404 of the Sarbanes Oxley Act. In a follow-up
      report dated December 4, 2007 titled "The Competitive Position of the U.S.
      Public Equity Market," it concluded that "by almost any meaningful
      measure, the competitiveness of the U.S. public equity market has
      significantly deteriorated in recent years. From 2006 to 2007, most
      measures either continued to decline or failed to substantially improve."
      The Committee renewed its call for action on the regulatory reduction front.
      See, Comm. on Capital Markets Regulation, The Competitive Position of the
      U.S. Public Equity Market (2007), available at http://www.capmktsreg. org/
      pdfs/The_Competitive_Position_of_the_US_Public_Equity_Market.pdf

25.   See, Duff Wilson & Michael S. Schmidt, Steroid Report Cites "Collective
      Failure," N.Y. TIMES, December 14, 2007; Josh Levin, Sports Nut: The
      Stadium Scene, The Rocket Under Fire; Congress investigates Jose
      Canseco's barbecue, a nanny in a peach bikini, and Roger Clemens' bloody
      butt, SLATE, Feb. 13, 2008.

      The problem, to be certain, is not one exclusive to baseball players. For
      instance, Olympic track and field champion Marion Jones was stripped of
      five medals won at the 2000 Summer Olympics in Sydney, and sentenced to
      six months in prison, inter alia, for lying to federal prosecutors about her
      use of performance enhancing drugs. See, Associated Press, Jones (six
      months), former coach (63 months) sentenced to prison, ESPN.COM,
      January 14, 2008. http://sports.espn.go.com/oly/trackandfield/
      news/story?id=3191954

      Floyd Landis, winner of the 2006 Tour de France was stripped of his
      championship, the first winner in the roughly 100-year history of the Tour
      to suffer that ignominy. He was dismissed from his riding team and sus-
      pended from competition for two years because of drug tests showing that
      he used performance enhancing drugs during a critical stage of the 2006
      event. See, Juliet Macur, Landis's Positive Doping Test Upheld, N.Y.
      TIMES, September 21, 2007.

      Nor is the problem one exclusive to U.S. athletes. Johann "Juanito"
      Muhlegg, the German born speed skater turned Spanish Olympian was
      disqualified from a race in which he'd won a gold medal and expelled from
      the 2002 Olympics in Salt Lake City for blood doping. See, Martyn
      Ziegler, Drugs in Sport: Caborn calls for tougher doping code, THE
      INDEPENDENT, January 25, 2003. He was banned from competition for
      2 years, and later stripped of two other gold medals won at the same
      Olympics. Ironically, Muhlegg was unavailable to receive a call of congrat-
      ulations from King Juan Carlos of Spain for winning his second gold

medal because he was being tested at that moment for drug use. The King sent a telegram that read: "This is a very important victory for Spanish sports." See, Staff, Olympics: Notebook; Record Run by Italian Threatens German Dominance in the Luge, N.Y. TIMES, February 11, 2002. Rather, it proved to be Spain's greatest sporting humiliation.

Canadian sprinter Ben Johnson forfeited a gold medal won at the 1988 Olympics in Seoul after testing positive for steroids. He'd won a greatly anticipated showdown with Carl Lewis of the United States, a burst for the ages in which Johnson actually had time to turn around and look at Lewis before stretching for the tape. Following a 2 year ban for that infraction, Johnson returned to international competition only to test positive again and be banned for life. See, Mark Kram, Ben Still Needs to Run, OUT-SIDE MAGAZINE, December, 1998.

Argentine soccer legend Diego Maradona was removed from the 1994 World Cup after testing positive for five variants of ephedrine, a substance banned by the sport. See, Sam Hovve Verhovek, World Cup '94; After Second Test, Maradona Is Out of World Cup, N.Y. TIMES, July 1, 1994.

26.   Staff, *Players listed in the Mitchell Commission report*, ESPN.COM, December 13, 2007, http://sports.espn.go.com/mlb/news/story?id=3153646

27.   Bonds was named *The Sporting News'* Baseball Player of the Decade in 1999 for winning three National League (NL) Most Valuable Player (MVP) awards, eight Gold Gloves and ranking in the top three players in home runs, runs batted in (RBI's), slugging percentage and walks in the '90s. In 1998, the season of America's infatuation with the "long ball" (see the discussion of McWire and Sosa, *infra*) he became the first player in the entire history of major league baseball to hit 400 home runs and steal 400 bases in a career. Few people outside of San Francisco, where he played, seemed to notice.

Though not apposite to the issue of his stature before allegedly beginning steroids use, Bonds became MLB's only 500–500 career player in 2003, and won four more NL MVP awards between 2001 and 2004. Altogether in his career, he won the award an unprecedented 7 times, finished second in balloting twice and in the top five players 12 times. He won the NL Hank Aaron Award in 2001, 2002 and 2004 and was named Major League Player of the Year in 1990, 2001 and 2004. He finished his career with scores of other awards, titles and honors.

28.   The career record had stood since 1974 when Aaron broke the legendary Babe Ruth's record of 714 career homers. *See*, John Donovan, *History maker: Bonds slugs No. 756 to pass Aaron as home run king*, SI.COM, August 8, 2007; *Sham? Maybe. Shame? Definitely: Bonds holds the home run record, but he's no hero*, SI.COM, August 8, 2007.

29.   Bonds finished the season with 73. His career total stands at 762. Barry Bond's Career Stats, http://mlb.mlb.com/stats/historical /individual_stats_player.jsp?c_id= mlb&playerID=111188 (last visited Nov. 18, 2008).

30.   Maris and teammate Mickey Mantle's pursuit of Babe Ruth's record 60 home runs (set in 1927) nearly 40 years earlier was celebrated in the movie

"61*." Maris's feat was accomplished in a 162-game season, while Ruth's was achieved in a 154-game season (though Ruth had more at bats, and hence opportunities than Maris in their respective record setting seasons). Baseball's commissioner Ford Frick determined that Maris's record should be marked in the books with an asterisk to denote his supposed advantage. It effectively deprecated and marginalized Maris's feat as being unfairly accomplished, and tainted the record with a patina of stigma. The asterisk was eventually removed from the record books, but not until after Maris's death. History has been kinder to Maris than were his contemporaries in the New York media. And Frick's act rather than Maris's record has come to bear the mark of injustice.

31.   David A. Kaplan & Brad Stone, *In baseball's season of redemption, two men go after the most fabled record in American sports—61 home runs*, NEWSWEEK, September 14, 1998.

32.   Gary Smith, *Sportsman of the Year 1998: Mark McGwire and Sammy Sosa*, SPORTS ILLUSTRATED, December 21, 1998.

33.   Ron Kroichick, *Book traces Bonds' steroids use to McGwire-Sosa HR race*, SAN FRANCISCO CHRONICLE, March 7, 2006.

34.   Andro was a substance banned by professional football, college basketball, the Olympics and professional tennis at the time, but not by professional baseball. *See,* Mike Bianchi, *Amid steroid scandal, it's time to apologize to AP's Steve Wilstein*, THE ORLANDO SENTINEL, December 27, 2004. It has subsequently been banned in baseball as well.

35.   JOSE CANSECO, JUICED: WILD TIMES, RAMPANT 'ROIDS, SMASH HITS, AND HOW BASEBALL GOT BIG, (Harper Entertainment) (2006).

36.   Dave Sheinin, *Baseball Has a Day of Reckoning In Congress: McGwire Remains Evasive During Steroid Testimony*, WASHINGTON POST, March 18, 2005, at A1.

37.   Staff, *Baseball under the microscope*, CBC SPORTS ONLINE, March 17, 2005. Canseco later apologized for naming players, an act he came to regret. "I never realized this was going to blow up and hurt so many people." He apparently named names in order to bolster his claims with the ring of truth, and wrote the tell-all because he wanted revenge on the sport for allegedly having black-balled him. "If I could meet with Mark McGwire and these players, I definitely would apologize to them.... They were my friends. I admired them. I respected them." *See,* Staff, *Canseco regrets naming names in his book about steroids*, ESPN.COM NEWS SERVICE, October 21, 2008, http://sports.espn.go.com/mlb/news/story?id=3655031& campaign=rss&source=MLBHeadlines

38.   Sheinin, *supra* note 37.

39.   Associated Press, *McGwire denied Hall; Gwynn, Ripken get in: Slugger with 583 HRs only gets 23 percent of votes; Gossage 21 short*, NBC SPORTS, January 10, 2007.

40.   Barry M. Bloom, *Transcript reveals Bonds' testimony*, MLB.COM, March 1, 2008.

41.   MARK FAINARU-WADA & LANCE WILLIAMS, GAME OF SHADOWS: BARRY BONDS, BALCO, AND THE STEROIDS SCANDAL THAT ROCKED PROFESSIONAL

SPORTS, (Gotham) (2007); Michiko Kakutani, *Barry Bonds and Baseball's Steroids Scandal*, N.Y. TIMES, March 23, 2006.

42.   Naturally, the problem of cheating in sport is hardly confined to the use of performance enhancing drugs, which is merely the variant-cum-flavor of the day. For instance, in the 2002 Olympics French figure skating judge, Marie Reine Le Gougne, confessed to scoring the Russian team preferentially due to pressure from Didier Gailhaguet, the French ice sports federation president. See, Staff, 3-year ban for skating judge, BBC SPORTS, April 20, 2002, http://news.bbc.co.uk/sport2/hi/other_sports/1959181.stm. In return, the French entrant in the upcoming ice dancing competition was expected to secure the Russian judge's preferential treatment. Unfortunately for the conspirators, the Russian pair of Yelena Berezhnaya and Anton Sikharulidze committed an obvious technical error during its performance. Le Gougne's high scores denied the gold medal to the crowd-darling Canadian pair, Jamie Salé and David Pelletier, which had skated flawlessly. The resultant uproar was quelled when a second gold medal was awarded to the defrauded Canadian team. Though Le Gougne later recanted her confession and shifted the finger of blame to pressure by the Canadian committee rather than to machinations by the Russian and French ones, she and Gailhaguet were found guilty of misconduct and banned from the sport for 3 years including the 2006 Olympics. See, Christopher Clarey, Figure Skating; Judge and Ice Official Face Accusers, N.Y. TIMES, April 30, 2002.

The National Football League's (NFL's) New England Patriots—winners of Super Bowls XXXVI in 2002, XXXVIII in 2004 and XXXIX in 2005, and the team universally recognized as the game's regnant dynasty—were fined $250,000 in 2007 and stripped of its coveted #1 pick in the 2008 college player draft. New England violated league rules by videotaping opposing New York Jets' coaches as they flashed defensive signals during a game thereby enabling the Patriots to break the Jets' code, giving them an unfair and dishonest advantage. See, Chris Mortensen, Sources: Goodell determines Pats broke rule by taping Jets' signals, ESPN.COM, September 13, 2007, http://sports.espn.go.com/nfl/news/story?id=3014677. The League's statement indicated that the Patriots had long been suspected of the anti-competitive practice, and that all teams had been strongly warned not to indulge in it. Patriots' coach Bill Belichick who is known for his exceptionally thorough and successful game plans, was fined $500,000 by the League, the largest fine ever paid by an NFL coach. Similar to the way that Bonds, McGwire, Sosa and Clemens' feats of athletic prowess are questioned due to the taint of cheating allegations, New England was accused on the eve of Super Bowl XLII in 2008 (won by the New York Giants in an improbable upset of the undefeated and heavily favored Patriots) of having videotaped its Super Bowl XXXVI opponent (2002), then defending champion and heavily favored Saint Louis Rams, during its final "walk-through" of plays in the Superdome the night before the game. See, Mike Fish, Ex-Ram Warner wants NFL to expand probe of Patriots, ESPN.COM, February 3, 2008, http://sports.espn.go.com/ nfl/news/story?id=3227592.

While acknowledging the Patriots' superiority that day, opposing Rams' quarterback in 2002, Kurt Warner, nevertheless commented that "anytime you have something like this go on, and you get caught doing that, it raises questions. And I think rightfully so." Regarding the violation, Patriot's backup quarterback in 2002, Drew Bledsoe, commented that "[l]ike in other realms in the world, in the business world, when you get into a highly competitive environment, people are going to try and do what they can get away with. [sic] That is not unique to football" (emphasis added).

43. Staff, *Baseball star Barry Bonds charged*, BBC SPORTS, November 16, 2007, http://news.bbc.co.uk/2/hi/americas/7097583.stm

44. Bonds' career total of 1,996 RBI's remains only four short of the magical 2,000 mark, a milestone reached by only two players in the history of the game: Hank Aaron and Babe Ruth. Bonds ranks third on the all-time list.

45. Ecko, a fashion designer, purchased the ball for $752,467 in an online auction. He put the question of whether the ball should be defaced in protest to a vote on the internet. The options were to brand it with an asterisk, do nothing to it, or shoot it to the moon. Almost half of the 10 million votes cast favored branding it. *See* Jack Curry, *Barry Bonds ball goes to the Hall, asterisk and all*, INTERNATIONAL HERALD TRIBUNE, July 2, 2008.

46. Mark Hosenball, *Roger Dodger v. The Feds*, NEWSWEEK, March 10, 2008, at 10.

47. For the record, this author is a lifelong fan of the San Francisco Giants, and has marveled at Bonds' nearly routine heroics on behalf of the team since his arrival in 1993.

48. It should be noted that the game's greatest home run hitters also rank among its greatest strikeout victims. For instance, Bonds hit more home runs than any player in history, and struck out more than all but 34 of them. His dual ranking is thus (#1-#35). Other players with notable home run-strike out career rankings are McGwire (#8-#29), Sosa (#6-#2), Ruth (#3-#88), Aaron (#2-#72) and Mantle (#15-#16). Additionally, all of these players enjoyed long and prosperous professional careers. The conclusion is that hard swingers will strike out more often. But, at the unusually high end of those who also connect often, longevity will ensure enough at bats to achieve notable success along with, and in spite of, notable failure.

49. *See*, CONNIE BRUCK, THE PREDATORS' BALL: THE JUNK BOND RAIDERS AND THE MAN WHO STAKED THEM, (The American Lawyer/Simon & Schuster) (1988); JAMES B. STEWART, DEN OF THIEVES, (Simon & Schuster) (1991).

50. *See*, MAXIMILIAN TORRES, ET AL., A VIRTUE-BASED BUSINESS ETHICS 131–148 (Samuel Gregg & Gerald Zandstra eds. 2005, Acton Center for Entrepreneurial Stewardship) (2005).

51. Arthur Levitt, Sec. and Exch. Comm'n Speeches & Public Statements, The 'Numbers Game' (Sept. 28, 1998) *available at* http://www.sec.gov/news/speech/ speecharchive/1998/spch220.txt

52. Sociability refers to the social nature of the person: his inclination towards, and need for, others. Aristotle gives the notion definitive expression in the *Politics*: "[H]e who is unable to live in society, or who has no need because he is sufficient for himself, must be either a beast or a god.... A social

instinct is implanted in all men by nature...." *See*, ARISTOTLE, BASIC WORKS OF ARISTOTLE 27-30, 1130, 1253 (Richard McKeon ed., Benjamin Jowett trans., 1941, Random House, New York) (1941).

53. ALASDAIR MACINTYRE, WHOSE JUSTICE? WHICH RATIONALITY? (University of Notre Dame Press) (1988).

54. Note that MacIntyre's focus on ends, or *telos*, identifies him as a philosopher in the Aristotelian, *virtue* tradition. Indeed, his book titled *After Virtue*, which immediately preceded *Whose Justice? Which Rationality?* in his *oeuvre* greatly contributed to the reestablishment of virtue ethics in the lexicon of academically respectable ethics. *See*, ALASDAIR MACINTYRE, AFTER VIRTUE (2nd ed., University of Notre Dame Press) (1984).

55. Note that either explanation or *final cause* of personal action might also serve to explain the aggregate of such action within a company or economic system. Hence, alternative answers to the question of what purpose a corporation ultimately serves might be *victory* (i.e., shareholder wealth maximization) or *excellence* (i.e., social welfare, or stakeholder well-being through the satisfaction of needs).

56. The latter analogy is admittedly unflattering to persons, insofar as people enjoy a freedom that sunflowers don't. It is precisely daily exercises of freedom that virtue guides. Freedom implies and requires a personal contribution in the setting of human orientations whereas the direction faced by a sunflower is determined by stimuli external to it. Freedom notwithstanding, human development partially depends upon something outside of oneself (some perceived good), which beckons and obliges a personal response. Naturally, people differ from sunflowers in too many other regards to name. Most importantly for the present purpose, each person selects her own end and by analogy chooses which sun to face.

57. MacIntyre, *supra* note 55, at 35.

58. Juan Antonio Pérez-López terms this necessary and indispensable quantum of goods of cooperative effectiveness (e.g., profitability) to which organizations must orient decision-makers "minimum effectiveness," not because decision-making in organizations should aim at *under*performance or mediocrity, but because the organization *must* achieve some necessary minimum of operating results in order to cover costs, engage in research and development, build reserves, provide a return on capital, and so forth, in a word, *flourish*. Beyond minimum effectiveness, Pérez-López contends that decision-making best aims at the achievement of other values, specifically "attractiveness" and "unity." *See*, discussion *infra*, and JUAN ANTONIO PÉREZ-LÓPEZ, TEORÍA DE LA ACCIÓN HUMANA EN LAS ORGANIZACIONES: LA ACCIÓN PERSONAL (THE THEORY OF HUMAN ACTION IN ORGANIZATIONS: PERSONAL ACTION), (Ediciones Rialp, Madrid) (1991); JUAN ANTONIO PÉREZ-LÓPEZ, FUNDAMENTOS DE LA DIRECCIÓN DE EMPRESAS (THE FOUNDATIONS OF BUSINESS MANAGEMENT), (Rialp, Madrid) (1993).

59. PLATO, THE REPUBLIC AND OTHER WORKS, (Benjamin Jowett trans., 1960, Dolphin Books, Doubleday and Company) (1960).

60. PLATO, GORGIAS, (Walter Hamilton trans., 1960, Penguin Books) (1960).

61. Note that "bad" necessarily refers to the self-selected end, which anchors the evaluation. It is a bad habit with respect to one that seeks excellence rather than victory.

62. JAAN ELIAS & J. GREGORY DEES, THE NORMATIVE FOUNDATIONS OF BUSINESS, (Harvard Business School Press) (1997).

63. Such costs consist of (1) monitoring expenditures by the principal, (2) bonding expenditures by the agent and (3) the residual loss. Monitoring expenditures include "efforts on the part of the principal to "control" the behavior of the agent through budget restrictions, compensation policies, operating rules, and so forth." *See*, Michael C. Jensen & William H. Meckling, *Theory of the Firm: Managerial Behavior, Agency Costs, and Ownership Structure*, 3 Journal of Financial Economics 305 (1976). Bonding expenditures would include audited financial statements, explicit bonding against agent malfeasance and a limitation of the agent's decision-making powers. *See*, generally ROBERTA ROMANO, FOUNDATIONS OF CORPORATE LAW, (Foundation Press, New York) (1993).

64. Shawn Young, Almar Latour & Susan Pulliam, *Burden of Proof: Linking Ebbers to the Fraud At WorldCom Proves Difficult; Ex-Finance Chief Sullivan Tells Of Meetings With the CEO, But Ambiguity Remains; 'We Have to Hit Our Numbers,'* WALL ST. J., Feb 18, 2005, at A1.

65. MacIntyre, *supra* note 55, at 40.

66. Enron was recognized as a "maximum-risk" engagement by senior Andersen partners, who met in February 2001 to discuss the pros and cons of retaining its business. They decided in favor because; *inter alia*, of their faith in Duncan's ability to manage it. *See*, AccountancyAge.com, *Andersen memo: Houston office to David Duncan*, ACCOUNTANCY AGE, January 18, 2002, http://www.accountancyage.com/accountancyage/news/2028778/andersen-memo-houston-office-david-duncan

67. Cynthia Cooper has received well-deserved plaudits for blowing the whistle at WorldCom including being named Time magazine's 2002 Co-Person of the Year along with Sherron Watkins of Enron and Coleen Rowley of the Federal Bureau of Investigation (FBI). Richard Lacayo & Amanda Ripley, *Persons of the Year 2002*, TIME, December 22, 2002, Cover. Less heralded have been the two selfless and faithful staffers who also risked their careers to ferret out the fraud: Gene Morse, a technology wonk, and Glyn Smith, a senior manager whose mother had been his and Ms. Cooper's high school accounting teacher.

68. Susan Pulliam, *Over the Line: A Staffer Ordered to Commit Fraud Balked, Then Caved—Pushed by WorldCom Bosses, Accountant Betty Vinson Helped Cook the Books—A Confession at the Marriot*, WALL ST. J., Jun 23, 2003.

69. Susan Pulliam & Deborah Solomon, Uncooking the Books: How Three Unlikely Sleuths Discovered Fraud at WorldCom—Company's Own Employees Sniffed Out Cryptic Clues And Followed Hunches—Ms. Cooper Says No to Her Boss, WALL ST. J., Oct. 30, 2002.

70. The defect was manifest at WorldCom as cheating and fraud, whereas at Lehman it took the form of something akin to gluttony. In both instances, action was marked by recklessness.

71.   HERBERT A. SIMON, ADMINISTRATIVE BEHAVIOR: A STUDY OF DECISION-MAKING PROCESSES IN ADMINISTRATIVE ORGANIZATION, (4th ed., 1976, The Free Press, Simon & Schuster Inc., New York: NY) (1976).

72.   Pérez-López, *supra* note 60.

73.   In Pérez-López's theory, the three questions correspond to diagnostic criteria, which address (1) the accomplishment of direct "results" (the "effectiveness" criterion), (2) the accomplishment of learning and distinctive competencies with which to produce future effectiveness (the "efficiency" criterion), and (3) the accomplishment of trust necessary to sustain effectiveness and retain efficiency (the "consistency" criterion). The discussion in this chapter will necessarily be limited to using the questions, and demonstrating their plausibility and operationality (i.e., usefulness, utility, usability).

The intricacies of how and why these questions and criteria address the character problems signaled by MacIntyre and throughout this chapter can be found in Pérez-López's work itself and elsewhere. See, JUAN ANTONIO PÉREZ-LÓPEZ & MARIA NURIA CHINCHILLA, BUSINESS OR ENTERPRISE? DIFFERENT APPROACHES TO THE MANAGEMENT OF PEOPLE IN ORGANIZATIONS, (IESE Business School Publishing, Barcelona, Spain) (1990); JUAN ANTONIO PÉREZ-LÓPEZ & MARIA NURIA CHINCHILLA, SOCIAL EFFECTIVENESS AND SELF-CONTROL, (IESE Business School Publishing, Barcelona, Spain) (1990); Maximilian B. Torres, Character and Decision-making (IESE Business School Publishing, Barcelona, Spain) (2001), http://www.iese.edu/research/pdfs/T_103.pdf; Maximilian B. Torres, Motivational Conflicts, (IESE Business School Publishing, Barcelona, Spain) (2001); Miguel A. Ariño, Toma de Decisiones y Gobierno de Organizaciones (Decision-making and the Governance of Organizations), (Deusto) (2005); Antonio Argandoña et al., Rethinking Business Management—Examining the Foundations of Business Education, 38-49 (Samuel Gregg & James R. Stoner, Jr. eds, 2008, The Witherspoon Institute) (2008); Antono Argandoña, Presentation delivered at the seminar entitled "Humanizing the Firm and the Management Profession" at IESE Business School: "Consistency in Decision-making in Companies" (June 30—July 2, 2008); Josep M. Rosanas, Beyond Economic Criteria: A Humanistic Approach to Organizational Survival, Journal of Business Ethics (2007) at 78:447–462; Josep M. Rosanas, (2008) Presentation delivered at the seminar titled "Humanizing the Firm and the Management Profession" at IESE Business School: "Towards a Humanistic Model of Decision-making in an Organizational Context" (June 30—July 2, 2008); Josep M. Rosanas & Manuel Velilla (2005) "The Ethics of Management Control Systems: Developing Technical and Moral Values," Journal of Business Ethics (2005) at 57:83–96.

74.   Pérez-López's theory of management in human organizations considers the human person a "problem solver" whose action is ordered to achieving satisfactions of various kinds, specifically, sense-related, cognitive and affective. *A priori* evaluations of expected satisfactions from the results of alternative action plans provide motives for action. Satisfaction depends

upon both the actual, *a posteriori* results of action, and a person's capacities for experiencing the full range of satisfactions. These capacities change according to evaluations made and satisfactions experienced in prior decisions. Every "problem" or event necessitating a decision is thus an opportunity to experience satisfaction or dissatisfaction, and for augmenting or eroding the capacities to experience them in the future. Each event presents the decision maker with an immediate objective, the accomplishment of which occasions the development of greater or lesser capacities (for experiencing across-the-board satisfactions in the future). As the person is a dynamic, changeable being at the level of "capacity," decision making has profound consequences for her and, derivatively, her organization, or *polis*.

75.   In addition to Ebbers and Sullivan, other accounting managers sentenced for misdeeds in the fraud were Buford "Buddy" Yates (1 year and a day in jail), David Myers (1 year and a day in jail), Betty Vinson (5 months in jail and 5 months of house arrest) and Troy Normand (3 years probation with no jail time, ostensibly because he'd attempted to resign his position at WorldCom).

CHAPTER 2

DOES CORPORATE SOCIAL RESPONSIBILITY AFFECT CONSUMER BEHAVIOR?

Larry W. Howard

Studies examining relationships between corporate social performance and economic performance are gathering. Hardly any of this research, however, relates corporate social performance to consumer attitudes and behaviors. I called 471 people randomly selected from mid-state telephone books in a Southeastern U.S. state to ask them about this relationship. The overwhelming majority indicated that information about a company's socially responsible actions would positively influence their intentions to purchase that company's products. Likewise, the vast majority indicated that socially irresponsible corporate activities would influence them to boycott the company. I discuss some implications and limitations of these findings. In the final analysis, it would seem that doing good can help a company do well.

What do Adelphia, Enron, Global Crossing, HealthSouth, Tyco, and WorldCom all have in common? Of course, these companies share recent histories of scandalous management. The details of each case might be a little fuzzy in the public mind. But the scoundrels who previously led these businesses have etched a public memory of corruption. A recent

Doing Well And Good: The Human Face of the New Capitalism, pp. 31–44
Copyright © 2009 by Information Age Publishing
All rights of reproduction in any form reserved.

Gallup poll indicates that people consider CEOs of large companies to be less trustworthy than politicians, lawyers, and stockbrokers, and only slightly more trustworthy than used car dealers. The fact is the term "business ethics" has long been in danger of becoming an oxymoron.[1]

In such a context of distrust, can an organization's reputation for doing good in society help it perform well? Are consumers more likely to purchase a company's products if they have specific information suggesting management is trying to be socially responsible? Or will information about a company's "dirty deeds" sway consumers to boycott the company? Or, would people simply not care? There is not much research that investigates these questions.[2]

I conducted a telephone survey to ask such questions. I wanted to find out if good deeds would lead people to be more likely to do business with a company. I also asked if bad deeds would make them less likely to do business with a company. Before reporting the results, in the next sections I clarify the concepts and study rationale.

WHAT IS CORPORATE SOCIAL RESPONSIBILITY?

The phrase "corporate social responsibility" is often misunderstood. It implies that nameless and faceless organizations are responsible to society. Instead, a company's managers are responsible. They choose the degree of responsibility they are going to demonstrate to their company's stakeholders. Stakeholders are groups that have something to gain or lose because of their relationship with the company. Some stakeholders are internal, like employees and stockholders/owners. Other stakeholders are external, including customers, suppliers, and people and entities representing the environment and society at large. Each stakeholder group retains certain rights to participate in and influence corporate actions that have relevance to the group.[3] Managers behave irresponsibly when they act merely in their own self-interest, or the interest of one favorite stakeholder at the expense of others. Kenneth Lay of Enron, Bernard Ebbers of WorldCom, and John Rigas of Adelphia, for example, have behaved irresponsibly. The actions of a single person in a company can shape the reputation of the entire organization.

As I see it, there are four different levels of social responsibility: economic, legal, ethical, and discretionary.[4] The first level refers to maximizing economic returns to the company. Managers are responsible when they operate "within the rules of the game."[5] These rules refer to competing fairly in the marketplace. Fair competition forbids monopolies, for instance, and prohibits what are called predatory practices. It is considered socially responsible to make an honest profit. This means that the company is providing a valued product or service and is maintaining employment. Those are positive outcomes for society. On the other hand, it is considered socially irresponsible to overcharge customers for the benefit of shareholders. For example, inflating phone bills by adding charges for services that would generally be covered by the basic contract is socially irresponsible The same goes for manipulating earnings statements and inflating stock prices to earn bigger executive bonuses.

The second level of social responsibility is the legal level. At this level, managers show a commitment to comply with all relevant laws. They follow the letter of the law even if it requires additional expense to the company. It would be considered socially irresponsible to gain some kind of competitive advantage by breaking the law. For example, hiring illegal immigrants at substandard wages to save money is illegal and socially irresponsible.

Some scholars argue that these first two levels should be taken for granted.[6] The public should expect such behaviors from all managers and all corporations. These scholars claim that the concept of social responsibility requires that managers further some good for society beyond the interests of the firm and the requirements of the law. In any case, consumers might still be affected by learning that a company cheated or broke the law.

The third level of social responsibility is the ethical level. At this level, managers show concern for what they believe is right or good for stakeholders. Rather than merely complying with the letter of the law, managers at this level follow the spirit of the law. For instance, managers of a manufacturing plant who installed updated technology that reduced polluting highly toxic by-products well below levels permitted by law could be considered as behaving socially responsibly. In addition, situations often arise that have consequences for stakeholders but are not covered by any laws. For example, when culprits tampered with Tylenol capsules in 1982, killing seven people in the Chicago area, there was no law telling managers how to respond. Since the incidents seemed to be localized, the FBI advised the company to recall capsules from the Chicago area only. Instead, managers at Johnson and Johnson, the makers of Tylenol, referred to company's credo that identifies their first responsibility as the users of their products. The company recalled all capsules nationwide. They also offered full refunds to customers who had any Tylenol capsules at home. The move cost the company about $180 million This generally is considered ethical because it was the right thing to do, in terms of the credo, and it was in the best safety interests of the company's customers. Most would consider it socially irresponsible, on the other hand, if the company had tried to cover up the incident and done nothing.

The fourth level of social responsibility is discretionary. Managers demonstrate discretionary social responsibility when they voluntarily take actions to improve society. Such actions may not be directly related to the company's normal operations. Managers at this level recognize that they control needed resources that are not available to the general public. They also recognize a public trust that allows the company to operate. They assume responsibility for returning that trust.

Ronald McDonald House is an example of discretionary social responsibility. Fred Hill, a football player with the Philadelphia Eagles in 1974, had a very sick child in Temple University Hospital. He met parents of other sick children at the hospital. Many of these other parents had no place in town to stay. Hotels were too expensive. With the help of fundraising by McDonald's franchise owners, he and other players fixed up a nearby tenement building and converted it into free housing for such parents. Since then, McDonald's has helped to open nearly 240 Ronald McDonald Houses in 25 countries. This program has nothing to do with McDonald's fundamental business, but it has helped more than 10 million families worldwide.

Exploiting victims of natural disasters, on the other hand, is an example of social irresponsibility. There were several such instances following recent hurricanes in the Southeastern United States. Some hotels quadrupled rates. Gas stations doubled gas prices. Construction companies increased prices of repairs multiples of the increased costs they faced for materials. Retailers of scarce and vital consumer products gouged customers. These examples do not illustrate the law of supply and demand. Rather, they illustrate greed and discretionary social irresponsibility Even in circumstances where escalated prices of some commodities attract additional suppliers, thereby eventually driving those prices back down, economic principles will not effectively govern humanitarian, and social responsibilities to avoid the price-gouging of vulnerable peoples. The essence of understanding social responsibility is the recognition that corporations are not merely economic institutions but they are also citizens of a broader social, political, and cultural community. It is up to the corporation's managers to enact that citizenship.

A company's social performance refers to the level of social responsibility reflected by the actions of that company's personnel—especially its managers. People disagree about the level of social performance managers should pursue. Some argue that shareholders own the company and managers should not spend the owners' money on social causes.[7] Others argue that a good reputation is essential. They claim that only socially responsible companies can survive in the long term.[8] This debate tends to emphasize the economic virtues only of social performance. It is not a moral debate. It is not even a philosophical debate. In fact, this debate would be largely moot if socially responsible actions were also good for business. But are they?

WHY WOULD CONSUMERS CARE ABOUT CORPORATE SOCIAL PERFORMANCE?

Information about a company's social performance should affect most consumers' intentions regarding buying the company's products or services.[9] Social responsibility issues tend to contain ethical content. That is, social performance often reflects choices in terms of right and wrong or good and bad.

According to theory, intention to purchase a company's product may be affected in two ways.[10] First, information about a company's social performance might directly affect the consumer's attitude toward buying the product. Many consumers will want to support companies that do right and do good deeds. And they will not want to support companies that do wrong and do bad deeds.

Second, if a person thinks that others either approve or disapprove of supporting the company by buying its products or services, they might be swayed to think accordingly. This influence often depends on who the other people are. Opinions of people more central in the individual's life will be more important. It also depends on how strongly others are perceived to believe the way they do. This influence also depends on how strongly the person feels obligated to agree with the others. Finally, it depends on whether or not the person believes he or she can freely decide one way or the other.

Some consumers may be more affected by social performance than others. In particular, women and older adults might tend to be more sensitive to such matters.[11] From an early age, women are conditioned in our culture to reason differently than men. They are taught to think more in terms of relationships than rules. Women are socialized to be more caring and are often reported to behave more ethically than men.[12]

Social performance is also more likely to affect older adults than young people. Ethical reasoning ability is related to cognitive ability in general. Both abilities develop over years. Although changes in cognitive functioning and moral reasoning will certainly occur throughout the lifespan, apparently most people plateau at their most mature level of moral reasoning by the time they reach age 30.[13]

Of course, some people may not be affected at all by a company's social performance.[14] Some people do not care about a company's policies or practices. They are only concerned with the product. Some people also do not care what other people think.

In summary, theories suggest that most consumers will be affected by social performance information. Most consumers will be more likely to form purchase or boycott intentions based on social performance information. By the same token, not everyone will be so influenced. Men and younger consumers will probably be less affected.

DO CONSUMERS CARE ABOUT SOCIAL PERFORMANCE?

We called 471 people randomly selected from phone books covering three mid-state counties of a Southeastern U.S. state. Most (368) were over 30 years old, and 53% (250) were women. We asked these consumers whether they would buy a hypothetical company's products under eight different conditions. Four conditions reflected positive social performance and four conditions reflected negative social performance. We created one "good" item for each of the four levels of social responsibility. Four "bad" items reflected four levels of irresponsible actions, respectively. Each time they were asked to indicate the likelihood that the social performance information would affect their decision on a scale of 1 to 5, where: 1 = definitely would not buy; 2 = probably would not buy; 3 = no effect; 4 = probably would buy; and 5 = definitely would buy. The items are presented in Table 2.1 below.

Table 2.1 also reports the proportions of survey respondents who indicated they would be more likely to buy a company's product, less likely to buy, or not effected by each of the eight social performance items. I conducted a series of analyses on the data. The results I summarize next were all supported by statistically significant effects.

For positive information regarding corporate social responsibility, 78.1% indicated that they would be more likely to buy the company's products. About 13.7% indicated their purchase decision would not be affected by favorable information about social performance. On a scale of 1-5, where 3 represented "no effect," the average scores for the "good" items were 4.50, 4.08, 4.20, and 4.14, for positive levels of social performance 1 through 4, respectively. The overall average of the good items was 4.23.

These scores all indicate that, on average, "good" deeds increased consumers' purchase intentions. The influence of good deeds generally declined as the level of social performance became increasingly abstract and distant from the consumer. Although purchase intentions were significantly higher for good item 1 than for good item 2, for instance, scores for the other good items were not significantly different.

For negative information regarding corporate social responsibility, 80.7% indicated they would be unlikely to buy the company's products

Table 2.1.   Proportions of Responses Across Social Performance Items

Item Label	Item "How would it affect your decision whether or not to buy a company's products if you knew that ..."	Definitely/ Probably Would Not Buy	No Effect	Definitely/ Probably Would Buy
Good 1	... the company responded quickly to customer complaints by paying full refunds.	5.3	5.9	88.5
Good 2	... the company complied with all legal requirements for waste disposal, even though many competitors did not.	8.5	16.6	72.8
Good 3	... the company had immediately recalled products it discovered were unsafe, even though they were not required to do so.	9.1	11.3	78.8
Good 4	... the company contributed generously to non-profit medical research.	5.8	20.8	72.4
Bad 1	... the company regularly faced accusations that it knowingly overcharged customers.	94.2	4.2	0.6
Bad 2	... the company employed illegal immigrants at sub-minimum wages.	79.8	14.4	4.6
Bad 3	... the company had used tax loopholes to pay bigger bonuses to top managers.	73.6	17.2	7.4
Bad 4	... the company had made huge profits from disaster relief funds.	75.2	15.1	5.5

and instead boycott the company. About 12.7% of respondents indicated that their purchase/boycott decision would not be affected by negative social performance information. Averages for the four levels of bad social performance were 1.18%, 1.58%, 1.75%, and 1.57%, respectively. The overall average for the bad items was 1.52%.

These scores indicate that, on average, "bad" social performance significantly increased these consumers' intentions to boycott the company's products. The effect of bad deeds also declined as those deeds became more abstract and distant from the consumer. Boycott intentions were significantly higher for level 1 of bad performance than for level 2, for instance, and they were significantly higher for level 2 than for level 3. Overall, the effect of bad information was stronger than the effect of good information. Previous research has also reported that people seem to be more sensitive to negative social performance than they are to positive social performance.[15]

On average, social performance information was more important to women than it was to men. Positive social performance was more likely to increase purchase intentions of women than it was men. Negative social performance was also more likely to increase boycott intentions of women that it was men.

Similarly, social performance information was more important to older adults, on average, than it was to younger consumers. Positive social performance was more likely to increase purchase intentions of people 30 and older than it was consumers under 30 years old. Negative social performance was also more likely to increase boycott intentions of people 30 and older than it was younger consumers.

I also found a combined effect of age and gender. Young men were the least likely to be influenced by information about either a company's good deeds or a company's bad deeds. In contrast, women who were at least 30 years old were the most likely to boycott a company's products because of irresponsible social performance. While these results were statistically significant, the effects of age and gender were quite small, associated with about four percent of the variance in either purchase or boycott intentions.

In summary, these consumers overwhelmingly indicated that corporate social performance would impact their purchase or boycott intentions. Good deeds encourage buying. Bad deeds discourage it. Women care more than men. Adults over 30 care more than younger consumers.

CONCLUSIONS, CAVEATS, AND LESSONS: DOING GOOD AND DOING WELL

We placed calls to nearly 500 people and asked them whether or not information about a company's social responsibility would influence their intentions to purchase products or boycott products from that company. About 13% of all respondents indicated that such information would not affect their purchase or boycott intentions. The overwhelming majority of respondents indicated that it would.

Of course, I did not measure actual consumer behavior. There are several reasons that an intention to buy or boycott might not translate into actual behavior. We are all familiar with adages about the futility of good intentions. We can neither assume with complete confidence that people will buy a company's products when they say they will nor that people are not going to buy a company's products even when they say they definitely won't. Furthermore, the companies and products in this study were all hypothetical, unbranded, and ostensibly immaterial. There is no obvious reason to presume that these consumers had any interest one way or the other in imaginary companies or their products. Furthermore, just as the examples given earlier represent single pieces of evidence regarding social responsibility, most companies probably present a mix of evidence, some good and some bad. Consequently, I wouldn't advocate bulking up inventory to meet increased demand simply because a manager gave a refund without arguing about it. Nor would I advise filing bankruptcy just because a salesperson got caught over-charging a customer.

By the same token, a sizable body of research documents the strong predictive validity of intentions as precursors of behavior.[16] In fact, the single best predictor of behavior is intention. Recognizing this, many marketing strategies are designed to arouse interest in and desire for their products, pushing eventually for action. Furthermore, an organization's reputation is rarely built upon a single incident or episode. Each incident represents a brick. It may take many bricks to build a solid reputation. Therefore, I recommend that managers learn to recognize and respond appropriately to all actions that might signal social performance to stakeholders. Encourage good deeds and discourage bad deeds.

The present results suggest that more proximal and concrete economic activities might be more influential in shaping buying or boycotting intentions. By the same token, more distal and abstract social performance activities also had impact. In either case, long-term effects are hard to predict. One of the reasons that research investigating relationships between firm social performance and financial performance has been inconsistent may be that there is a correspondence between the level of social performance and the type—short-term versus long-term—of financial performance. This issue is sometimes referred to as the "bandwidth-fidelity" problem. In the future, social performance scholars need to pay more attention to this issue.

The primary finding of this study is straightforward. Socially responsible behavior at all levels of social responsibility helps shape consumer purchase intentions. It may or may not be sufficient. It may or may not be necessary. But it helps. Likewise, irresponsible behavior hurts. Results of this study contribute additional useful insights.

I opened this chapter by alluding to the reprehensible behavior of some high-profile executives. That might have been a little misleading. Certainly the Bernie Ebbers, Kenneth Lays, and John Rigases of the world are scoundrels capable of single-handedly ruining entire companies. In addition, we know that the single biggest influence on the ethical or unethical behavior of employees is the behavior of their bosses. Therefore, calling attention to and punishing the bad deeds of such persons is vital. But the subject of corporate social responsibility is not merely the actions of executives.

Social responsibility is the business of all people in business. Workers and managers at any level of the organization's hierarchy can commit "good" or "bad" social performance. A company's representatives who actually deliver its products and services need to be made aware of their roles as ambassadors for their firms. It does not matter what their hierarchical level may be. These ambassadors need training. They need guidance. They need help. Companies that seek to build their reputations for positive social performance need to begin by building corporate cultures of good deeds.

Results of the current study suggest that people over 30 may be more likely to recognize the moral, ethical, or socially-responsible content of information. They may also feel more compelled to use this information in forming purchase or boycott intentions. A corresponding argument is that older adults may feel more compelled than younger adults to behave socially responsibly. Younger people may be less likely to recognize the value in "good" deeds. They may be less likely to recognize the costs in cheating.

I am not suggesting that young people are inherently unethical. Rather, I am saying that the results of this study are consistent with an extraordinary body of evidence that younger adults have not yet had the time to fully develop their moral compasses There is also emerging evidence, thanks to technological developments in functional magnetic resonance imaging, that the human brain has not fully developed until their early twenties. Neuroscientists now know that the frontal cortex, that part of the brain that governs impulsiveness, judgments, foresight of consequences, and other characteristics that make people morally responsible is the last part of the brain to mature.[17] Thus, managers in organizations need to ensure that their younger employees (especially) receive social responsibility training. Internal systems, including performance appraisals, compensation, and promotions must reinforce socially responsible behaviors. These systems also need to associate irresponsible behaviors with undesirable outcomes and make bad deeds less desirable and more difficult.

Women in our study were more affected than men by social performance information. Perhaps women have a higher sensitivity toward the ethical content of corporate social performance. Maybe they considered the social implications of business practices more important criteria for shaping purchasing and boycotting intentions. The neuroscience cited above also indicates that there are indeed differences in the rates of brain maturation between males and females. The frontal cortex of womens' brains tends to mature a little earlier than men. Previous theory and research suggests that some gender differences might constitute an artifact of socialization processes embedded in the culture. Consequently, some attitudinal and behavioral differences associated with gender may be the combined product of differences in neurology, genetics, and culture. Therefore, some gender differences may be subject to change over time, and there may be cross-cultural differences. For the time being, however, these results indicate that managers need to spend extra energy steering male employees in the right direction. They also imply that more women might be more effectively positioned to manage social responsibility and social marketing programs.

I also need to note that, while we found differences between age groups and genders, these differences were rather small. Recall that between 78% and 81% of all people called indicated that social performance information would influence their purchase or boycott intentions, respectively. Gender and age differences affected these proportions by about 4%, plus or minus. Consequently, gender and age differences led to extremes but did not shape the direction of attitudes. The fundamental conclusions remain the same:

- Socially responsible behavior affects consumers' intentions.
- Good deeds increase purchase intentions.
- Bad deeds increase boycott intentions.
- Every member of the organization has
- social responsibility.
- Every member of the organization needs to be trained in social responsibility.
- Doing good can help a company do well.

NOTES

1. Alsop, R. J. 2004. *The 18 Immutable Laws of Corporate Reputation.* New York: Free Press.
2. Meijer, M. & Schuyt, T. 2005. Corporate social performance as a bottom line for consumers. *Business & Society, 44*: 442–461.
3. Evan, W. M., & Freeman, R. E. 1988. A stakeholder theory of the modern corporation: Kantian capitalism. In T. Beauchamp & N. Bowie (Eds.), *Ethical Theory and Business*, pp. 101–105. Englewood Cliffs, NJ: Prentice-Hall.
4. Carroll, A. 1979. A three-dimensional conceptual model of corporate performance, *Academy of Management Review, 4:* 497–505.
5. Friedman, M. 1962. *Capitalism and Freedom.* Chicago: University of Chicago Press.
6. McWilliams, A., & Siegel, D. 2001. Corporate social responsibility: A theory of the firm perspective, *Academy of Manaagement Review, 26:* 117–126.
7. Friedman, *ibid.*; Connolly, T., Conlon, E. J., & Deutsch, S. J. 1980. Organizational effectiveness: a multiple constituency approach. *Academy of Management Review 5:* 211–217; Evan & Freeman, *ibid*; Lachman, R., & Wolfe, R. A. 1997. The interface of organizational effectiveness and corporate social performance. *Business and Society, 36:* 194–214; Quinn, R. E., & Rohrbaugh, J. 1983. A spatial model of effectiveness criteria: Towards a

competing values approach to organizational analysis. *Management Science, 29:* 363–377.

8.   Connolly, Conlon, & Deutsch, *ibid*; Evan & Freeman, *ibid*; Lachman & Wolfe, *ibid*; Quinn & Rohrbaugh, *ibid*; Fombrun, C. J. 1996. *Reputation: Realizing Value from the Corporate Image.* Boston, MA: Harvard Business School Press; Goldsmith, R. E., Lafferty, B. A. & Newell, S. J. 2000. The impact of corporate credibility and celebrity credibility on consumer reaction to advertisements and brands. *Journal of Advertising 29*(3): 43–54; Lafferty, B. A., & Goldsmith, R. E. 1999. Corporate credibility's role in consumers' attitudes and purchase intentions when a high versus a low credibility endorser is used in the ad. *Journal of Business Research 44*(2): 109–116; Roberts, S. 2003. Supply chain specific? Understanding the patchy success of ethical sourcing initiatives, *Journal of Business Ethics, 44:* 159–170.

9.   See, for example, Vyakarnam, S. 1992. Social responsibility: what leading companies do. *Long Range Planning, 25:* 59–67; Park, J., Lyon, L., & Cameron, G. T. 2000. Does reputation management reap rewards: A path analysis of corporate reputation advertising's impacts on brand attitudes and purchase decisions, *Web Journal of Mass Communication Research, 4:1* (December) http://scripps.ohiou.edu/wjmcr/; Mohr, L. A., & Webb, D. J. 2005. The effects of corporate social responsibility and price on consumer responses. *Journal of Consumer Affairs, 39:* 121-147; Follows, S. B., & Jobber, D. 2000. Environmentally responsible purchase behavior: a test of a consumer model, *European Journal of Marketing 34*(5/6): 723–746. Fombrun, C. J. 1996. *Reputation: Realizing Value from the Corporate Image.* Boston, MA: Harvard Business School Press.

10. Alsop, *ibid*; Fombrun & Riel, *ibid*; Ajzen, I. 1991. The theory of planned behavior, *Organizational Behavior and Human Decision Processes, 50:* 179–211; Ajzen, I., & Fishbein, M. 1970. The prediction of behavior from attitudinal and normative variables, *Journal of Experimental Social Psychology, 5:* 400–416; Fishbein, M., & Ajzen, I. 1975. *Belief, Attitude, Intention, and Behavior: An Introduction to Theory and Research.* Reading, MA: Addison-Wesley.

11. Kohlberg, L. 1969. Continuities and discontinuities in childhood and adult moral development, *Human Development, 12:* 3-120; Kohlberg, L. 1984. The psychology of moral development: The nature and validity of moral stages. San Francisco, CA: Harper & Row; Meijer & Schuyt, *ibid*; Gilligan, C. 1982. *In a Different Voice: Psychological Theory and Womens' Development.* Cambridge, MA: Harvard University Press; Dawson, L. 1997. Ethical difference between men and women in sales, *Journal of Business Ethics, 16:* 1143–1153.

12. Betz, M., O'Connell, L., & Shepard, J. M. 1989. Gender differences in proclivity for unethical behavior, *Journal of BusinessEthics, 8:* 321–324; Dawson, *ibid*; Glover, S, Bumpus, M., Sharp, G., & Munchus, G. 2002. Gender differences in ethical decision making, *Women in Management Review, 17*(5/6): 217–228; Kohut, G., & Corriher, S. 1994. The relationship of age, gender,

experience and awareness of written ethics policies to business decision making, *SAM Advanced Management Journal, 59*, 1 (Winter): 32–40.

13.   Colby, A., Kohlberg, L., Gibbs, J., & Lieberman, M. 1983. A longitudinal study of moral judgment, *Monographs of the Society for Research in Child Development, 48* (1-2, Serial No. 200).

14.   Brown, T. J., & Dacin, P. A. 1997. The company and the product: Corporate associations and consumer product responses, *Journal of Marketing, 61:* 68-84; Haijat, M. M. 2003. Effects of cause-related marketing on attitudes and purchase intentions: The moderating role of cause involvement and donation size, *Journal of Nonprofit & Public SectorMarketing 11*(1): 93–109; Babin, B. J., Griffin, M., & Boles, J. S. 2004. Buyer reactions to ethical beliefs in the retail environment, *Journal of Business Research, 57:* 1155–1163; Giacolone, R. A., & Jurkiewicz, C. L. 2003. Right from wrong: The influences of spirituality on perceptions of unethical business activities, *Journal of Business Ethics, 46:* 85–97; Butterfield, K. D., Treviño, L. K., & Weaver, G. R. 2000. Moral awareness in business organizations: Influences of issue-related and social context factors, *Human Relations, 53:* 981–1018.

15.   Becker-Olsen, K. L., Cudmore, B. A., & Hill, R. P. 2006. The impact of perceived corporate social responsibility on consumer behavior. *Journal of Business Research, 59:* 46–53; Graham, P., & Fearn, H. 2005. Corporate reputation: What do consumers really care about? *Journal of Advertising Research 45:* 305–313; Meijer & Schuyt, *ibid;* Mohr, L. A., Webb, D. J., & Harris, K. E. 2001. Do consumers expect companies to be socially responsible? The impact of corporate social responsibility on buying behavior. *Journal of Consumer Affairs, 35:* 45-72.

16.   See, for example, Bagozzi, R. P. 1982. A field investigation of causal relations among cognitions, affect, intentions, and behavior, *Journal of Marketing Research 19*(4): 562–583; Bagozzi, R. P., Baumgartner, J., & Yi, Y. 1989. An investigation into the role of intentions as mediators of the attitude-behavior relationship, *Journal of Economic Psychology 10*(1): 35–62; Follows, S. B., & Jobber, D. *ibid;* Hrubes, D., Ajzen, I., & Daigle, J. 2001. Predicting hunting intentions and behavior: An application of the theory of planned behavior, *Leisure Sciences 23*(3): 165–178; Reinecke, J., Schmidt, P., & Ajzen, I. 1996. Application of the theory of planned behavior to adolescents' condom use: A panel study, *Journal of Applied Social Psychology 26* (9): 749–772.

17.   E.g., Blakemore, S. J. 2008. Development of the social brain during adolescence. *The Quarterly Journal of Experimental Psychology 61*(1): 40–49; Conklin, H. M., Luciana, M., Hooper, C. J., & Yarger, R. S. 2007. Working memory performance in typically developing children and adolescents: Behavioral evidence of protracted frontal lobe development. *Developmental Neuropsychology 37*(1): 103-128; Crone, E. A., Donohue, S. E., Honomichl, R., Wendelken, C., & Bunge, S. A. 2006. Brain regions mediating flexible rule use during development. *Journal of Neuroscience 26:* 11239-11247; Lewis, M. D., & Todd, R. M. The self-regulating brain: Cortical-subcortical feedback and the development of intelligent action. *Cognitive Development 22:* 406-430; Romine, C. B., & Reynolds, C. R. 2005. A model

of the development of frontal lobe functioning: Findings from a meta-analysis. *Applied Neuropsychology* 12(4): 190–201; Waber, D. P. De Moor, C., Forbes, P. W., Almli, C. R., Botteron, K. N., Leonard, G., Milovan, D., Paus, T., & Rumsey, J. 2007. The NIH MRI study of normal brain development: Performance of a population of healthy children aged 6 to 18 years on a neuropsychological battery. *Journal of the International Neuropsychological Soceity 13:* 729–746.

CHAPTER 3

FACING THE
STAKEHOLDER TRUST GAP

Michael Pirson

"Business as usual" has come under heavy scrutiny. Current business organizations are facing a predicament that Jackson and Nelson compare to a perfect storm. They argue that in addition to the traditional pressures of competition and short term financial performance no major company can ignore the following threats to long-term corporate success and viability: the crisis of trust, the crisis of inequality, and the crisis of sustainability. In this article I lay out a framework that can help managers to face the current trust crisis and systematically measure and build trust with their stakeholders. Doing well by doing good seems a promising strategy with regard to managing stakeholder trust sustainably.

BUSINESS AS USUAL FACES PROBLEMS

"Business as usual" has come under heavy scrutiny. Public outrage over crooked corporate officers, the looting of pension funds, the defrauding of stockholders, and the wholesale firings of hardworking employees have reached a new high.[1, 2] Not only the anti-globalization movement of the

Doing Well And Good: The Human Face of the New Capitalism, pp. 45–66

far left but also more traditional thinkers and the public are increasingly uncomfortable with corporate power and influence. In September 2000 (even before Enron's collapse), over 70% of Americans surveyed said that business had too much power over important aspects of their lives and too much political influence. Only 4% agreed that companies should have only one purpose, namely to make the most profit for shareholders. Ninety five percent agreed that American corporations should have more than one purpose and additionally, that they owe something to their workers and the communities in which they operate.[3, 4] International surveys on trust in corporations also demonstrate that trust in big business continues to decrease. According to GlobeScan,[5] in 2006, trust in multinational and global companies reached its all time low. In the eyes of bestselling author William Greider,[6] the avatars of capitalism are meeting deeply rooted anger and are blamed for the erosion of family life, the decreased sense of personal and professional security, corroded communities, impoverished spiritual lives, and a devastated natural environment. Overall, the criticism leveled at current capitalism is that it fails to be life-conducive. It is insufficiently set up to fulfill authentic human needs,[7] or in humanistic terms, it fails to make "humans the measure of all things" (Protagoras).

As a result current business organizations are facing a predicament that Jackson and Nelson compare to a "perfect storm." They argue that "despite the ongoing pressures of relentless competition, and the need to deliver short-term financial performance, no major company can ignore and fail to respond to the following threats to long-term corporate success and viability:

- the crisis of trust
- the crisis of inequality
- the crisis of sustainability."

In the following, I will focus on the crisis of trust. I will outline why a trust gap has developed, what trust is and how managers can focus on the causes of low trust levels to effectively build trust. Doing well by doing good is the most sustainable way to close the trust gap and secure ongoing competitiveness.

THE DEVELOPMENT OF A TRUST GAP

Trust has been widely recognized as a key enabler of organizational success. [8] Trust has been shown to facilitate efficient business transactions,[9–11] increase customer satisfaction,[12–14] and enhance employee motivation and commitment.[15, 16] More generally, trust promotes cooperative behavior within organizations[17–19] and between organizational stakeholder groups,[20–22] as it fosters commitment,[14, 23] motivation,[24] creativity, innovation, and knowledge transfer.[25–28] As such, by strengthening relationships between the firm and its various stakeholders (e.g., employees, customers, investors, etc.), trust can serve as a source of competitive advantage for the organization.[22, 29, 30]

The positive effects of trust are only gaining relevance. In a globalizing world the complexity for managers is increasing, more strangers than ever meet and teamwork and networks become more prevalent. Traditional mechanisms of coordination such as power and coercion lose their effectiveness and trust is becoming more important.

The current state of affairs, however, looks bleak in terms of stakeholder trust levels. A global public opinion survey carried out for the World Economic Forum 2006 in 20 countries, for which researchers interviewed more than 20,000 citizens, "paints an alarming picture of declining levels of trust."[31] 1

The survey shows that trust over a range of institutions has dropped significantly since January 2004 to levels not seen since the months following the 9/11 terrorist attacks.

The research conducted by GlobeScan shows that trust in organizations has dramatically declined in 14 countries even after 2001.[2] After recovering trust in 2004 to pre-Enron levels, trust has since declined for both

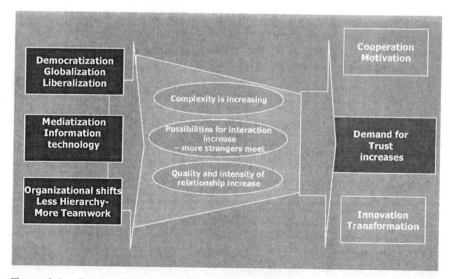

Figure 3.1.   Demand for trust is increasing.

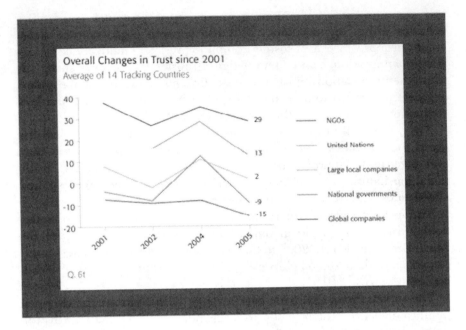

Figure 3.2.   Trust is declining according to World Economic Forum data 2006.

large national companies and for global companies. As of 2005, trust in global companies had reached its lowest level since the tracking began in 2001.[31] 3

A survey conducted by Harris International[32] corroborates these findings. Both in the U.S. and the EU people view big companies by far as the least trustworthy with an average of 65% mistrusting big companies, while the same percentage say they trust the police.[see also other surveys 32, 33, 34, 35]

Many attribute the decline in trust to corporate misconduct and unethical behavior. [33] On an interpersonal level, lack of integrity as well as an increasing opportunism, acquisitiveness, and greed[4] are deplored.[36] Trust on an organizational level is also falling because of an increased shortsightedness and an attitude that only seeks to make a "quick dollar."[33] Harvard Business School professor Lynn Sharp Paine views an increasing discrepancy between external demands and internal demands as the problem. In her book *Value Shift* [4] she argues that stakeholders are increasingly aware of corporate conduct and demand more responsibility and social awareness. Bakan[37] also argues that there is a fundamental problem in the capitalistic system that leads to ever decreasing trust. A growing number of citizens mistrust the capitalist system since it seems unable to solve social problems, but multiplies them instead.[36]

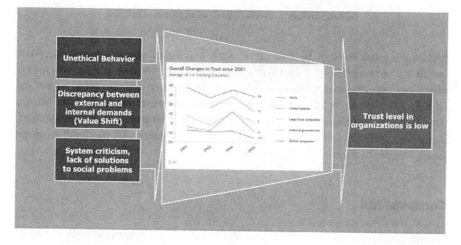

Figure 3.3.   Reasons for trust decline.

On the one hand, political, economic, societal, and technical developments lead to more need for trust, on the other hand, organizations,
especially corporations, do not possess much trust, and in fact are continually losing stakeholders' trust. Hence, a trust gap is emerging which is
likely to impair successful corporate development.

Thus, the question is: How can organizations reestablish and maintain
trust in order to close their trust gap and thereby secure long-term
survival?

WHAT IS TRUST?

Trust is a complex phenomenon that can take various forms. There is general trust and situation-specific trust, emotion-based trust and rational
trust. Luhmann[38] argues that the onset of a trusting relationship is based
on a situation characterized by uncertainty, the risk of personal loss, and
freedom of choice. Seifert[39] views a trust decision based on routine, emotion or rationality. Mayer, Davis and Schoorman and Ripperger claim that
when actors trust, they are making themselves vulnerable to the trustee,
risking that the trustee will behave opportunistically.[40, 41] Many scholars
argue that trust is based on attributions of benevolence, integrity, reliability, competence, openness, and identification. Trust here is thus viewed as
a willingness to become vulnerable to a person, a group, or an organization
based on expectations of trustworthiness along the dimensions of competence, reliability, integrity, transparency, and identification.[40, 42]

MEASURING ORGANIZATIONAL TRUST

Although trust cannot be managed with an input-output equation, trust sensitive management can take decisions that do not harm and even improve the trustworthiness of the organization. To become aware of stakeholder trust, management needs to measure trust levels. To do so, the current literature suggests focusing on competence, benevolence, integrity, transparency, reliability and identification. All of these dimensions I explain in more detail below.

Competence

Organizations are trusted because they deliver a certain service or good that fulfils a need or solves a problem. If the organization is not skilled or competent to do so trust will be low, since good intentions are not enough. Competence is a generalized perception that assumes the effectiveness of the organization's ability to survive in the marketplace. Competence induced trust can include faith in the ability to deliver quality products or services, to compete dynamically, to survive in an ever-changing global economy, or to embrace disruptive technological developments, such as e-business.[43–45]

Reliability

Reliability refers to the expectation of consistent and dependable behavior. Reliability describes the notion of benevolent predictability.[46] Predictability with regard to opportunistic behavior does not constitute reliability.[47] Consistency and congruency between words and actions build trust across stakeholder groups;[48] inconsistencies and incongruence diminish trust.[43]

Integrity

Integrity highlights the moral aspects of trust. Traits that are commonly described as character, honesty, or authenticity constitute an important factor of trust.[46, 49, 50]

Mishra and Spreitzer[51] emphasize, that openness is not enough; an organization that is open about its illegal behavior will not earn trust. To create trust organizational behavior needs to be rooted in ethical behavior.

Ad hoc integrity is seen to lead to mistrust; rather, a historical foundation, that is, a "track-record," needs to be established to maintain or to create trust.[52]

Transparency

Many authors view accountability, openness, and transparency as a key construct of organizational trust. Especially after the corporate scandals in the wake of Enron,[53, 54] openness or transparency describes the extent to which relevant information is not withheld.

Benevolence

Benevolence is seen as the confidence that one's well-being or something one cares about will be protected or not harmed by the trusted party. This constitutes faith in the altruistic and moral disposition of the other. Organizational stakeholders perceive benevolence when concern, care, and interest are expressed by the respective organization.[28] As a result, they have more trust in the organization.

Identification

Another proposed dimension of organizational trust is identification.[43, 46, 55] Pavlou views familiarity and similarity as the basis for identification. Parkhe states that being similar leads to attraction and evokes positive attitudes. Identification in the context of trust especially relates to value congruence. Shockley and Ellis emphasize the importance of shared goals, values, norms, and beliefs.[56–59] With deep identification, organization trust and organizational effectiveness prosper.[43, 60]

MANAGING TRUST

Based on current research I am proposing that managers are on the look out for general managerial behavior that endangers the overall trust climate. In the following I outline several of these within the trust dimensions outlined above. Following these findings managers can deliberate which trust hazards are driving current trust levels in their own organizations and determine how they can be elevated.

Competence

As Shaw argues, in most people's understanding of trust competence does not matter; still, it is a central aspect and needs to be taken into consideration when building trust.[61] The products and services offered by an organization are communicative elements that establish a relationship between clients and an organization. Poor product and service quality directly affects the trust levels of customers. However, poor quality levels will not only affect customers' perception, but also the perception of the company as a whole, and investors, employees and suppliers will trust the organization less as a consequence. Investors in their due diligence process focus strongly on service and product quality, before they invest[62, 63] and employees are more likely to join an organization when quality levels of services and products offered match general expectations.[64]

Some organizations are technically very competent, but lack the capability to change when necessary. Adaptation to markets and flexibility in response to new circumstances is critical to gaining and maintaining the trust of investors as well as of employees. Trust in an organization is coupled with the perceived competence of management and its flexibility to respond to competitive demands.

Trust building essentials		
	Menaces to Trust	Trust Enablers
Competence	low product and service quality	committment to quality
	managerial inflexibility	flexibility
	consistent underperformance	accountability
Reliability	inconsistent messages	clear strategy/clear priorities
	inconsistent standards	simple rules/adherence to rules
	broken promises	choosing promises wisely
Integrity	hidden agendas	value based culture
	opportunism	ethical role models
	machiavellism	
Transparency	opacity	clear communication
	rumors	timely communication
		relevant communication
Benevolence	lack of concern	authentic concern
	autism	stakeholder empowerment/stakeholder dialog
	misplaced benevolence	confronting problems
Identification	value incongruence	value congruence
	profit maximization	merging social and economic imperatives
	organizational setup	different organizational setup
Overall	mistrust	trust

Figure 3.4. Trust building essentials.

Reliability

In the realm of reliability, trust is endangered by (1) inconsistent messages, (2) inconsistent standards, and (3) broken promises. Inconsistent messages are one of the most critical hazards to building and maintaining trust. These inconsistent messages can be either verbal or behavioral. In the example below one critical barrier to trust was the perceived inconsistency in messages by top management.

Asking the middle managers in the organization how they perceived the current change processes, many expressed their skepticism towards top management.

> Interviewer: So, why are you skeptical?
> Manager: You know, I have been here for 15 years and we have had many attempts at trying to change the situation. They never worked. The boss says one thing and then does another. I don't believe that this time it will be different. We will come up with a plan to change and then continue as usual.

Top management declared it supported the changes middle management had proposed, but top management's actions undermined these changes.

> Manager: Well you know, at first it seemed like he supported the new team structure, but all the decisions we agreed on in our team, he just doesn't care about. He decides his way, like always.

According to respondents, teamwork was encouraged and more active participation by all employees demanded. However, when middle and lower management took decisions, senior management interfered and sometimes reversed outcomes. Consequently, trust was quickly dissolved and motivation and commitment lowered. Inconsistent messages can occur anywhere in an organization, from senior managers on down.

The second problem and source of mistrust is an inconsistency of standards across stakeholders and within stakeholder groups. As Slavio, an immigrant cab driver in Boston remarked:

> I do not trust my employer, because he prefers white, American-born cab drivers. He gives the good rides to the guys he knows, not to anybody else.

Similar reactions are expressed by employees of a nursing home, who mistrust their leadership because they employ different standards.

Interviewer: What incident destroyed your trust?

Employee: Scheduled vacations were not granted to the employees, not because there was a lack of personnel, but because leadership went on vacation.

Inconsistent standards for leadership and employees are a common cause of mistrust. Galford and Drapeau claim that employees keep score relentlessly and that any type of preferential treatment engenders cynicism in the rest of the organization.

Broken promises are a third major factor leading to losses in trust. According to Elangovan and Shapiro,[52] the issue of broken promises concerns not only promises that are made explicitly, but extends to all violations of societal norms or social contracts. Task or value-related violations of expectations can cause trust to disappear especially when these expectations are personal and pivotal to the relationship.[52] If the expectations are not pivotal, then their violation is not significant to the relationship and will most likely be excused, ignored, or viewed as a disappointment.[65] But in situations where violated expectations have serious consequences, such as not receiving a contract because technical gear was not delivered in time, trust is broken and future cooperation endangered.

Integrity

Hazards to trust are many in the field of integrity but can be categorized under the rubric of (1) hidden agendas, (2) opportunism, and (3) Machiavellism.

Some organizations are not trusted since a hidden agenda is assumed.

Interviewer: Okay and what do you associate with trustworthiness?

Respondent: ... some institutions are more trustworthy than others. I would never trust scientology for example, or, sects or, companies that work with global systems, with details that are not communicated in the sales pitch; that now are written in the small details of the contract, fitness studios with long periods to give notice. These things are not trustworthy.

Interviewer: Okay, ... scientology or sects because of what exactly ...
               you don't trust...?

Respondent: Hidden agenda. Manipulations. Not acting in the inter-
               est of the individual, financial gains, no win/win/ strate-
               gies.

Manipulations and hidden agendas are assumed for some organizations, but also concern relationships with teammates or leaders.

Employee: ... the important thing is that you can trust people in
               your team. Some people are not reliable and they just
               abuse you, they play a "false game' just trying to look
               good in front of superiors.

In many organizations trust is low because people do not trust the motivation of peers, subordinates, superiors or partners. In many cases hidden agendas are assumed; employees question motives of their leaders, managers the motivation of investors, while members of society question the motivation of companies in general. Whatever the communicated goal of an organization, most stakeholders I interviewed assume profit maximization is the real motivation behind a business.

Interviewer: So, would you say you trust businesses in general?

Respondent: ... for businesses in general [my trust] would be quite
               low.

Interviewer: Because?

Respondent: Because, well they're profit motivated, and a lot of them,
               actually with those businesses that you only have a one
               time relation with, those I believe [are] just, ... basically,
               out to maximize profit from you.

Profit maximization, seen as the real motive for many businesses, lowers stakeholder trust. It is interesting to note that respondents who were intensively exposed to business practices are more mistrusting than less informed respondents.

A second hazard to trust is opportunism. Opportunism as Williamson defined it is "self-interest seeking with guile." Respondents often describe their environment as one based on a philosophy of opportunism that leads to a heightened sense of betrayal. In a very drastic case of opportunism, one respondent reported that he was removed as CEO of his own company, because other employees expected better compensation with a new CEO. He recounted the story:

The guy entered the company through a capital increase. He took care of distribution [within the company] and negotiated with banks. I took vacations for the first time after 4 and ½ years and the business was debt free by then. Somehow, when I was gone, the supervisory board decided that the situation was very terrible, even though the protocol says everything was fine.... However, when I came back from the vacation, the same guy was CEO and then I knew they played a "false game." Shortly after the new CEO took office the payment for all who supported him was increased, but only after 6 months they filed for bankruptcy.

A staged takeover led to the CEO's replacement and indeed compensation packages were drastically increased but resulted in filing for bankruptcy the following year. This maneuver had drastic long-term consequences for employees' trust in the organization.

One employee said:

At first we felt it was strange that the founder of the company and the person who owns most of the shares, can be kicked out that easily by someone who only joined the firm six months ago. But my trust was only really decreased when we saw how the new leadership just spent money on all these unnecessary things such as logos or company cars etc. while we were cash strapped in the technology area, which was core of our business.

Self-interest seeking with guile by the new CEO led to a tremendous decrease in trust within the company. It also led to the creation of two rival firms by former employees, who left the company because they could not identify with the organization anymore.

This might be an extreme case of personal opportunism, but according to Hogan and Hogan[66] opportunistic betrayals in everyday life, ranging from failing to return a phone call to deliberately sabotaging another person's reputation, are relatively common. In a study by Jones and Burdette [65] focusing on betrayal in the workplace, 25.4% of men and 9.4% of women identified work-related episodes in which their coworkers or bosses had betrayed them. According to Elangovan and Shapiro,[52] betrayal episodes in the workplace are not only prevalent, but their effects are lasting. Opportunistic betrayal menaces trust, motivation and commitment in the very long term. Stakeholders do not build trust when they believe they are a resource or pawn in a political game. While "playing politics" and "shrewd maneuvering" are often touted as great business skills, they do not lead to a heightened sense of integrity. Macchiavellistic maneuvering, playing politics and treating stakeholders as a means rather than an end are behaviors that menace trust.

Transparency

Opacity and its ensuing rumors are hazards to achieving trust through transparency. Bakan claims that corporations are often rightly mistrusted since they are not open about their activities and try to conceal negative actions. In many organizations leadership does not communicate relevant information in a timely fashion. When relevant information is withheld stakeholders are left in a "guessing game." Galford and Drapeau posit that insufficient communication leads to over-interpretation of available facts.

> Employees know that something important is going on, but if they don't know the full story (maybe the full story doesn't exist yet), they'll quite naturally overinterpret any share of information they get their hands on. Rumors circulate, and, in most cases, they'll be negative rather than positive.[67]

Benevolence

Hazards to trust in the realm of benevolence are many. Concern and the lack thereof are often viewed as reasons for mistrust. Management autism often causes lack of concern, and misplaced benevolence also seriously undermines organizational trust.

As shown in the 1995 Brent Spar case, Shell had acquired a reputation as an environmental polluter. When they announced that sinking the drilling platform was economically and ecologically the best alternative (which later proved to be true), the German public mistrusted these statements and massive boycotts ensued. Shell learned the hard way that lack of concern fuels mistrust, and is now actively engaging in stakeholder dialog to demonstrate concern and build trust.

Lack of concern and "autism" often go hand in hand in organizations. In many business organizations, for example, top management is unidimensionally interested in catering to shareholders. Many businesses are often accused of only caring about shareholders. Critics argue that they cut themselves off from societal dialogs. Autism can be highly beneficial when firms only seek short-term results (see Deutsche Bank). However the lack of connection achieved through societal discourses regarding decisions hurts reputations and undermines trust.

In many other cases misplaced benevolence destroys trust. Galford and Drapeau report:

> Anyone who has spent time in business has encountered at least one person who is, simply and sadly, so out of his league that everyone is stupefied that

he's in the position at all. His colleagues wonder why his supervisors don't do something. His direct reports learn to work around him, but it's a daily struggle. Because the person in question isn't harming anyone or anything on purpose, his supervisor is reluctant to punish him. But incompetence destroys value, and it destroys ... trust.

Removing such people from their positions of responsibility can enable trust within organizations, and keeping such people out of misplaced concern will undermine it.

Identification

While current literature does not focus on value incongruence as a reason for mistrust very much, I find in my research that it is crucial. Many interviewees indirectly question the organizational setup that requires businesses to maximize profit and forces firms to think short term.

Many interviewees doubted the motivations and values of business organizations. A central issue that was consistently raised across the interviews was a lack of identification with business organizations because of profit maximization goals.

> Interviewer: So can you tell me why you don't trust any bank?
> Client: that's a difficult question. I think they only care about the money which is on the account and how they can use the last dollar of every customer. But, it's not really about your money, 'cause you don't get really a lot of interest on your savings account either. And, you actually pay more interest if you overcharge your account, ... I don't think this is the way it should be.

A former employee of a consulting firm states that he hedges a general mistrust towards the organization because it is profit motivated.

> Former Employee: ... I trust [organization X] less, because what I don't like about the organization is that they are basically profit motivated.

Many respondents placed trust in business organizations rather low, while trust in churches, NGOs, or several state-run organizations, such as the police was quite high.

Interviewer: Which societal organizations do you trust the most and which the least?

Respondent: ... trust in the church and NGOs is high, business I trust much less, for example the pharma industry is only interested in making profit. They are aligned in a way that they have to screw you over...

Another respondent argued in a similar fashion.

Interviewer: So, would you say you trust businesses in general?

Respondent: ... for businesses in general [my trust] would be quite low.

Interviewer: Because?

Respondent: Because, well they're profit motivated ...

Many respondents rate trust in organizations with a social purpose much higher and could not identify with the profit maximization objective pursued by most businesses. Interestingly, especially respondents with considerable business experience and management insight reported a high level of disconnect with the values of business organizations. Judging from my sample it seems that profit maximization, the central objective of shareholder capitalism, severely undermines trust in business organizations. Hart[68] concurs and posits the short-term focus of businesses and lack of concern about environmental destruction are common reasons for mistrust. Some respondents argued that family businesses or NGOs do not succumb to the pressures of the financial markets and hence can be more socially responsible. Bakan[37] blames pressures generated by financial markets for detrimental effects on society and argues that the setting up of the corporations as organizations with limited liability as a basic reason for justifying mistrust.

Mistrust—the Biggest Enemy of Trust

Another hazard of trust which receives very little attention in the management literature is *mistrust*. From my findings I posit that mistrust is the biggest enemy of trust and when focusing on building trust, signs of mistrust need to be understood. Ripperger and Luhmann argue that mistrust generates a downward spiral effect. Signs of mistrust create mistrust as a self-fulfilling prophecy. Malhotra and Murnighan[69] report that signals of mistrust such as highly specified contracts, result in lower levels of cooperation. Sprenger states organizations that monitor employee attendance, report lower levels of productivity. Shaw recounts the story of Bill

Packard who noticed that at his former employer, General Electric, tools were safely locked up so that nobody could steal them. This signal of mistrust somehow created a challenge for employees and it became a sport to overcome security controls and soon every worker had a toolset at home. When founding Hewlett & Packard, management decided to trust their employees and not lock anything away; in fact, they encouraged people to take tools home, so they could work on their ideas more. The high levels of innovation experienced at HP are often attributed to the high level of trust.

In most companies control practices undermine trust. Pervasive signals of mistrust, such as detailed contracts, camera monitoring, or incentive schemes based on external motivations undermine trust. The signals of mistrust are often very subtle but powerful and destructive. Trust is undermined by mistrust, a finding that sounds rather banal, but has immense repercussions for management.

Trust as a Self-Fulfilling Prophecy

On the other hand, trust is also a self-fulfilling mechanism, meaning that it grows the more it is employed.[38, 70] Trust is one of the resources that does not adhere to the economic logic: It *increases—not decreases—* when used.

In several interviews respondents powerfully demonstrated the impact of trust on trust. When asked about an incident in which his trust had increased, one employee recounted that his trust increased immensely when leadership expressed their confidence in him to manage a complex project.

> Interviewer: Can you tell me of an incident that increased your trust?
> Respondent: ... I felt it was very positive when in a general meeting leadership said, "Yeah, we think you are the man for the job. We trust you to do that." I just grew about 2 meters. My motivation increased dramatically.

In another incident an employee reported that his trust skyrocketed when he was given responsibility for a small business branch.

> Interviewer: ... and can you tell me of an incident in which your trust increased?
> Respondent: Guess it was when I was working for my first employer, which was a big, traditional Japanese company; and they

usually don't give their younger people too much
responsibility, or too much ... leeway. But, once they
actually gave me the responsibility to run a small, [a]
very small portion of the business.... I felt quite good. I
felt that they trusted me with that, even though it wasn't
really spectacular....

Interviewer: So your trust went up?

Respondent: My trust went up, yeah.

In both incidents employees felt trusted which increased their trust in the
organization tremendously. Luhmann and others thus postulate more
trust in trust and Hoehler[71] views trust as the most effective control.
Many organizations, however, build their processes on the philosophy of
theory X,[72] which basically assumes the negative self-serving nature of
human beings. In recent times organizations based on theory Y, for example Ebay or AES, have continually proven that trust creates trust and
results in higher levels of success.

CONCLUSION

Lack of trust caused by the enemies of trust has serious consequences.
Simons (see also this volume) studied the effects of mistrust in organizations in the hotel industry and found a stunning ripple effect. Hotels
where employees strongly believed that the organization and their managers were trustworthy were substantially more profitable than those that
were not. A one-eighth point improvement in a hotel's score on a 5-point
scale could be expected to increase the hotel's profitability by 2.5% of revenues which translated to a profit increase of more than $250,000 per
year per hotel.

If stakeholders don't trust the organization and its leaders, they'll dis-
engage their cooperative efforts. Clients switch brands, investors
reallocate their funds and suppliers will not deliver their best service.
Employees will look for another job or succumb to inner resignation in
their current job. Organizational confusion, decline in productivity, and
decrease in competitiveness become the norm.

To successfully manage the current trust crisis, a new management
paradigm is therefore needed. "Doing well by doing good" seems a
promising alternative to "business as usual" and can help rebuild trust
lost while restoring much needed competitiveness. When extrapolating
the results presented above, we can envision organizations that are
much better fit to engender high levels of stakeholder trust. As the

opportunistic profit motive is a true barrier to sustained high trust, we need to look at potential alternatives. Non-profit organizations are enjoying much higher levels of trust, because they serve a cause larger than financial profit. Over the time businesses did indeed feel the need for higher level vision/mission statements but those are rarely believed. But how about creating business organizations that actually serve a higher purpose and use financial means to that end? Such organizations do indeed exist: look at for example the Grameen Bank in Bangladesh, the Wainwright Bank in the United States, Mondragon in Spain, and other cooperatives around the world. The new movement to social entrepreneurship also leads the way in creating organizations that are structurally setup to solve social problems and create profit towards that end. A trust based economy needs to restructure its institutions to not reward systemic trust decrease, but even within the current system there are many ways to build and rebuild businesses to enjoy higher levels of stakeholder trust.

DATA SOURCES

1. The survey asked respondents how much they trust each institution "to operate in the best interests of our society." Identical questions were asked in most of the same countries in January 2004, August 2002 and January 2001. Net trust levels are presented here—the difference between the percentage of respondents who express trust and those who express no trust in a given institution. A full report, including charts illustrating all findings, is available at: http://www.weforum.org/trustsurvey.

2. The 14 countries that were tracked are: Argentina, Brazil, Canada, Germany, Great Britain, India, Indonesia, Italy, Mexico, Nigeria, Russia, Spain, Turkey and the United States.

3. These findings are based on a global public opinion poll involving a total of 20,791 interviews with citizens across 20 countries ($n = 1,000$ in most countries), conducted between June and August 2005 by respected research institutes in each participating country, under the leadership of GlobeScan. (A full list of participating institutes, with contact details, is available at: www.weforum.org.) Each country's findings are considered accurate to within 3 percentage points, 19 times out of 20.

4. Tyco Boss Denis Kozlowsky or Richard Grasso of NYSE, who left their respective companies with US$140 million, are cited as examples.

NOTES

1. Pirson, M., *Facing the Trust Gap: How Organizations can measure and manage stakeholder trust.* Dissertation. 2007, St. Gallen: University of St. Gallen.

2. Jackson, I. and J. Nelson, *Profits with Principles- seven strategies for delivering value with values.* 2004, New York: Currency Doubleday.

3. Bernstein, A., *Too much corporate power?*, in *Business Week.* 2000.

4. Sharp Paine, L., *Value Shift: Why Companies Must Merge Social and Financial Imperatives to Achieve Superior Performance.* 2003, New York: McGraw-Hill.

5. Forum, W. E., *Decline in Trust.* 2006, World Economic Forum. http://www.weforum.org/site/homepublic.nsf/Content/Trust+in+Governments,+Corporations+and+Global+Institutions+Continues+to+Decline

6. Greider, W., *The soul of capitalism- opening paths to a moral economy.* 2003, New York: Simon & Schuster.

7. Diener, E. and M. E. P. Seligman, *Beyond money: Toward and economy of well-being.* Psychological Science in the Public Interest,, 2004. *5*: p. 1-31.

8. Davis, F. D., et al., *The trusted general manager and business unit performance: empirical evidence of a competitive advantage.* Strategic Management Journal, 2000. *21*(5): p. 563-576.

9. Noteboom, B., *Trust, opportunism and governance: a process and control model.* Organizational Studies, 1996. *17*(6): p. 985–1010.

10. Williamson, O.E., *Calculativeness, trust, and economic organization.* Journal of Law and Economics, 1993. *36*(1): p. 453-486.

11. Williamson, O.E., *Corporate finance and corporate governance.* Journal of Finance, 1988. *XLIII*(3): p. 567-91.

12. Doney, P. M. and J. P. Cannon, *An examination of the nature of trust in buyer-seller relationships.* Journal of Marketing, 1997. *61*: p. 35-51.

13. Morgan, R.M. and S.D. Hunt, *The commitment-trust theory of relationship marketing.* Journal of Marketing, 1994(58): p. 20-38.

14. Ganesan, S., *Determinants of long-term orientation in buyer-seller relationships.* Journal of Marketing, 1994(April): p. 1-19.

15. Brockner, J., et al., *When trust matters: the moderating effect of outcome favorability.* Administrative Science Quarterly, 1997. *42*.

16. Tyler, T. R., *Cooperation in groups : procedural justice, social identity, and behavioral engagement.* 2000, Philadelphia, PA: Psychology Press.

17. Dirks, K. T. and D. L. Ferrin, *The role of interpersonal trust in organizational settings.* Organization Science, 2001. *12*(4): p. 450-467.

18. Gulati, R. and J.D. Westphal, *Cooperative or controlling? The effects of CEO-board relations and the content of interlocks on the formation of joint ventures.* Administrative Science Quarterly, 1999. *44*: p. 473-506.

19. Williams, M., *In whom we trust: Group membership as an affective context for trust development.* Academy of Management Journal, 2001. *28*(3): p. 377-396.

20.   Gulati, R., *Does familiarity breed trust? The implications of repeated ties for contractual choice in alliances.* Academy of Management Journal, 1995. *38*(1): p. 85-112.

21.   Uzzi, B., *Social structure and competition in interfirm networks: The paradox of embeddedness.* Administrative Science Quarterly, 1997. *42*: p. 35-67.

22.   Jensen, M., *The role of network resources in market entry: Commercial banks' entry into investment banking, 1991-1997.* Administrative Science Quarterly, 2003. *48*: p. 466-497.

23.   Mayer, R. C. and M. B. Gavin, *Trust in management and performance: who minds the shop while the employees watch the boss?* Academy of Management Journal, 2005. *48*(5): p. 874-888.

24.   Dirks, K. T., *The effects of interpersonal trust on work group performance.* Journal of Applied Psychology, 1999. *84*: p. 445-455.

25.   Clegg, C., et al., *Implicating trust in the innovation process.* Journal of Occupational and Organizational Psychology, 2002. *75*(4): p. 409-423.

26.   Tsai, W. and S. Ghoshal, *Social capital and value creation: the role of intrafirm networks,.* Academy of Management Journal, 1998. *41*(4): p. 464-477.

27.   Politis, J. D., *The connection between trust and knowledge management: what are its implications for team performance.* Journal of Knowledge Management, 2003. 7(5): p. 55-66.

28.   Edmondson, A., *Psychological safety and learning behavior in work teams.* Administrative Science Quarterly, 1999. *44*: p. 350-383.

29.   Barney, J. B. and M. H. Hansen, *Trustworthiness as a source of competitive advantage.* Strategic Management Journal, 1994. *15*: p. 175-190.

30.   Nahapiet, J. and S. Ghoshal, *Social capital, intellectual capital, and the organizational advantage.* Academy of Management Review, 1998. *23*(2): p. 242-266.

31.   Forum, W. E., *Decline in Trust.* 2005. p. http://www.weforum.org/site/home-public.nsf/Content/Trust+in+Governments,+Corporations+and+Global+Institutions+Continues+to+Decline

32.   Harris, I., *Trust in Institutions.* 2005.

33.   Jenkins, R. L., *Crisis in confidence in Corporate America.* Mid - American Journal of Business., 2003. *18*(2): p. 5.

34.   Gallup, *Trust in professions.* 2005.

35.   Harris, I., *Trust in professions.* 2002(The Harris Poll. Nov. 14-18, 2002).

36.   von Oetinger, B., *Interview mit Bolko von Oetinger: "Es geht um Vertrauen."* in *Brand Eins.* 2004. p. 60-66.

37.   Bakan, J., *The Corporation : The Pathological Pursuit of Profit and Power.* 2004: Penguin Books, Canada.

38.   Luhmann, N., *Vertrauen: ein Mechanismus zur Reduktion sozialer Komplexität.* 4. ed. 2000, Stuttgart: Lucius& Lucius.

39.   Seifert, M., *Vertrauensmanagement in Unternehmen- eine empirische Studie über Vertrauen zwischen Angestellten und ihren Führungskräften.* 2001, München und Mering: Reiner Hampp Verlag.

40. Mayer, R. C., J. H. Davis, and F. D. Schoorman, *An integrative model of organizational trust*. Academy of Management Review, 1995.

41. Ripperger, T., *Ökonomik des Vertrauens*. Die Einheit der Gesellschaftswissenschaften. 1998, Tübingen: Mohr Siebeck.

42. Pirson, M. and D. Malhotra. *Stakeholder trust, what matters to whom?* in *Academy of Management Conference*. 2006. Atlanta.

43. Shockley-Zalabak, P., K. Ellis, and R. Cesaria, *Measuring Organizational Trust—Trust and Distrust across cultures—The Organizational Trust Index*. 1999, IABC Research Foundation.

44. Jarvenpaa, S. L. and N. Tractinsky, *Consumer trust in an internet store: a cross-cultural validation*. Journal of Computer-Mediated Communication, 1999. 5(2).

45. McKnight, D. H. and N. L. Chervany, *What trust means in e-commerce customer relationships: an interdisciplinary conceptual typology*. International Journal of Electronic Commerce, 2002. 6(2): p. 35-53.

46. Pavlou, P. A., *Institution-based trust in interorganizational exchange relationships: the role of online B2B marketplaces on trust formation*. Journal of Strategic Information Systems, 2002. 11: p. 215-243.

47. Baier, A., *Vertrauen und seine Grenzen*, in *Vertrauen - die Grundlage des sozialen Zusammenhalts*, M. Hartmann and C. Offe, Editors. 2001, Campus: Frankfurt/Main. p. 37-84.

48. Mishra, A. K., *Organizational responses to crisis: The centrality of trust.*, in *Trust in Organizations: Frontiers of Theory and Research*, R. M. Kramer & T. R. Tyler (Eds), Editor. 1996, Sage: Thousand Oaks, CA. p. 261-287.

49. Hoy, W. K. and M. Tschannen-Moran, *Five Faces of Trust: An Empirical Confirmation in Urban Elementary Schools*. Journal of School Leadership, 1999. 9: p. 184-207.

50. Whitener, E. M., et al., *Managers as initiators of trust: An exchange relationship framework for understanding managerial trustworthy behavior*. Academy of Management Review, 1998. 23(3): p. 513-531.

51. Mishra, A. K. and G. M. Spreitzer, *Explaining how survivors respond to downsizing: The roles of trust, empowerment, justice, and work redesign*. Academy of Management Review, 1998. 23(3): p. 567-588.

52. Elangovan, A. R. and D. L. Shapiro, *Betrayal of trust in organizations*. Academy of Management Review, 1998. 23(3): p. 547-567.

53. Turnbull, S., *A new Way to Govern- Organizations and Society after Enron*. 2002, London.

54. Dervitsiotis, K. N., *Beyond stakeholder satisfaction: aiming for a new frontier of sustainable stakeholder trust*. Total Quality Management, 2003. 14(5): p. 511-524.

55. Lewicki, R. J. and B. B. Bunker, *Developing and maintaining trust in work relationships*, in *Trust in organizations: Frontiers of theory and research.*, R. M. Kramer and T. R. Tyler, Editors. 1996, Sage Publications, Inc.: Thousand Oaks, CA,. p. 114-139.

56.   Schein, E. H., *Organizational culture and leadership: A dynamic view*. 1985, San Francisco: Jossey-Bass.

57.   Shockley-Zalabak, P. and D.D. Morley, *Creating a culture: A longitudinal examination of the influence of management and employee values on communication rule stability and emergence*. Human Communication Research, 1994. *20*: p. 334-335.

58.   Shockley-Zalabak, P., D. D. Morley, and R. Cesaria. *Organizational influence processes: Perceptions of values, communication and effectiveness*. in *Organizational Communication at the National Communication Association Convention*. 1997. Chicago.

59.   Ellis, K. and P. Shockley-Zalabak. *Communicating with management: Relating trust to job satisfaction and organizational effectiveness*. in *National Communication Association Convention*. 1999. Chicago, IL, November, 1999.

60.   Lewicki, R. J. and B. B. Bunker, *Trust in relationships: A model of trust development and decline*, in *Conflict, Cooperation, and Justice*, B. B. Bunker and J.Z. Rubin, Editors. 1995, Jossey-Bass: San Francisco, CA. p. 133-173.

61.   Lewis, J. D., *Trusted Partners- How companies build mutual trust and win together*, ed. T. F. Press. 1999, New York: Simon & Schuster Inc.

62.   Aaker, D. A. and R. Jacobson, *The Financial Information Content of Perceived Quality*. Journal of Marketing Research, 1994. *31*(2): p. 191-201.

63.   Stoughton, N. M., K. P. Wong, and J. Zechner, *IPOs and Product Quality*. The Journal of Business, 2001. *74*: p. 375-408.

64.   Fombrun, C. J., *Reputation: Realizing Value from the Corporate Image*. 1996, Boston: Harvard Business School Press.

65.   Jones, W. and M. P. Burdette, *Betrayal in relationships*, in *Perspectives on close relationships*, A. Weber and J. Harvey, Editors. 1994, Allyn and Bacon: Boston.

66.   Hogan, J. and R. Hogan, *The mask of integrity*, in *Citizen espionage:Studies in trust and betrayal*, C. E. R. Carney, Editor. 1994, Praeger: Westport, CT. p. 107-125.

67.   Galford, R. and A. S. Drapeau, *The Enemies of Trust*. Harvard Business Review, 2003: p. 1-7.

68.   Hart, S., *Capitalism at the Crossroads : The Unlimited Business Opportunities in Solving the World's Most Difficult Problems*, ed. W. S. Publishing. 2005.

69.   Malhotra, D. and J. K. Murnighan, *The effects of contracts on interpersonal trust*. Administrative Science Quarterly, 2002. *47*(3): p. 534-559.

70.   Sprenger, R.K., *Vertrauen führt- worauf es im Unternehmen wirklich ankommt*. 2002, Frankfurt am Main: campus.

71.   Hoehler, G., *Die Sinn- Macher. Wer siegen will, muss führen*. 2002: Econ.

72.   McGregor, D., *The human side of business*. 1960.

73.   Galford, R. and A. Seibold Drapeau, *The Enemies of Trust*. Harvard Business Review, 2003: p. 1-7.

PART II

A NEW FOR-PROFIT PARADIGM

CHAPTER 4

BEING SERIOUS ABOUT BEING GOOD

Eugene Heath

Is it possible to live well and to be good? Two popular theories of business ethics, the theory of social responsibility and the stakeholder theory, suggest that commerce must be properly reformed if it is to be ethical. However, neither of these theories is compatible with the actual practice of business as essentially exchange for profit. There is however an alternative account: A life in commerce may be embedded within the virtues of common life, and in this way business and morals will function in tandem.

Is it possible to do well and to be good? Such a question is not peculiarly modern or contemporary, for it was put forth by the ancient Hebrews or Greeks. In its contemporary guise this question is about the moral status of commerce: Is the life of business compatible with a moral life, a life of virtue? For some the clear and obvious answer is "yes." Those who so respond may know or recall specific persons who are both successful and virtuous. However, others may hesitate, perhaps because they know of no such examples or because they do not think that a few examples could resolve the more general question. An even deeper reason for such hesitation may rest on the belief that commerce and morality draw us in

Doing Well And Good: The Human Face of the New Capitalism, pp. 69–85

different, if not opposing, directions. Business and ethics cannot be yoked together so as to enable a person to embark along a path of prosperity and morality—living well and being good.

Many scholars who think and write on business ethics seem to fall into this hesitant group. For them, business or commercial practices are ethically deficient. Unless properly regulated, constrained or channeled, the participants in business will engage in morally dubious conduct, aspire to endeavors that are ethically questionable, or fail to manifest some basic qualities of human moral excellence. According to another (and similar) perspective, commerce and goodness are incompatible because business, like a game, operates within a sphere constituted by practices that are neither moral nor immoral.[1] On this perspective—which is not especially popular with business ethicists—commercial practices acquire a moral justifiability insofar as they generate greater productivity than alternative economic systems. The everyday practices of commerce have no moral worth except for the fact that they are necessary or sufficient for producing goods and services.

It is notable that each of these critical views suggests that commerce and morality diverge. The first assumes that commerce and moral goodness are compatible only if the practice of business and exchange is altered or reformed. The second maintains that business people are engaged in amoral practices justifiable only because these activities generate goods and services otherwise desirable. However, neither characterization offers a fair portrayal of business, at least not in its typical or historical formation in most Western societies. Nor do these characterizations offer an adequate formulation of how commercial practice might reasonably be understood as compatible with moral goodness. There is an alternative conception of business, one that reveals how a person may live a commercial and yet virtuous life. One may live well and be good. How this is possible is the subject of this essay.

A life in commerce may be situated or embedded in the moral virtues of common life.[2] Such a perspective on business and morals also demonstrates a seriousness about business and the moral life that is missing from the critical construals, noted above. To rethink the compatibility of doing well and being good, it is necessary to rediscover how business can be situated within a larger moral life, embedded within an existing moral foundation. In order to grasp the appeal of this conception of commerce, let us first consider the nature of business. We then consider two theories of how to moralize the practice of commerce, the theory of social responsibility and the stakeholder theory. These theories are popular and almost ubiquitous, but in fact neither theory is compatible with business; therefore, neither theory provides an adequate account of how commerce and morals may function in tandem. Such an incompatibility of moral ideal and commerce bears similarity to a thesis broached in the eighteenth century, by Bernard Mandeville, regarding the incompatibility of prosperity and ethical ideal. In the subsequent section we set forth a conception of commerce as compatible with, or embedded within, virtue. In the penultimate section, we take up two objections to this view, followed by some brief concluding remarks.

UNDERSTANDING BUSINESS

In order to consider carefully the compatibility of commerce and goodness, we ought first to acquire an understanding of business. Business is buying and selling, but it is also discovering, producing, growing and creating. These activities reflect the simple truth that human beings have ends or goals and they seek to satisfy these ends or goals through their own labor or by exchange. The activities of business take place within a legal framework of permissions, prohibitions and requirements. Such a framework permits individuals (and groups of individuals) to hold property, including property in one's labor, mind or talents, and allows individuals to satisfy their goals either through their own endeavor or by trade. Laws permit the exchange of property (among other activities), prohibit other deeds (such as forced exchange or fraud), and require yet other actions (adherence to regulation, payment of taxes). These permissions, prohibitions and requirements establish the conditions in which individuals join together for some endeavors (business firms) or work alone; in so doing, individuals produce, create, and innovate, and more generally respond to changing circumstances, new opportunities, and incentives.

The goods and services created by individuals or firms are exchanged with other individuals or firms. Such transactions do not occur only at the level of finished products but also at the early stage of the retrieval of raw materials and during production and manufacture. When two individuals exchange a good each has a stronger preference for the good received than for the good relinquished: If I give you a lemon for your lime, then I value your lime more than my lemon. The amount of any good that I must relinquish in order to attain some other good is the *price*. Since exchange is founded on the preferences of individuals, then so are prices reflective of these preferences. When there is more than one buyer and seller of a good or service, there will be competition among them and a unitary price will emerge. In general, if the price of an item falls, then the demand for that item increases; and if the price rises, then the supply grows. Both buyers and sellers compete with (and among) one another to get the best deal; this competition introduces efficiency into both the production and the marketing of goods and services. Competition, innovation and creativity ensure a growth in productivity, and as productivity rises, so do wages and salaries (as employers compete for the best workers).

From this discussion we discern two important elements of business activity: Profits and prices. Individuals seek to satisfy preferences by trading something of lesser value for something they deem of greater value. In this sense, all production, manufacture, and trade involves a quest for profit, the acquisition of greater value than what was expended. Thus, commerce is transaction for profit. The exchange need not require *monetary* profit, though that is its typical form, but it should involve exchange in order to satisfy the preferences of the traders.[3] How will individuals make their decisions about which preferences to satisfy (and how and when)? In the myriad of trades and decisions about trades, individuals will use prices to guide their choices as to the best means of realizing their ends. Prices inform decisions in the sense that they affect our conduct, but they also inform us in another way: They manifest the preferences of others. Prices move in accordance with preferences, which themselves do not remain constant but vary in relation to changing circumstances and shifting beliefs and desires. The movement of prices signals to us where we might most effectively place our resources or time. Indeed, by conveying a wealth of information not otherwise attainable by single individuals, prices help to coordinate the activities of numerous and often anonymous persons.

With this brief and schematic account, we can grasp more fully how business or commerce is a practice of exchange (for profit) that takes place within a legal framework of property relations and other laws. The characteristics of the market participants, including their beliefs and desires, affect the overall character of business interaction. Dispositions, habits, customs and beliefs affect the conduct of buyers and sellers, creators and consumers, owners and workers—the participants in markets and businesses. However, there is another element of human society that influences commerce: Morals. Before we discuss how commerce might be embedded within morality, let us turn to two popular theories for reconciling commerce and ethics, the theory of social responsibility and that of the stakeholder.

SOCIAL RESPONSIBILITY

The popularity of the concept of social responsibility extends from business ethicists to corporations and the public.[4] Some of this popularity may arise from the assumption that a socially responsible firm is an ethical firm. In other words, social responsibility reconciles commerce with goodness. Indeed, some discussions of social responsibility seem to identify it with ethical action in such a way that a firm is ethical only if it is socially responsible. Other discussions suggest that a firm may be ethical without being socially responsible but that such responsibility would enhance or improve the moral standing of the firm and legitimate it as a corporation.[5] In either case, if businesses engage in socially responsible endeavor, then, according to the theory, so are the practices of commerce rendered ethical. Of course, there are clear counterexamples to the notion that social responsibility will either absolve or prevent sin, as the case of Enron has demonstrated so clearly.[6] Nonetheless, the rhetoric of many business ethicists suggests that business ethics and corporate responsibility refer to the same thing.[7] The identification of the ethics of business and social responsibility may provide but one more barometer of the popularity of the idea of social responsibility but, as argued below, it is a mistaken identification nonetheless.

There exists a fairly wide range of activities to which the appellation "social responsibility" has been affixed. George Brenkert explains how social responsibility may refer to " 'public welfare deficiencies'" including "problems of the inner city, drug problems, poverty, crime, illiteracy" among others.[8] Richard De George describes how the various appeals to social responsibility includes "a grab bag of obligations, some moral and some not."[9] More recently, William C. Frederick has expressed both the expansive nature of the concept and the enthusiasm that it generates:

> In the end, CSR [corporate social responsibility] is about more than business. It is about the nourishment of humane values that sustain societies around the globe. In the most literal sense it is about the future of life on this planet. It is what peoples [sic] everywhere seek for themselves and for humanity. CSR is 'realer' than the business profession knows.
>
> Listen up, business! Corporation, be good![10]

Despite the sweeping range of the concept of social responsibility, it is possible to construe it a bit more narrowly and carefully. A socially responsible business or corporation expends some portion of its revenue (or its equivalent) in order to ameliorate (or assist in the amelioration of) some problem of society or to provide some public benefit. Examples of such could include the expenditure of revenue towards the reduction of drug use in a section of a city, or a corporate effort to sponsor a new wing in a municipal museum. A crucial feature of social responsibility is that the firm is not itself causally responsible for the problem or state of affairs to which it responds.[11] This condition illuminates how social responsibility is not, in any strict sense, a form of compensation for some prior act. Moreover, the socially responsible endeavor is not part of any specific exchange relationship or nor is it intended to complete some trade or agreement.[12]

What occurs when a manager (including the manager who is also the proprietor) embarks upon some socially responsible endeavor? In such an instance, the manager is making a decision about how to disburse the firm's revenue. Of course, managers often engage in such deliberations. After all, it is the responsibility of a manager to determine whether funds ought to be used to purchase new equipment, to hire and train new employees, to advertise more widely and so on. What distinguishes, therefore, an instance of socially responsible decision-making from other sorts of managerial choices? In cases of managerial decision-making, the individual is thinking about how to allocate scarce resources with an eye to profit-making: If I produce this good and inform people about it, then I may be able to exchange it for an amount of money that will cover its production costs and allow some profit. However, when the manager is deliberating about how to disburse revenue for endeavors deemed socially responsible, he is not deliberating with any eye to the criteria of profit, but with something else in mind. The manager is no longer seeking to use the revenues of the firm for production, service or exchange; rather, he is attempting to employ revenue without any attention to profit-making. (One might object, of course, that many instances of socially responsible endeavor are not, in fact, what they seem: they are in fact instances of profit-making under the guise of social responsibility. Without doubt this is often the case, but our inquiry is about the *idea* or *concept* of social responsibility, rather than its actual applications.)

In reminding ourselves that socially responsible decision making is not concerned with the same parameters or standards as business decision-making, we are brought up short: For social responsibility is, in effect, trying to render business ethical by eviscerating commerce from itself. In this sense, socially responsible endeavors have little to do with business at all. Indeed, the argument that social responsibility bestows some sort of ethical imprimatur on business is, in fact, an argument that business is improved only insofar as it ceases to be business! Even if an individual becomes a better person through socially responsible activity, the improvement is not gained as a result of business practice but as an effect of setting commerce aside and acting with an eye to something other than exchange for profit.

Stakeholder Theory

Advocates of the stakeholder theory contend that the recognition of and attention to stakeholders provides a means of rendering the practice of business more ethical. However, this sort of theory falls victim to the same problem that afflicts the theory of social responsibility: For the stakeholder theory also suggests that the moral improvement of business is achieved when commerce becomes something other than exchange for profit. Perhaps it is not surprising that the stakeholder theory comes to this conclusion, for an exercise of stakeholding is, in a sense, a species of social responsibility. According to advocates of the stakeholder theory, the managers of a corporation or firm have ethical duties to "those groups who have a stake in or claim on the firm," and these are "groups and individuals who benefit from or are harmed by, and whose rights are violated or respected by corporate actions."[13] Thus, within stakeholder theory the responsibilities of the firm are extended not so much to specific projects, endeavors or activities as they are to groups or individuals who have some "stake" in the activities of the firm.

We need not address all of the criticisms of stakeholding in order to discover the fatal flaw in the theory, at least in relation to business and goodness.[14] The stakeholder theory suggests that businesses must attend to the interests and needs of stakeholders. The list of stakeholders typically includes parties or persons with whom the firm is already engaged in exchange relations: employees, customers, suppliers, as well as the larger public (perhaps even "competitors!"[15]). What should be readily apparent is that a firm already has (or seeks to have) relations with at least some of these parties or persons. However, these are the economic relations of business in which each party—owner and employee, salesperson and customer, manager and supplier—seeks to enjoy an exchange in order to gain some profit. In these economic relations each party responds to the other by seeking to secure the best price for a good or service: The employee prefers the larger salary, the owner the smaller; the customer seeks the lowest price, the firm hopes to sell at the higher. The prices that emerge out of this on-going process of bargaining convey information about which resources, products, skills, or modes of production or service are in greatest demand. As described in section I, the pricing mechanism offers a signal to participants alerting them as to where to invest money, time and effort in order to satisfy their desires (or those of the wider community). The movement of prices reflects changes in preferences that would otherwise be nearly impossible for any one person or group of persons to discern.

However, the stakeholder theory contends that managers should attend to the interests and needs of stakeholders rather than to the signals of trade. Attending to stakeholders, it is argued, will help to realize the moral imperatives otherwise wanting in the practice of business. All the same, if managers heed the call of stakeholders, then managers will be attending to and responding to signals other than price. This is not to say that price becomes irrelevant, but it no longer has a priority over the interests of the stakeholders. Moreover, within the theory of stakeholding, it is unclear under what conditions prices should have priority. The implication of stakeholder theory, therefore, is that business can be moral but only if business does not adhere to the basic determinant of commercial exchange: price.

It might be suggested that our conclusion is shortsighted: After all, when a firm takes into account the needs and interests of those affected by its conduct then that firm not only enhances its image but ensures its longevity. Therefore, stakeholder theory does not contradict the essence of business. However, this objection fails to consider whether the enhancement of image is anything other than a short term advantage inconsistent with business exchange. After all, a positive image will prove helpful to a firm only so long as customers purchase its products. And this last point suggests a more significant problem with this objection: The longevity of a firm is determined by whether its products or services are demanded by consumers willing to pay for them. However, when a firm accedes to the requests and interests of stakeholders—such as suppliers, employees, or representatives of the public—then the firm will, in all likelihood, increase its costs of production, thereby increasing the price of its product. Unless one particular group of stakeholders, the consumers, are willing to pay higher prices, then the firm may place itself at a competitive disadvantage. The sustainability of a firm is, in fact, determined by how well it meets the demands of consumers, not the varied groups of stakeholders some of whom may not actually contribute to the revenue of the business.

An Historical Aside

If business is to be rendered moral through either social responsibility or stakeholding, then the practice of business must be redirected from activities of exchange for profit to other forms of endeavor. Whether or not these other endeavors will bring about the moral transformation of business people, or bring to fruition some greater overall good, is not part of my concern. My point is more minimal: The theories of social responsibility and stakeholding seek to save business by foreclosing its essential element: exchange for profit. Thus, the ideals of social responsibility and stakeholding are, in their essence, incompatible with business. Perhaps it is worth recalling that the incompatibility of ideals and institutions was a crucial thesis developed by one of the early defenders of markets, Bernard Mandeville.

In the early eighteenth century, Mandeville penned a sardonic poem, "The Grumbling Hive," in which he tells the tale of a bustling hive of commercial and entrepreneurial bees. The prosperity of the hive depends, alas, on the bees' failure to live up to an ideal of morals. Nonetheless, out of the self-interested activities of the bees, a greater good is generated: "Private Vices, Publick Benefits." Once he published his poem, Mandeville acquired some notoriety, and he was accused of defending vice. So, in a preface appended to the poem, some 8 years after its publication, Mandeville maintains that he is merely revealing the incompatibility of prosperity with the practice of a moral ideal:

> For the main Design of the Fable ... is to shew the Impossibility of enjoying all the most elegant Comforts of Life that are to be met with in an industrious, wealthy and powerful Nation, and at the same time be bless'd with all the Virtue and Innocence that can be wish'd for in a Golden Age.[16]

If we take Mandeville at his word—that he is not defending vice but only revealing the incompatibility of a moral ideal with empirical circumstance[17]—then we have an illustration of an important lesson. Even if a moral aim is laudable in abstract, its application to society may reveal its incompatibility with circumstances and institutions that we otherwise wish to preserve.

In recounting this lesson from the early eighteenth century, we find a parallel to the theories of social responsibility and stakeholding. Just as Mandeville pointed out how certain forms of morality might be incompatible with the prosperity of markets, so are the ideals of social responsibility and stakeholding incompatible with the essential element of commerce: exchange for profit. Social responsibility and stakeholding generate moral improvement by eliminating essential elements of business. Yet, according to defenders of social responsibility and of stakeholding, commerce is morally deficient without the reformation wrought by socially responsible endeavor or by attending to the interests of stakeholders. It would seem as if we are at an impasse.

Is there a way out?

BUSINESS: EMBEDDED WITHIN VIRTUE

Business is an activity that involves production and exchange among individuals, but the participants always exist within historical and social circumstances that affect the springs and contours of daily life—the manners, dispositions, habits, and expectations that guide conduct. Therefore, as an alternative to the theories of social responsibility and the stakeholder theory, we may consider business as a practice or set of activities embedded within a larger historical, social and moral context. In particular, we are born into a moral world in which there are normative expectations about conduct and self. We aspire to develop qualities of character, including such traits as honesty, integrity, generosity, courage, prudence, and individual responsibility. Commerce is moral when its practices and activities do not stray from the virtues that render one a good person. Of course, even if business is embedded within a larger historical, social and moral background, this fact need not entail that business *must* be understood through virtue, rather than, say, rules or rights. However, many of us do conceive our moral lives in terms of qualities of character (virtues), and virtue provides the best understanding of how individuals not only *do* right actions but live as *good* persons. Moreover, the ethics of virtue and its relation to business has some conceptualizations worth considering and developing. Let us turn to several of these before undertaking a discussion of some specific virtues.

In the eighteenth-century, the philosopher David Hume sought to articulate qualities of "common life," distinguishing between useful and agreeable traits of character. Benevolence, generosity, courage, honesty, and loyalty are useful to the wider public; industry, frugality, honesty, and fidelity, as well as discretion, caution, enterprise, and industry are useful primarily to the individual agent. These virtues of common life, Hume insisted, are radically distinct from the "monkish virtues," all of which are "everywhere rejected by men of sense, but because they serve to no manner of purpose; neither advance a man's fortune in the world, nor render him a more valuable member of society."[18] In the nineteenth century, the writer and moralist Samuel Smiles, situated a more explicit account of business qualities within a larger understanding of moral character, contending that along with honesty, the traits of self-reliance, attention, application, accuracy, method, punctuality, dispatch, discretion, and perception were essential to successful commerce. Yet, as Smiles notes, these traits are also required, "for the successful conduct of any important undertaking."[19] A contemporary list of market virtues is offered by the economist, Deirdre McCloskey. In a spirited and wide-ranging work, she elucidates the significance and value of "bourgeois virtue." One may live virtuously as a peasant, an aristocrat or an artist but one may also live virtuously as a bourgeois citizen. Virtues not only sustain commercial practices but are encouraged and required by capitalism. Her wide-ranging account of commercial morals seeks to counter the widespread view of markets as antithetical to virtue, community, friendship and a life lived well.[20]

Each of these thinkers, embeds business within a setting of human dispositions (moral and cultural), and thereby offers a catalogue of virtues applicable to markets and trade. Their conceptualizations offer a plausible outline of how a life of commerce is compatible with a virtuous life. To illuminate, further, how one may engage in business and hew, nonetheless, to virtue, let us take up the traits of honesty, integrity, generosity, and prudence.[21]

Without doubt, honesty is the best policy. However, even if honesty is essential to commerce, business success is not the *reason* a person is honest. Rather the honest businessman is, first, the honest man, and, second, the man who engages in commerce. The person of honest character seeks to avoid exaggeration and overstatement. For example, the honest salesperson will present a product without misleading a customer or withholding information that the customer would find relevant. Honesty is a matter of word *and* deed: The honest person adheres to a contract or promise and otherwise seeks to do that which could reasonably be expected in the specific circumstances. In sum, the honest person is trustworthy, and trust is one of the most sought after qualities in all endeavors.

A trait allied to honesty is that of integrity, living one's life as an integrated whole in which one remains steadfast to one's commitments and ideals. The person of integrity is not simply truthful but also loyal to his highest aims. In business the person of integrity seeks to ensure that the very activity of work as well as its products remain true to his highest ideals. One's work should manifest an adherence to the best practices and standards of the industry, profession or craft. Of course, in commerce, a person functions within a competitive framework. The individual of integrity should also seek to uphold the institutions and principles that are presupposed in production and exchange. The person of integrity will, therefore, be wary of using the political process to gain competitive advantage. To lobby the legislature or an administrative agency for a law or regulation that will give one's business a competitive advantage would be alien to one's commitment to the principles of free exchange.[22]

Generosity is another of the traditional virtues. A business transaction is not an exchange of gifts, but commerce may nonetheless express generosity. This expression may be indirect, in the sense that business may function as the means to acquire the wealth requisite for generous giving. However, generosity encompasses more than the giving of money. The activities of production and exchange may themselves be shaped directly by this virtue. The manner in which one treats an inexperienced employee, honors an ambiguous element of a contract, or assists a customer may reflect a disposition to give appropriately of one's time, attention, consideration, and effort. The willingness to give to colleagues, customers, employees, and others without seeking remuneration, recognition or reward manifests a generous disposition that is good in itself.

Although often allied with self-interest, prudence is a virtue eminently suitable to business, for commerce demands that one weigh objectives, circumstances, and risks with an eye to long-term material security. The prudential business person is not necessarily successful but is more likely to be so. Yet prudence does not come without other traits in train. For prudence requires responsibility and thrift, as well as self-control, the very trait that Adam Smith suggested gives "luster" to all the other virtues.[23] The exercise of self-control, or temperance, entails that one acts with the long-term in mind, prioritizes work over leisure, and organizes one's labor and effort so that one's own time and that of others is used well.

These are but four traditional virtues in which commerce may be situated. Without doubt, there are others, including loyalty, courage, and fairness. What the discussion should show, however, is that virtue and commerce are not contradictory, for the engagements of business need not be isolated events, brief episodes, but extensions of character. Whereas theories of social responsibility and stakeholding suggest that goodness is acquired insofar as one relinquishes the practices of commerce, the theory of virtue requires only that one's exchanges exist within virtue's scope.

Two Objections

At this point in the narrative, one might object that the very idea of embeddedness misconstrues the practice of business. It might be argued, for example, that within business all that really matters is the pursuit of self-interest. The features of markets (its structure of conditions, permissions, and incentives) are such that anyone engaged in market exchange will pursue self-interest. If commercial motives are self-interested and if virtue requires something other than the pursuit of self-interest, then it is idle folly to think that business could be embedded within virtue.

To make a long story very short, it is not at all obvious that self-interest is or must be the single or prime motive of those engaged in commercial exchange. Without doubt, some may think that business conduct is motivated by self-interest because economic theory utilizes, in most of its standard models, an assumption that agents will act in rational and self-interested ways. However, a postulate of economic theory should not be assumed to be descriptive of actual conduct. A more plausible but qualified assumption exists: Each person acts, typically, to acquire his or her highest value, but action is often guided as much by social and moral disposition as by explicit and rational deliberation.

Even if agents act, in deliberate and intentional ways, to achieve their highest value, that alone does not imply selfishness or self-interest. For an agent's strongest interest might lie in helping others, caring for his or her family, or earning money to contribute to a social, religious, or political cause. In fact, as Philip Wicksteed pointed out some 75 years ago, an economic exchange should be understood as a "non-tuistic" (from the Latin *tu*, you) relation: Each party to the trade excludes the interest of the other trader (*tu*), even as each may be acting for the good of others. According to Wicksteed, the traders in an exchange each consider the other as a means to an end, even though that end need not be selfish or self-interested.[24] However, even Wicksteed's insight may be too strong, for in a number of exchanges—especially those that are repeated regularly among the same individuals—parties do consider the interest of the other. Moreover, even in those exchanges that are purely non-tuistic the parties ought to be guided nonetheless by virtues of honesty and fair-dealing.

A second reason for rejecting the embeddedness of business in virtue lies in the notion that theories of virtue are more applicable to small societies with common aims than to large commercial societies with divergent ends and purposes. This objection assumes not only that the practice of virtue requires a substantive and common end across society but that the forces economic liberalism—with its embrace of free and equal spheres of action—have weakened, if not swept away, any substantive agreement on ends. It is argued that the very societies in which business flourishes lack the agreement necessary for virtue, so it will prove difficult to embed the practices of business within the traditional moral virtues.

Such an objection assumes that theories of virtue demand a strong notion of a communal end, or *telos*. Aristotle, it is said, held a teleological ethic in which there exists an *end* (happiness or *eudaimonia*) to the things that we do; virtue is to be understood in relation to this end or goal. However, it is important to understand how the *end* of our lives is found in a manner or mode of activity, and not in some goal extraneous to the activity. This point, of course, is made in the very first paragraph of Aristotle's *Nicomachean Ethics*:

> Every art and every inquiry, and similarly every action and pursuit, is thought to aim at some good; and for this reason the good has rightly been declared to be that at which all things aim. But a certain difference is found among ends; some are activities, others are products apart from the activities that produce them.[25]

Any claim that our moral lives must have a common substantive purpose must be understood in light of how the end of virtue need not exist apart from the very activity of being virtuous. The point of morality is not to serve some agreed goal but to provide the condition for the pursuit of our other ends, and these need not be held in common. In other words, one does not so much aim to be honest, courageous, or generous, as one seeks to do other things (to hire a new employee, to buy equipment, to meet a colleague for lunch) and to do these virtuously. Morality serves to modify what one does, so that one performs one's actions in a courageous manner, a generous way, an honest fashion. Therefore, it is not necessary to set forth any substantive or thick conception of an end if one is to forward a theory of the virtues. As Iris Murdoch has suggested, morality is "good for nothing."[26]

Yet it may still be objected, even by defenders of business, that market societies, exhibiting less reliance on common ends (moral or otherwise) than non-market societies, do not sustain virtue. For example, F. A. Hayek (and Michael Oakeshott, among others) have characterized modern and liberal societies as purpose- or end-independent orders, within which operate any number of smaller organizations with their particular ends and disparate beliefs and values.[27] Within these societies, Hayek contends, there is a diminution of solidarity, benevolence, and loyalty, and an increasing sense of impersonality.[28] If there is less reliance on substantive virtues than on impersonal norms (and if these serve less to *embed* our buying and selling than to *regulate* it), then, despite what has been argued here, the market itself proves inhospitable to virtue.

This is a serious objection, yet it may be too quick: It is not obvious that liberal market societies render the life of virtue difficult. In fact, there may be another explanation for Hayek's observations regarding commercial societies. The sociologist Robert Nisbet points out how the centralization of the modern state serves to diminish the function and authority of numerous voluntary social groups, mutual-aid societies, charitable associations, and business and professional organizations, all of which may serve to foster benevolence, friendship, responsibility and to enforce, informally, qualities of civility, honesty, and trust.[29] Intermediary between the state and the citizen, these societies and institutions encourage individuals to relate to each other in ways other than commercial exchange, thereby counteracting any putative tendency of the market to valorize efficiency or self-interest over the bonds of neighborhood, community, and society.

CONCLUDING REMARKS

Neither the theory of social responsibility nor that of stakeholding is compatible with the practice of commerce. However, there is a plausible case to be made that genuine goodness *is* compatible with commerce and precisely because we can cast the practices of business within the traditional virtues. Such a task is both theoretical and practical, and much remains to be done. But to uphold this aspiration is to forsake neither morality nor business. We are, in fact, demanding genuine, not spurious, goodness— the reality rather than the appearance. This is what is entailed in being serious about being good.

NOTES

1. I thank Reva Wolf for her comments on an earlier draft of the essay and Julian Friedland for his editorial assistance and generous patience. The amoral view of business may be found in Albert Z. Carr, "Is Business Bluffing Ethical?" *Harvard Business Review* (January–February 1968): 143–153. Carr also contends that business is analogous to a game such as poker. A deeper and more nuanced view of business as a game was offered by the great economist Frank H. Knight, who held that the rules and practices of the game of business sometimes conflict with the moral and religious tenets of society. See his essay, "The Ethics of Competition" [1923] in *The Ethics of Competition and Other Essays*, new introduction by Richard Boyd (New Brunswick, NJ: Transaction, 1997), 33–67.

2. On the idea of "embeddedness," see Mark Granovetter, "Economic Action and Social Structure: The Problem of Embeddedness," *American Journal of Sociology* 91: 3 (November 1985): 481–510.

3. This account is compatible with that offered by Alexei M. Marcoux in his essay, "The Concept of Business in Business Ethics," *Journal of Private Enterprise* 21:2 (2006): 50–67. He contends that business involves "transactions" that are "self-sustaining" or profitable. In her book on business ethics, Elaine Sternberg also emphasizes the nature of business, defining the purpose of business as "maximizing owner value over the long term by selling goods or services." *Just Business: Business Ethics in Action*, 2nd edition (Oxford: Oxford University Press, 2000), 32. My account seems consistent with hers, though I do not think that the practice of business requires the *maximization* of owner value.

4. Not only are there university chairs devoted to the subject of social responsibility or social responsibility and ethics, but the American Association of Collegiate Schools of Business (AACSB) has endorsed six "Principles of Responsible Management Education," including the recommendation that the "values of global social responsibility" be incorporated into "academic activities and curricular" (Principle 2) and the stipulation (Principle 5) that educators "interact with managers of business corporations to extend our knowledge of their challenges in meeting social and environmental responsibilities." See the "Principles for Responsible Management Education" at www.unprme.org (the AACSB Web site is: www.aacsb.edu). Some institutions even offer their graduating students the opportunity to make a "Graduation Pledge" of social responsibility: "I pledge to explore and take into account the social and environmental consequences of any job I consider and will try to improve these aspects of any organizations for which I work." See the Web site: www.graduationpledge.org/new. For one view of the popularity and efficacy of social responsibility, see the feature article, "The Good Company: A Survey of Corporate Social Responsibility," in The Economist 374: 8410 (January 22–28, 2005): 3–22 (esp. 3–4)

5. Discussions of corporate social responsibility have traditionally focused on *corporations*, and it is sometimes implied that social responsibility is a necessity of the corporation rather than the privately held firm.

6. See for example Robert L. Bradley, Jr. "Epilogue: Surreal Enron; Real Capitalism" in *Capitalism at Work: Business, Government and Energy* (Salem, MA: M & M Scrivener Press, 2008), 292–319.

7. In his history of corporate social responsibility, Willam C. Frederick suggests that the new wave of CSR theorizing must be normative and ethical and that it might be best understood as "Corporate Social Rectitude."

Corporation, Be Good! The Story of Corporate Social Responsibility (Indianapolis: Dog Ear Publishing, 2006), 89–94.

8. Brenkert, "Private Corporations and Public Welfare," *Public Affairs Quarterly* 6:2 (April 1992), 155.

9. Richard De George, *Business Ethics*, 4th ed (Englewood Cliffs, N. J.: Prentice Hall, 1990), 199.

10. Frederick, *Corporation, Be Good! The Story of Corporate Social Responsibility*, 3.

11. Brenkert makes this clear in, "Private Corporations and Public Welfare," 155.

12. Another form of social responsibility entails that a business or firm *refrain* from undertaking some activity. For example, it might be deemed socially responsible for a company to refrain from expanding its production facilities if the expansion would destroy a plot of beautiful and undeveloped land. This second type of social responsibility may, in most cases, be akin to attending to the rights or interests of stakeholders.

13. R. Edward Freeman, "Stakeholder Theory of the Modern Corporation," in W. Michael Hoffman, Robert E. Frederick, and Mark S. Schwartz, *Business Ethics: Readings and Cases in Corporate Morality*, 4th edition (New York: McGraw-Hill, 2001), 161 and 163, respectively. Another defense of the theory may be found in R. A. Phillips, *Stakeholder Theory and Organizational Ethics* (San Francisco: Berrett-Koehler, 2003).

14. See, for example, Alexei M. Marcoux's argument for the "special moral status" of shareholders, "A Fiduciary Argument against Stakeholder Theory," *Business Ethics Quarterly* 13:1 (2003), 1–24.

15. As Freeman suggests himself: "competitors and government would be the first to be included in an extension of this basic theory," "Stakeholder Theory of the Modern Corporation," 164.

16. Mandeville, "The Preface," *The Fable of the Bees, or Private Vices, Publick Benefits*, intro. F. B. Kaye (Oxford: Oxford University Press, 1924; reprint, Indianapolis: Liberty Fund, 1988), pp. 6–7.

17. For a discussion of Mandeville's real intention, see the introductory remarks by F. B. Kaye, in *The Fable of the Bees*, esp. pp. xxxviii–lxxvi; M. J. Scott-Taggart, "Mandeville: Cynic or Fool?" *Philosophical Quarterly* 16 (July 1966): 221-232. See also, E. J. Hundert, *The Enlightenment's Fable: Bernard Mandeville and the Discovery of Society* (Cambridge: Cambridge University Press, 1994), and M. M. Goldsmith, *Private Vices, Public Benefits: The Social and Political Thought of Bernard Mandeville* (Cambridge: Cambridge University Press, 1985). Selections from Mandeville's contemporaries may be found in J. Martin Stafford, ed., *Private Vices, Publick Benefits? The Contemporary Reception of Bernard Mandeville* (Solihull, UK: Ismeron, 1997).

18. Hume, *Enquiries Concerning Human Understanding and Concerning the Principles of Morals*, edited by L. A. Selby-Bigge, revised by P. H. Nidditch (Oxford: Clarendon Press, 1975), 270. The list of qualities can be found in Section VI, part I (242–243).

19. Smiles, "Business Qualities," in *Self-Help; with Illustrations of Character and Conduct* (New York: Harper and Brothers, 1860), 208. For a study of Smiles, see Adrian Jarvis, *Samuel Smiles and the Construction of Victorian Values* (Stroud, UK: Sutton, 1997).

20. McCloskey, *The Bourgeois Virtues: Ethics for an Age of Commerce* (Chicago: University of Chicago Press, 2006).

21. Some of the discussion of these four virtues was first developed in my text, *Morality and the Market: Ethics and Virtue in the Conduct of Business* (New York: McGraw-Hill, 2002), 320–22 (honesty), 365–6 (integrity), 291–2 (generosity), and 282–3 (prudence).

22. The attempt to secure a competitive advantage through law, regulation or public policy is typically referred to as "rent-seeking." The morality of

rent-seeking behavior is complicated, especially when a firm is facing a field of competition in which there are numerous laws and regulations that already benefit some at the expense of others. For an economic discussion of rent-seeking, see Gordon Tullock, *The Economics of Special Privilege and Rent Seeking* (Boston: Kluwer, 1989). Business ethicists have devoted little attention to the question of rent-seeking. One of the few essays is that of Michael E. DeBow, "The Ethics of Rent-Seeking?: A New Perspective on Corporate Social Responsibility," *Journal of Law and Commerce* 12 (Fall 1992): 1–21.

23.   Smith, *The Theory of Moral Sentiments,* edited by D. D. Raphael and A. L. Macfie (Oxford: Oxford University Press, 1976; reprint, Indianapolis: Liberty Fund, 1982), VI.iii.11 (p. 241)

24.   Wicksteed, "Business and the Economic Nexus," in *The Common Sense of Political Economy* (London: Routledge and Kegan Paul, 1933), 162–181.

25.   *Nicomachean Ethics,* tr. W. D. Ross, in *The Basic Works of Aristotle,* ed. Richard McKeon (New York: Random House, 1941), 1094a1–5.

26.   "The only genuine way to be good is to be good 'for nothing' in the midst of a scene where every 'natural' thing, including one's own mind, is subject to chance, that is, to necessity." Murdoch, *The Sovereignty of Good* (New York: Schocken Books, 1971), 71.

27.   F. A. Hayek, "The Market Order or Catallaxy" in *Law, Legislation and Liberty*, vol. 2, (Chicago: University of Chicago Press, 1976), 107–132; Oakeshott elaborates the purpose-independent "civil association," in *On Human Conduct* (Oxford: Clarendon Press, 1975), 108–184.

28.   Elizabeth Anderson also characterizes market relations as impersonal. See her discussion in *Value in Ethics and Economics* (Cambridge: Harvard University Press, 1993), esp. chapter 7 ("The Ethical Limitations of the Market"), 141–167.

29.   See, for example, "The Loose Individual" in *The Present Age: Progress and Anarchy in Modern America* (New York: Harper Collins, 1988), esp. 84–89. The more developed account is in Nisbet's great work, *The Quest for Community: A Study in the Ethics of Order and Freedom* (New York: Oxford University Press, 1953).

CHAPTER 5

TRANSFORMING THE ETHICAL CULTURE OF ORGANIZATIONS

Steve May

Major ethics scandals have tarnished a remarkably wide range of social institutions in recent years, including accounting fraud at dozens of corporations, torture at Abu Ghraib, sexual abuse in the Catholic Church, cheating and plagiarism at schools, colleges, and the New York Times, sweatshop labor in the apparel industry, steroid use in sports, and conflicts of interests in a variety of industries, such as pharmaceutical research, brokerage houses, auditing firms, and insurance companies. Each scandal has prompted demands for institutional change and various strategies for accomplishing such change, from increased government oversight and regulation to stronger professional codes of conduct to creating institutional incentives to encourage ethical behavior and legal compliance. This chapter argues that several common practices are often found in ethically engaged organizations that enable constructive cultural change. Drawing upon scholarly research, popular literature, and empirical data from several organizations, I suggest that ethically engaged organizations: (1) align personal, professional, and organizational aspirations and behaviors; (2) foster dialogic communication; (3) encourage participation in decision making; (4) establish transparent structures, policies and procedures; (5) emphasize accountability for anticipating and responding to ethical crises; and (6) promote courageous efforts to identify and resolve ethical dilemmas.

Doing Well And Good: The Human Face of the New Capitalism, pp. 87–111
Copyright © 2009 by Information Age Publishing
All rights of reproduction in any form reserved.

In an era of widespread organizational scandals, it is important that we study organizational ethics more closely, given the misconduct in both the for-profit (e.g., Enron, WorldCom, Tyco, Arthur Andersen, Adelphia), and non-profit (e.g., Catholic Church, U.S. military and government, universities) sectors. Worldwide, there is growing interest in business ethics in general and corporate social responsibility, in particular.[1] Especially since 2001, businesspersons, politicians, scholars, and citizens alike have called for greater responsibility among businesses. Certainly, recent U.S. scandals have intensified media attention on irresponsible corporate actions and have placed the decision-making integrity of America's corporate leaders on the national agenda. At the same time, organized discussions of issues of ethics, corporate social responsibility, corporate citizenship, and sustainable business have advanced in various parts of the industrialized world.[2]

Undoubtedly, there is growing, if not renewed, interest in organizational ethics.[3] For a time, the recent scandals intensified the media scrutiny of organizations and their leaders. Each new scandal seemed to produce additional clamor for organizational change, with strategies that included improved legal compliance, stronger sentencing penalties for white collar crime, more rigorous professional codes of conduct, and more stringent government oversight and regulation. The scandals also raised serious questions about our trust in corporate America, in particular, and have produced lawsuits, criminal trials, and legislation.[4] In several cases, the scandals have produced the decline, if not the destruction, of several well-known organizations—notably Arthur Andersen.

Over the years, attention to such ethical scandals appears to ebb and flow between the well-publicized, most egregious acts of misbehavior and the mundane, naturalized, and often overlooked practices of everyday organizational life. Ethics, however, has found its way back onto the agenda of organizational leaders.[5] Business executives, for example, have launched ethics programs, mission-driven strategies, values initiatives, and cultural change efforts. In addition, companies have created ethics officers, high-level ethics committees, ethics ombudspersons, codes of ethics, and ethics task forces. Finally, companies have attempted to strengthen their relationships with various stakeholders, developing programs on the environment, human rights, work-family balance, corporate volunteerism, community assistance, product safety, customer service, and philanthropy, among others.

This shift in focus has left many observers asking: Why the renewed emphasis on ethics? The obvious answer is that the leaders of organizations have realized that a lack of legal compliance can produce disastrous results. But organizational scandals alone don't explain the change. There are several additional reasons for the shift in focus toward ethics among organizational leaders: (1) reasons related to risk management; (2) reasons related to organizational functioning; (3) reasons related to market positioning; and (4) reasons related to civic positioning.[6]

Each reason, alone, offers scholars and businesspersons a legitimate rationale for further emphasizing a transformation of the ethical culture of organizations. Perhaps, most notably, there is growing evidence that organizational ethics also makes good business sense. Regardless of the many compelling reasons for the renewed focus on organizational ethics, though, business ethics has continued to have a marginal status in the theory and practice of organizational studies. Even in applied ethics, itself considered a marginal branch of moral philosophy, business ethics remains peripheral.[7]

The purpose of this chapter is to propose a new, alternative framework that moves business ethics "beyond the fringe," both theoretically and practically. The chapter argues that scholars have not adequately addressed the common tensions of past business ethics research, including prescriptive/descriptive, individual/organizational, and ethics/performance. For business ethics to be a viable project, in the long-term, it must account for these dialectical tensions and seek a synthesis that integrates them into a single framework. In response to this need, the chapter proposes a series of principles/practices of effective ethical engagement that enable and/or constrain ethical behavior in organizations. It is my hope that it will satisfy both ethicists and practitioners alike who seek to create organizations that will simultaneously do well and good, as the title of this volume proposes.

DIALECTICAL TENSIONS IN ORGANIZATIONAL ETHICS

My exploration of the dialectical tensions in organizational ethics is based on the presumption that any organizational phenomenon implies and generates its opposite. Organizational opposites are interconnected and interdependent in a state of tension that also produces a sense of harmony and habit in organizational practice. Dialectical tensions, then, may serve as the basis for either organizational stability or transformation. For the purposes of this chapter, I am most interested in the ways in which opposing forces in organizations—and, by extension our research and practice--may drive change. The challenge for many organizations seeking to transform their cultures, though, is that ethical opportunities will necessarily create resistance from the status quo. Therefore, it may be helpful to examine some common dialectical tensions in organizational ethics in order to discover a new path through habit and resistance to change. The most relevant of these tensions for transforming the ethical culture of organizations are: (1) prescriptive/descriptive; (2) individual/community; and 3) ethics/performance.

Prescriptive/Descriptive Tension

The first dialectical tension that poses difficulties for organizational ethics scholars and practitioners is prescriptive versus descriptive ethics.

As Parker explains, "the tension between theorizing what people should do (prescriptive ethics) and explaining what people actually do (descriptive ethics), is a fracture that threatens the project from the start."[8] This prescriptive/descriptive tension is one that must be addressed if business ethics scholars and practitioners are to make any improvements in either theory or practice. As Parker and others have noted, philosophers and business ethics scholars have debated the relative merits of various prescriptive, theoretical frameworks with little consensus. Scholars have considered Aristotle's virtues, Rawls' social contract, Kant's categorical imperative, Mill's greatest good for the greatest number, among others, with limited agreement regarding foundational prescriptions for businesspersons.

However, the disagreement and—in some respects, confusion—has certainly not stopped academics from writing about business ethics. For example, business scholars have explored Western philosophical ethics, in general, as well as more specific strands of existentialism, virtue, utility, social contract theory, cognitive philosophies, sophism, relational ethics, and social justice.[9] In fact, the writings of a range of noted scholars in the human (e.g., Bauman, Derrida, Foucault, Giddens, Habermas, Levinas, Lyotard, Said) and the political (e.g., Rorty, Taylor, MacIntyre) sciences have moved ethics to a central position in the academy. Their emphasis on the "interpretive" and "critical" turns has been readily translated for organizational studies in recent years.[10] The result has been a steady but growing interest in questions of interpretation and judgment, particularly as it relates to ethics.

To move forward, however, business ethics scholars and, in turn, practitioners need a more comprehensive, yet specific, conceptual foundation that is not necessarily beholden to many of the common philosophical perspectives of ethics. It should be conceptually sound, but also practical by integrating meta, meso, and micro levels of theory.

At a practical level, business ethics research and practice is needed in order to address a range of business-related issues, not the least of which have been the recent organizational scandals, noted above. However, business ethics should not be—and has not been—limited to scandals and crises alone. Scholars and ethics officers, for example, have pursued a broader range of ethically-oriented issues such as legal compliance, globalization and labor conditions, equal opportunities (e.g., sex, race, age, disability) in the workplace, corporate governance, social and environmental responsibility, employee control and discipline, fair wages and benefits, customer redress for accidents and product malfunctions, advertising and marketing misrepresentation, philanthropy and community involvement, and whistle-blowing, among others. Any new developments in business ethics should, ideally, accommodate both the highly visible examples of ethical misconduct and also the more mundane, yet incredibly important features of organizational life and its impact on various stakeholders.[11]

The future state of business ethics research and practice also has significant implications for business education. A number of edited volumes have sought to explore organizational ethics for teaching purposes, yet business ethics remains, in most cases, a fringe discipline in business schools.[12] When an ethics course is established, it is typically an elective or is attached toward the conclusion of more mainstream subjects such as organizational behavior or strategic management. Some scholars have even suggested that business educators rethink the place of "business as a humanity."[13]

Individual/Organizational Tension

A second tension that needs to be addressed in any new approach to business ethics is the individual/organizational tension. To date, most business ethics scholars and practitioners have focused on either the individual actor/employee or organizational features/structures. This should not necessarily be surprising since the agency/structure pair is the central tension in organizational theory and research.[14] Several authors, for example, have argued that this dualism is the defining characteristic of modern Western social and organizational studies.[15] For the purposes of business ethics, one focuses on the multiple factors that determine employee behavior and the other focuses on the processes through which employee decision making is circumscribed by the characteristics of organizational context. This common dualism raises key questions not only for ethics research, but also for the primary focus of ethics interventions in organizations. For example, should the primary focus of organizational transformation be an individually-based form of ethics training and development or should it be an organizationally-based form of structural change in corporate governance, accounting, and incentive systems, among others? Or both?

On the individual side of the continuum, scholars interested in business ethics have studied moral development, decision making, personal values, honesty, emotion, and reasoning, among others.[16] Guided by a doctrine of "social action," these studies focus on subjective experience and voluntary and/or creative action (if not precursors to action). By contrast, another set of scholars has focused on the organizational side of the continuum. They have studied organizational values, ethics codes, corporate governance, organizational structure, performance appraisals, stakeholders, organizational culture, dialogue, and organizational environment.[17] Guided by a doctrine of "social system, these studies focus on structural configurations and objective externalities.

Future business ethics research and practice needs to integrate, if not transcend, these often competing and incompatible views of agency and structure in organizations. Any new conceptual framework for business ethics, then, must be able to account for both human agency and institutional constraints. Occasionally, scholars have sought to bridge the gap by examining, for example, professions, both organizational and individual constraints on decision making, and individuals' perceptions of work climate on judgment.[18] However, the research to date that seeks to address the individual/organizational tension has been neither comprehensive nor systematic.

Ethics/Performance Tension

A final, yet crucial tension that has limited business ethics research and practice is between ethics and organizational performance. This is partly because past research has suffered from a conceptual narrowness and from a fixation on the corporate form of organization.[19] Even the recent arguments regarding the need for "triple bottom line" reporting retain the taken-for-granted assumption of economic performance.[20] That is, many business ethicists, in particular, entirely overlook the question of whether capitalism, as a form of economic organization, is ethically defensible. Fundamental assumptions regarding the role of business in society set many ethicists and businesspersons apart from the start. For example, many businesspersons take for granted that free enterprise, market mechanisms, and shareholder value should guide and drive business decision making whereas ethicists more frequently ask how, if at all, such business assumptions create broader sets of social "goods."

A second challenge regarding the seeming divide between ethics and organizational performance is simply that relationships between academic ethicists and businessperson are uneasy, if not combative. Both the means and the ends of business can seem problematic to ethicists outside of business schools, whereas they are more likely to accept the moral grounds for other realms of work, such as medicine, law, and even politics. As Sorell explains, "mainstream business goals can look dubious to ethicists," while the pronouncements of ethicists seems "self-righteous or utopian" to businesspersons and mainstream academics in business schools.[21] He describes this fundamental separation between ethicists and practitioners the "alienation problem." I agree with him that, unless it is solved, the ultimate goal of ethically affecting behavior in organizations is in danger of being compromised—certainly more so than other areas of applied ethics (e.g., medical ethics, legal ethics) in which scholars and practitioners collaborate to engage in both dialogue and intervention. Yet, much of the business ethics research also suffers from a second, but related, dilemma: "the over-rationalization problem." On this side of the ethics/performance tension, business ethics scholars have been perhaps overzealous in arguing for the importance of shareholder returns on investment in order to gain legitimacy in business circles.[22] To overcome both problems, a conceptual framework is needed that focuses not on "business as usual" but on businesses that are ethically out of the ordinary and profitable. Fortunately, scholars have begun to uncover empirical evidence that ethics has an impact on longer-term financial consequences, but we currently lack a framework that is true to both ethics and performance.[23] As Stark has described, ethicists in other professions—medicine, law, and government—have provided real and welcome assistance to their practitioners. However, business ethics has not "taken" in the world of business practice, he explains, because it has focused on "prescriptions that, however, morally respectable, run so contrary to existing managerial roles and responsibilities that they become untenable."[24] For example, businesspersons do not necessarily see the relevance of many of the "foundational" principles (e.g., duty, rights) of behavior that business ethicists claim should guide business decisions, regardless of context. Especially in a global economy, businesspersons need to be responsive, adaptable, and innovative in a range of cultures with diverse values and practices and, as a result, ethical principles appear to constrain "doing business" effectively. One of the common middle grounds between business ethicists and businesspersons has been the company ethics code, which often identifies key values and/or behaviors. Even in organizations with strong, widely followed ethics codes, though, members are rarely given guidance on the range of difficult ethical dilemmas they may face.

TRANSFORMING ORGANIZATIONAL CULTURE VIA EFFECTIVE ETHICAL ENGAGEMENT

Organizational ethics research need not be unrealistic or utopian, as some of its critics have suggested.[25] Similarly, the practice of ethics in organizations need not be solely compliance driven, as is commonly believed to be true by some practitioners. I propose that organizations can turn compliance regulations into a competitive advantage by leveraging the basic mechanisms that underlie trust, identity, and commitment. Accordingly, I put forth the term "effective ethical engagement," using "ethical" as a term to refer to ethical theory, "engagement" as a term to refer to ethical practice, and "effective" as a supra term that applies to both. Through my discussion of effective ethical engagement, the goal is to bridge theory and practice through the application of ethical theory to organizational functioning.

Effective ethical engagement involves the practice of ethical principles in the search for greater ethical awareness, the deliberate process of ethical decision making, and the aim for ethical behavior in organizations. In this chapter, I identify five ethical principles that play a significant role in the creation of effective ethical engagement in organizations: Participation, Dialogic Communication, Transparency, Accountability, and Courage. I propose that these five principles are dynamic, theoretically interdependent, and provide a cumulative influence on organizational performance. In practice, these principles are what enable companies to target specific areas for intervention in ways that increase their overall level of effective ethical engagement.

I argue that a low level of effective ethical engagement creates a culture where leaders and employees fear delivering bad news, fail to explain decisions, disregard stakeholders, dismiss ethical dilemmas, and hide mistakes. By contrast, a high level of effective ethical engagement creates a culture where leaders and employees speak up without fear of retribution, align policies and principles, account for stakeholders, integrate ethical concerns into decision making, and take action to uphold values.

Effective ethical engagement fundamentally reflects the level of ethical awareness, ethical decision-making skills, and ethical behavior in the organization. These three levels of ethical engagement can be found in business ethics research, which has defined and refined similar concepts such as ethical intent, ethical recognition, ethical judgment, ethical orientation, and ethical reasoning.[26]

Effective Ethical Engagement

In the following sections, I outline how five principles—Participation, Dialogic Communication, Transparency, Accountability, and Courage—create effective ethical engagement with a focus on the potential organizational outcomes produced from the practice of each principle. I also include several examples to describe how the principles, in practice, either enable or constrain organizational ethics.[27] Throughout my discussion, I propose how these principles interact and build on one another to facilitate ethical awareness, ethical decision making, and ethical behavior.

Participation
Ethically engaged organizations practice the principle of Participation when they position ethical behavior as a core component of their

business. In these organizations, leaders provide ethical guidance to employees, creating an ethical climate that enhances employee identification with, and loyalty to, the organization. Employees participate in ongoing efforts to sustain and improve the ethical culture of the organization. Their commitment to the organization's purpose allows them to make independent decisions in working towards collaborative objectives. An opportunity to participate in the organization's future direction enables employees' commitment to ethical principles. As a result, employees tend to be proud to associate themselves with the organization and are more likely to remain. At the organizational level, incentive systems are designed to encourage employees to address ethical concerns and integrate ethical considerations into their decision making.

Employee participation tends to be related to organizational commitment, including perceptions of shared values, loyalty to a supervisor, organizational vision, or professional values.[28] Commitment is an outcome of behaviors and communicative interactions that is facilitated through identification with the organization.[29] This organizational identification promotes a "global organizational understanding"—that is, a sense of ownership that prompts an understanding of other areas of the organization and how an individual's work impacts others. This in turn, creates a connection or sense of oneness with the organization; it promotes the tendency to experience the organization's successes and failures as one's own, and defining oneself by the distinctive qualities of the organization.[30] Thus, organizational commitment is best understood as a byproduct of the organizational member's participation, which as discussed above, can be a difficult enterprise to direct, but extremely beneficial to effective ethical engagement.

Commitment to one's organization is associated with several positive organizational outcomes, such as reduced absenteeism, reduced turnover and innovativeness of paid employees.[31] Commitment has also been associated with increased job performance and pro-social behaviors.[32] It has been repeatedly shown to be an important factor in understanding the work behavior of employees. Organizational commitment has also been linked to extra-role behavior, satisfactory job performance, and lower rates of employee turnover.[33] It has been argued that employees who are committed to the organization also believe their organization is a good place to work, are not looking for another employer, and believe that their current employer best fits their needs.[34] This interest in organizational commitment is further motivated by the understanding that employees who are committed are more likely to support organizational goals, require less supervision, and are willing to put forth extra effort on behalf of their organizations.[35]

One of the classic examples of a participatory organization that fosters employee commitment is W. L. Gore and Associates. Best known as the maker of GORE-TEX, Gore is well-known for its ability to motivate its employees through participation. Gore has developed a variety of rules that focus on providing the resources and opportunities for a work environment in which employees participate and, as a result, take greater responsibility for their work. For example, Gore has become a successful innovator in its field by requiring managers to act more like coaches than bosses by: (1) listening to employees' concerns; (2) avoiding close supervision; (3) trusting employees to work within a framework of clear direction; and (4) being responsive to employees' feedback. In addition to Gore, companies such as 3M, the Grameen Bank, the Donnelly Corporation, Ashoka, Working Assets Long Distance, and the Mondragon co-operatives in Spain have been praised for their participatory workplace cultures.

By contrast, NASA has been less successful in its efforts to involve employees in important decisions, even those that affect the safety of its astronauts. For years, NASA was well-known for a variety of its successes, particularly the Apollo missions. However, in recent years, they have been better known for the visible, public failures in the Challenger and Columbia disasters. Although NASA has blamed technological problems (e.g., the O rings) for the disasters, oversight commissions have indicated that a lack of participation in decision making is at least one of the causes. Still fairly hierarchical in its structure, NASA employees were aware of the technical problems with both shuttles. However, there were few, if any, mechanisms in place for persons with the knowledge to fully participate in launch decisions. This lack of participation at all levels of NASA is particularly troubling since the Rogers Commission (in its review of the Challenger disaster) had noted that experienced engineers were discouraged from providing negative feedback about the O rings. The Columbia disaster suggests that, although feedback mechanisms were later put in place, they were not used. Other well-documented cases include the Ford Pinto and its exploding gas tanks and A. H. Robins and its Dalkon contraceptive IUD, which apparently produced various illnesses for the women who used it. In the case of the Ford Pinto, more extensive participation in product design and manufacturing of the gas tanks might have produced both a more cost-effective and safe automobile. However, leaders of the company focused, instead, on a short-term, cost-benefit analysis which limited participation of knowledgeable employees who might have created an innovative alternative that was both ethical and met business needs. In the case of A. H. Robins, key medical experts—both inside and outside of the organization—who expressed concerns about the IUD's safety, were excluded from participation in decision making. Once the product was being "brought to market," scientific data regarding safety risks was either ignored or omitted from decision-making processes.

Dialogic Communication

Ethically engaged organizations practice the principle of Dialogic Communication when they have open, honest and reciprocal communication among their workforce. In these organizations, leaders actively seek out and provide feedback on important issues from employees at all levels of the organization. They value the perspectives of all employees and facilitate their employees' ability to voice their opinions and concerns by demonstrating care and respect for their employees' point of view. Employees actively participate in the decision making processes of their departments and organization, providing leaders pertinent information without fear of retribution. Management and employees alike understand that in order to have effective, reciprocal communication, they must take personal responsibility for creating this dialogue. In short, a dialogic organizational culture is characterized by mutual trust within its workforce. For example, organizations that foster dialogic communication provide opportunities for candid discussions regarding ethical dilemmas in the workplace and how they may be addressed by employees. Similarly, performance appraisal processes (e.g., 360 degree performance assessment) that integrate ethics and/or integrity as a basis of employee evaluation are likely to prompt more open, honest, and reciprocal conversations regarding ethical behavior in organizations.

Managers exhibit Dialogic Communication through open communication, sharing of information, and delegation of control. Specifically, when managers delegate tasks or share control, they encourage employees' participation in decisions, demonstrating significant trust in and respect for their employees.[36] Similarly, open communication emphasizes the sharing and exchanging of ideas and information between manager and employee.[37] Both of these processes make the manager somewhat vulnerable but also affirm the employees' standing and worth in the organization.[38]

The trust built within an employee-manager relationship is also greatly influenced by fair treatment practices and associated perceived fairness of the manager by the employee. Employees are more likely to support management decisions that have been reached through a fair process.[39] By the same token, employees are more likely to subvert decisions that benefit particular groups at the expense of the organization as a whole. In this way, Dialogic Communication facilitates ethical behavior by helping to minimize the risk of ethical scandals; because unless employees believe they can deliver bad news to management without fear of repercussions, they may be unwilling to inform management of developing ethical risks or problems until it is too late.

The trust created between organizational members through Dialogic Communication could potentially lead to other beneficial, tangible organizational outcomes. For example, trust in the legitimacy of a manager has been shown to generalize to the organization, acting as a key factor in building long-term commitment.[40] Employees are more likely to take pride and feel ownership in their organization when they perceive top management to have high credibility and a coherent set of values. Also, leaders' effective communication can produce clear expectations that may improve both employee satisfaction and performance. The mutual trust between leaders and employees mitigates the risk involved in speaking up in situations where there are moral wrongdoings; for that reason, honest, open, and reciprocal communication is essential for employees to hold each other accountable.

There are a number of organizations that foster dialogic communication, including Levi-Strauss, Hanna Anderson Clothing, and Patagonia, among others. However, one company has developed an ethics training program that is quite extensive and might be considered dialogic, Bell South. For example, the company has integrated its ethics and compliance training materials into multiple delivery sources to demonstrate to employees that ethics is integral to every part of the business and to leverage existing infrastructure. Using media such as CD-ROMS, videos, and the company's Intranet, BellSouth has blended its ethics and compliance training into new employee orientations, general management courses, sales training, and other learning modules. The ethics and compliance team sees Human Resources as a key partner in its work, and continually looks at ways to include ethics and compliance topics in other employee training programs. In addition, each operations unit has a compliance executive and a coordinator responsible for ethics and compliance oversight in that operating division. These managers draw information from "the bottom up," conduct risk assessments, and report back to the compliance office when gaps in training or communication are discovered. If the subject can best be handled on a small scale, the compliance coordinator will take care of it. However, if the corporate compliance office sees that many areas are addressing similar issues, time and money can be saved by creating cross departmental programs. Examples of this include antitrust and environment training. While the company uses technology to deliver the message, it views that the most productive work comes from face to face meetings, where employees are giving the time to sit and discuss the nuances of various ethical dilemmas.

By contrast, there are many organizations that still suffer from monologic communication that limits candor, fosters secrecy, and manages communication and information in a top-down manner. One well-known example includes the Sears Auto scandal in the early 1990s. In June of 1992, the California Bureau of Auto Repairs (BAR) revoked the operating permits of 72 auto centers in that state. The decision was based on 18 months of undercover investigation into repair practices at 35 centers. The California BAR accused Sears of fraud and willful departures from accepted trade standards and launched a sting effort in 1990 after receiving 250 customer complaints. According to BAR, in 42 of 48 visits, Sears employees performed unnecessary services or repairs. On average, customers were bilked of $250, by replacing new parts that were not necessary and, in some cases, cars emerged in worse condition. The problem was caused by the company's efforts to improve lagging profits after the recession of the 1980s that had hurt Sears. As a result, a new compensation policy was created to give commissions to auto mechanics which, in effect, provided an incentive for the mechanics to provide additional services. Employees were instructed to sell a certain number of services in an eight hour day. If they failed to meet the goals, employees received a cutback in their hours or were transferred. When confronted with the allegations, however, Sears communicated an angry denial. It was not until the story became news that the company began to communicate more directly and honestly with its customers, placing full-page ads to apologize to them. Even then, though, the chairman of Sears only admitted that "mistakes may have occurred." Similar claims might be made about Nike and secrecy surrounding its sweatshops in Asia, as well as both Ford and Firestone in the case of the rollover deaths of drivers of Ford Explorers, which included each company blaming the other.

Transparency

Ethically engaged organizations practice the principle of Transparency when they have clear and visible structures of governance, mission statements, policies, and procedures. These structures, statements, and policies reflect and support the culture of the organization. In these organizations, employees understand their role in achieving the values and goals of the organization and how their performance will be evaluated. Leaders explain how and why decisions are made, enabling employees and other stakeholders to more fully support those decisions when they agree with the result. Transparency also provides employees the necessary information to disagree with, or resist, organizational decisions that may be unethical and/or illegal. As a result, transparency may simultaneously create support for ethical decision making and resistance to unethical behavior, providing an internal feedback mechanism within the organization. At the same time, employees and leaders make public information, externally, that enhances legal compliance and public confidence. For stakeholders, both internal and external to the company, transparency provides greater confidence that the organization is being managed effectively and is acting responsibly.

Two central aspects of Transparency are behaviors that facilitate coherence and coordination (i.e., providing clear and visible structures of governance, mission statements, policies and procedures). Specifically, coherence is built through a shared understanding of the organizational mission, goals, and purpose; coordination is facilitated through policies and procedures that correspond and are in line with the shared understanding of the company's purpose.[41] Clear role expectations and knowledge of the organizational mission and goals facilitates the identification of situations that require ethical decision making.

Transparency and Dialogic Communication are mutually reinforcing. Through the establishment and communication of clear, explicit, coherent governance structures, goals, and policies across the multiple levels of the organization Transparency creates employee trust in the institution. Additionally, actions that give the work coherence by building a shared understanding of the goals and issues are likely to decrease the likelihood of misunderstanding and, thus, will remove some powerful threats to trust. Greater confidence in the way the institution is being governed reinforces the confidence of the employee that leaders are doing what they say they are doing. Similarly, rules, procedures, and practices that assist coordination delineate accountability and, thus, facilitate hand-offs and joint work efforts which necessitate trust.[42]

Although companies such as Ben and Jerry's, Free Trade Coffee, and Tom's of Maine are best known for their transparency, there are less visible examples, as well. One example is Baxter International. The company's medical therapies are used by health care providers and their patients in more than 100 countries. Because Baxter's 40,000 employees are located throughout the world (with more than half outside the United States), the company has approached the challenge of communicating its business practice standards to a global workforce by decentralizing its ethics training programs. All new employees—and in many cases, prospective employees—are given a copy of the company's business practice standards, which have been translated into 14 different languages. Each new employee takes part in mandatory training conducted by managers who have been designated as ethics trainers. Additional training programs and training schedules are left up to each region and business unit, with headquarters providing resources. For example, the team responsible for the company's Asian operations has developed a yearly training program, based on real-life scenarios, that is designed to encourage group discussion and participation. In Latin America, the company's employees develop and present their own scenarios as part of the training. In addition to the large library of case studies, Baxter is developing Web-based vehicles to supplement existing communication channels of ethical standards. These efforts suggest that, at least internally, Baxter is seeking to infuse ethics in a transparent manner.

A much more visible case, Enron, is evidence of the risks of a non-transparent organization when it comes to ethics. The level of secrecy (and related risk) upon which Enron was built, and upon which it failed, cost the jobs and retirement incomes of thousands, contributed to a slump in the stock market, and may have exacerbated California's 2000-to-2001 energy crisis. The collapse of the company, the largest bankruptcy in U.S. history, was followed by several criminal and civil lawsuits against the executives of the company. These lawsuits have suggested that the arrogance and greed of Enron's leaders was related to the lack of transparency in decisions made at the highest level of the company. In short, since rank and file employees did not necessarily realize their jobs and the company were at risk, they could not hold leaders accountable for their decisions. It appears that they had limited information about the specific decisions that were being made and, when criticisms were raised within the company, employees were reprimanded for making their concerns public. Similar, related examples include R. J. Reynolds and Tobacco Industry, the Catholic Church, and WorldCom.

Accountability

Ethically engaged organizations practice the principle of Accountability when they embrace the responsibility they have to each of their stakeholders. In these organizations, leaders and employees consider the impact of their actions on both internal and external stakeholders, taking into account potential stakeholder concerns in their decision making process. As a result, accountable organizations experience fewer unanticipated internal ethical crises and successfully execute strategies for engaging external critics in ways that mitigate conflicts. Leaders are accountable for the responsibilities they delegate to employees; employees, in turn, are accountable for their own actions. Organizational members do not view business units independent from each other; rather they view the organization as interdependent. Each employee takes personal responsibility for their own part of the job in an ethical manner and expects others to do the same.

Transparency and Accountability are closely related: While Transparency implies the existence of clear structures and policies that enable employees to act independently in service of the organization and its stakeholders. Accountability is more closely related to the levels of disclosure by an organization and the responsibility taken for providing honest disclosure. It follows that the two main components of Accountability are the concern for all stakeholders and the need to take personal responsibility for organizational actions. Accountability builds on Transparency to achieve credibility. Other principles such as Dialogic Communication and Participation facilitate Accountability through their emphases on trust, openness, and employee engagement.

The central theme of the Accountability Principle is interdependence. The more workers believe that everyone else is competent and taking responsibility for their own part of the job, the more trusting and the more cooperative the organization will be.[43] Workers will also be more confident in knowing that if they do their own part, others will do theirs. Accountability is a clear expression of interdependence, feeling "we're in this together," and is consistent with a social contract in which employees are guided by a shared vision, mission, and value system. Finally, an organization with a high degree of Participation creates the context for employees who will also view accountability as a day-to-day part of their work. When that Participation is Transparent, employees are more likely to hold the organization accountable to them and to hold co-workers and, on occasion, stakeholders accountable to them, as well.

The Body Shop, created by Anita Roddick, is known for its accountability to its employees, its suppliers and, ultimately, the environment. The Body Shop has grown world-wide and is an example of a company that "does good business by doing good." Believing that both employees and customers are hyped-out, the Body Shop seeks to educate both employees and customers, producing greater accountability for decision making. In addition, The Body Shop is well-known for its stewardship of the environment and its support of local, indigenous groups through programs such as "Trade Not Aid." Through a series of interrelated programs, Roddick has sought to be responsible to various stakeholders throughout the supply chain. As a result, employees are also able to hold one another accountable for their actions and to hold the company accountable for its decisions, as well. As she explains, "I think you can trade ethically.... It's showing that you forsake your values at the cost of forsaking your work force."

Arguably the worst corporate disaster provides a stark contrast to the Body Shop. In 1984, the Union Carbide pesticide plant in Bhopal, India released a dangerous chemical, methyl isocynanate gas (MIC), creating the worst industrial accident in history. As a result of the accident, at least 10,000 people were killed, over 300,000 became ill, and nearly 500,000 were displaced. In time, it became clear that the plant was neither safe nor efficient and had been located in India to take advantage of cheap labor and limited regulations. In addition, most employees and citizens had not been told that they would be working and living amidst toxic chemicals. Once among the top 50 companies in the U.S., Union

Carbide's reputation was further tarnished when it fought lawsuits against it to compensate the victims of the disaster. Although the lawsuits have been settled, the Indian government and citizens still seek the full compensation required under the law. Another example during the 1980s was the Manville Corporation and its use of asbestos in various products, consistently denying accountability for its negative health effects on persons exposed to it. A more recent example of a lack of executive accountability, in particular, can be found in Adelphia.

Courage

Ethically engaged organizations practice the principle of Courage when they willingly undertake risk to uphold their values, confront moral wrongdoings, and create opportunities for constructive organizational change. In these organizations, leaders encourage employees to make difficult decisions and take appropriate action in service of organizational values and to challenge those values when necessary. They personally admit mistakes in order to identify and solve problems. Employees have the skills to identify and assess the relevant ethical principles, as well as the tools that enable them to create a plan of action when facing tough situations. When addressing and resolving ethical issues, they accept the professional and personal consequences of their actions. Courageous organizations demonstrate a willingness to break from established practice in order to uphold their values and change course for ethical reasons even if financial risk is involved.

Courage is deeply rooted in not only ethical awareness but also the willingness to take difficult action. Courage means "daring to challenge the conventional models of working behaviors;"[44] it is freely undertaking dangerous or difficult action in pursuit of a valued end and must be coupled with the interconnection between people.[45] In order to foster Courage, a leader must make room for highly individual thought and action, at the same time communicating a strong sense of the vision, mission and sense of the organization as a whole. Dialogic Communication and Participation provide the foundation for employees' willingness to accept the professional and personal consequences of their actions; when employees are able to speak openly and they identify with the organization, they are more likely to confront ethical dilemmas directly. An experience of extraordinary action in an organization can change the quality of connection between people, often building on and deepening people's trust and respect in their dealings with others. Transparency and Accountability of organizational practices makes mistakes self-evident and the ability to provide honest feedback allows them to be discussed in a collaborative environment and, as a result, solved effectively.

Johnson & Johnson is perhaps best known for its ethical courage. In response to tainted Tylenol capsules, Johnson & Johnson strengthened its standing as one of the leading health care companies by pulling the capsules off the shelves and addressing consumers' concerns about the capsules, truthfully and quickly, via the media. Although the company suffered short-term financial losses, it also affirmed its commitment to patient health and consumer safety, which have remained features of its organizational culture. As a result, it has been lauded as one of the country's most ethical and successful companies. Similarly, the owner of Malden Mills suffered financial loss in order to retain jobs for his employees. In addition, various whistleblowers at Enron, in the tobacco industry, in the FBI and CIA, and in numerous attorneys general offices across the country have showed ethical courage to protect the public.

As a contrast to Johnson & Johnson, accounting firm Arthur Andersen made one of the quickest and most devastating falls from grace in corporate history. Despite a long-standing reputation as one of the most objective and responsible accounting firms, Arthur Andersen employees signed off on earnings statements for Enron (and other clients such as Waste Management) that were, according to industry observers, "aggressive and unique at best, "misleading or irresponsible" at worst. The failure of Arthur Andersen came after a series of reports in the 1990s by the Government Accounting Office that noted the growing conflict of interest between auditor/client relationships in the accounting industry. In response to numerous concerns expressed over auditor independence, Arthur Andersen argued before the SEC that "a broad scope of practice" was necessary and that "the future of the accounting profession is bright and will remain bright—as long as the commission does not force us into an outdated role trapped in the old economy." Court documents filed in a 2002 trial for "deceptive practices" indicated that Arthur Andersen had been warned about its practices and that many employees were aware of the practices and the warnings. The response of many mid-level managers was to shred company documents. The result has been the unexpected and incredibly fast decline of one of the most well-known and successful companies in the United States. Additional example, as of this writing in 2008, include new pressures placed on the pharmaceutical industry and the Food and Drug Administration to come forward with more details regarding drug risks for patients.

Effective Ethical Engagement and Organizational Performance

Effective ethical engagement is a process that involves the negotiation between differing dialectical tensions in organizations. It is practiced through ethical awareness, ethical decision making, and ethical behavior as delineated by five ethical principles: Participation, Dialogic Communication, Transparency, Accountability, and Courage.

In sum, ethically engaged organizations demand high levels of Participation to confront both everyday and extraordinary ethical dilemmas. Leaders set the tone that ethics is a core component of the business, not an add-on. When individuals are committed to the organization and its values, they are able participate in ongoing efforts to sustain and improve its culture. A "collective mindfulness" emerges, facilitated through Dialogic Communication, where individuals understand the perspective of others in ways that promote understanding among different constituencies and make managing diverse perspectives possible. Equally important, an individual's personal sense of investment in and commitment to the ethos of the organization is enhanced by Transparency, which facilitates their ability to make independent decisions. Members of transparent organizations better understand the rationales for decision making and, as a result, learn to make effective and ethical decisions.

The cumulative outcome of Participation, Dialogic Communication, and Transparency is Accountability. Members of accountable organizations understand how their decisions affect others in the organization and develop strategies for disseminating ethical best practices across various groups. In short, individuals take responsibility for anticipating and responding to ethical challenges because they value the interdependence that exists within the organization and its members.

Finally, the sustaining ethical force of these principles and moral conscience of the organization is Courage. Ethically engaged organizations have a bias toward action that prompts member involvement and learning. Courage prevents stakeholders from becoming complacent with regards to their ethical awareness, ethical decision making skills, and ethical behavior; the objective of an ethically engaged organization is continual improvement in these dimensions in order to sustain its effectiveness.

Taken together, in practice, ethically engaged organizations avoid difficult dilemmas and deal with them effectively when they do arise. They encourage cooperation, inspire commitment, and nurture innovation. They earn customer trust, build brand equity, and attract and retain talented employees. They create value by deepening trust within the organization and enhancing the organization's reputation in the marketplace.

In the current analyses, we sought to bridge ethical theory and practice through the notion of effective ethical engagement. Our review of the dialectical tensions in ethical research and practice and the function of and relationships that exist between five basic principles of effective ethical engagement begin to carve out a framework for conceptualizing ethics in a way that asserts clear implications to organizational performance.

NOTES

1. See, for example, Parker, M. (Ed.). (1998). *Ethics and organization*. London: Sage for a discussion of organizational ethics in general; See, for example, May, S., Cheney, G., & Roper, J. (Eds.). (2007). *The debate over corporate social responsibility*. New York: Oxford University Press for a discussion of CSR, specifically.

2. See, for example, the recent special issue of *Business Ethics Quarterly, 18*(1), for a discussion of corporate citizenship. Similar journals now frequently include special issues on organizational ethics, corporate social responsibility, and sustainability.

3. See, for example, Donaldson, T., & Dunfee, (1994). Toward a unified conception of business ethics: Integrative social contracts theory. *Academy of Management Review, (19)*2, 252–284; Freeman, R. E. (1991). *Business ethics: The state of the art*. New York: Oxford University Press; Goodpaster, K. E. (2006). *Conscience and corporate culture*. Oxford, UK: Blackwell; Jackall, R. (1988). *Moral mazes: The world of corporate managers*. New York: Oxford University Press; Reich, R. B. (2007). *Supercapitalism: The transformation of business, democracy, and everyday life*. New York: Alfred A. Knopf.

4. Lorsch, J. W., Berlowitz, L., & Zelleke, A. (Eds.). (2005). *Restoring trust in American business*. Cambridge, MA: American Academy of Arts and Sciences.

5. Bagley, C. (2005). The ethical leader's decision tree. *Harvard Business Review, 81*(2), 18–19; Thompson, M. (2002). Marketing virtue. *Business ethics: A European Review, 11*(3), 354–362.

6. Paine, L. S. (2003). *Value shift: Why companies must merge social and financial imperatives to achieve superior performance*. New York: McGraw-Hill.

7. Sorell, T. (1998). Beyond the fringe? The strange state of business ethics. In M. Parker (Ed.), *Ethics and organization* (pp. 15–29). London: Sage.

8. Parker, M. (Ed.). (1998). *Ethics and organization*. London: Sage., p. 1

9. For a discussion of Western philosophical ethics, in general, see Carlin, W. B., & Strong, K. C. (1995). A critique of Western philosophical ethics: Multidisciplinary alternatives for framing ethical dilemmas. *Journal of Business Ethics, 14*(5), 387–396. For a discussion of more specific strands of existentialism, virtue, utility, social contract theory, cognitive philosophies, sophism, relational ethics, and social justice, see Argawal, J., & Malloy, D. (2000). The role of existentialism in ethical business decision-making. *Business Ethics: A European Review 9*(3), 143–154; Solomon, R. (1992). *Ethics and excellence*. New York: Oxford University Press; Goldman, A. H. (1980). Business ethics: Profits, utilities, and moral rights. *Philosophy and Public Affairs, 9*(3), 260–286; Donaldson, T., & Dunfee, T. W. (1994). Towards a unified conception of business ethics: Integrative social contracts theory. *Academy of Management Review, 19*(2), 252–284; McDonald, G., & Pak, P. (1996). It's all fair in love, war, and business: Cognitive philosophies in ethical decision-making. *Journal of Business Ethics, 15*(9), 973–996; Michaelson, C. (2001). Is business ethics philosophy of sophism? *Business Ethics: A European Review, 10*(4), 331-339; Pelton, L. E., Chowd-

hury, J., & Vitell, S. J. (2004). A framework for the examination of relational ethics: An interactionist perspective. *Journal of Business Ethics, 19*(3), 241–253; Shminke, M., Ambrose, M., & Noel, T. (1997). The effect of ethical frameworks on perceptions of organizational justice. *Academy of Management Journal, 40*(5), 1190–1207.

10. For discussions of the interpretive and critical turns, see Rabinow, P., & Sullivan, W. M. (Eds.). (1979). *Interpretive social science: A second look.* Berkeley: University of California Press; Calhoun, C. (1995). *Critical social theory.* Oxford, UK: Blackwell. For discussions regarding how they have been translated for organizational studies, see Alvesson, M., & Deetz, S. (2000). *Doing critical management research.* London: Sage; Conrad, C. (Ed.). (1993); *Ethical nexus.* Norwood, NJ: Ablex. Putnam, L. L., & Pacanowsky, M. R. (Eds). (1983). *Communication and organization: An interpretive approach.* Sage: Beverly Hills, CA.

11. Deetz, S. (2007). Corporate governance, corporate social responsibility, and communication. In S. May, G. Cheney, & J. Roper (Eds.), *The debate over corporate social responsibility* (pp. 267–278). New York: Oxford University Press.

12. For an initial review of textbooks on organizational ethics see, Conrad, C. (2003). The corporate meltdown. *Management Communication Quarterly, 17*(1), 5–19; Donaldson, T., & Gini, A. (Eds.). (1996). *Case studies in business ethics* (4th edition). Upper Saddle River, NJ: Prentice Hall; Malachowski, A. (Ed.). (2001) *Business ethics: Critical perspectives on business and management (volume IV).* London: Routledge; May, S. (Ed.). (2006). *Case studies in organizational communication: Ethical perspectives and practices.* Thousand Oaks, CA: Sage; Micholas, A. C. (1995). *A pragmatic approach to business ethics.* Thousand Oaks, CA: Sage; Peterson, R. A., & Ferrell, O. C. (Eds.). (2005). *Business ethics: New challenges for business schools and corporate leaders.* Armonk, NY: M. E. Sharpe; Seeger, M. W. (2002). *Ethics and organizational communication.* Cresskill, NJ: Hampton Press.

13. Donaldson, T., & Freeman, R. E. (1994). *Business as a humanity.* New York: Oxford University Press.

14. Conrad, C., & Haynes, J. (2001). Development of key constructs. In F. M. Jablin & L. Putnam (Eds.), *The new handbook of organizational communication* (pp. 47–77). Thousand Oaks, CA: Sage.

15. See, for example, Clegg, S. (1989). *Frameworks of power.* Newbury Park, CA: Sage; Dawe, A. (1978). Theories of social action. In T. Bottomore & R. Nisbet (Eds.), *A history of sociological analysis* (pp. 362–417). New York: Basic Books; Giddens, A. (1979). *Central problems in social theory.* Berkeley: University of California Press; Giddens, A. (1984). *The constitution of society.* Berkeley: University of California Press; Reed, M. (1985). *Redirections in organizational analysis.* London: Tavistock.

16. See, for example, Wimbush, J. (1999). The effect of cognitive moral development and supervisory influence on subordinates' ethical behavior. *Journal of Business Ethics, 18*(4), 383–395; Beu, D., Buckley, M., & Harvey, (2003). Ethical decision-making: A multi-dimensional construct. *Business Ethics: A European Review, 12*(1), 88–107; Fritzsche, D. (1995). Personal

values: Potential keys to ethical decision-making. *Journal of Business Ethics*, *14*(11), 909–922; Quinn, J., Reed, J., Browne, M., & Hiers, W. (1997). Honesty, individualism, and pragmatic business ethics: Implications for corporate hierarchy. *Journal of Business Ethics, 16*(12–13), 1419–1430; Gaudine, A., & Thorne, L. (2001). Emotion and ethical decision-making in organizations. *Journal of Business Ethics, 31*(2), 175–187; Nell, O. (1975). *Acting on principle: An essay on Kantian ethics*. New York: Columbia University Press.

17.   For a discussion of values, see Daft, R.L., Conlon, E.J., Austin, J., & Buenger, V. (1996). Competing values in organizations: Contextual influences and structural consequences. *Organization Science, 7*(5), 557–576; Donaldson, T. (1996). Values in tension: ethics away from home. *Harvard Business Review*, Sept.- Oct., 48-62; For a discussion of ethics codes, see Coughlan, R. (2005). Codes, values, and justifications in the ethical decision-making process. *Journal of Business Ethics, 59*(1-2), 45–53; Warren, R. (1993). Codes of ethics: Bricks without straw. *Business Ethics: A European Review, 2*(4), 185–191; Willmott, H. (1998). Towards a new ethics? The contributions of poststructuralism and posthumanism. In M. Parker (Ed.), Ethics an organizations (pp. 76–121). London: Sage. For a discussion of corporate governance, see Spira, L. (1999). Independence in corporate governance: The audit committee role. *Business Ethics: A European Review, 8*(4), 262–273; Deetz, S. (2007). Corporate governance, corporate social responsibility, and communication. In S. May, G. Cheney, & J. Roper (Eds.), The debate over corporate social responsibility (pp. 267-278). New York: Oxford University Press. For a discussion of organizational structure, see James, H. S. (2000). Reinforcing ethical decision making through organizational structure. *Journal of Business Ethics, 28*(1), 43–58; White, L. P., & Lam, L. W. (2000). A proposed infrastrural model for the establishment of organizational ethical systems. *Journal of Business Ethics, 28*(1), 35–42. For a discussion of performance appraisals, see Banner, D., & Cooke, A. (1984). Ethical dilemmas in performance appraisal. *Journal of Business Ethics, 3*(4), 327–333. For a discussion of stakeholders, see Harrison, J., & Freeman, E. (1999). Stakeholders, social responsibility, and performance: Empirical evidence and theoretical perspectives. *Academy of Management Journal, 42*(5), 479–485. For a discussion of organizational culture, see Douglas, P., Davidson, R., & Schwartz, B. (2001). The effect of organizational culture and ethical orientation on accountants' ethical judgments. *Journal of Business Ethics, 34*(2), 101–121; Nicotera A., & Cushman, D. (1992). Organizational ethics: A within-organization view. *Journal of Applied Communication Research, 20*(4), 437–462. For a discussion of dialogue, see Morrell, K., & Anderson, M. (2006). Dialogue and scrutiny in organizational ethics. *Business Ethics: A European Review, 15*(2), 117–129; Nielsen, R. (1990). Dialogic leadership as ethics action (praxis) method. *Journal of Business Ethics, 9*(10), 765–783. For a discussion of organizational environment, see Sims, R., & Keon, T. (1999). Determinants of ethical decision making: The relationship of the perceived organizational environment. *Journal of Business Ethics, 19*(4), 393–401.

18.   For a discussion of professions, organizational and individual constraints on decision-making, and individuals' perceptions of work climate on judgment, see Arnold, D., Bernardi, R., Neidermeyer, P., & Schmee, J. (2005). Personal versus professional ethics in confidentiality decisions: An exploratory study in Western Europe. *Business Ethics: A European Review, 14*(3), 277–289; Buchan, H. (2005). Ethical decision making in the public accounting profession: An extension of Ajzen's theory of planned behavior. *Journal of Business Ethics, 61*(2), 165–181; Aquino, K., & Becker, T. (2005). Lying in negotiations: How individual and situational factors influence the use of neutralization strategies. *Journal of Organizational Behavior, 26*(6), 661–679; Barrett, T., & Vaicys, C. (2000). The moderating effect of individuals' perceptions of ethical work climate on ethical judgments and behavioral intentions. *Journal of Business Ethics, 27*(4), 351–362.

19.   Werhane, P. H. (2007). Corporate social responsibility/corporate moral responsibility: Is there a difference and the difference it makes. In S. May, G. Cheney, & J. Roper (Eds.), *The debate over corporate social responsibility* (pp. 459–474). New York: Oxford University Press.

20.   Ganesh, S. (2007). Sustainable development discourse and the global economy: Promoting responsibility, containing change. In S. May, G. Cheney, & J. Roper (Eds.), *The debate over corporate social responsibility* (pp. 379–390). New York: Oxford University Press; Zorn, T., & Collins, E. (2007). Is sustainability sustainable? Corporate social responsibility, sustainable business, and management fashion. In S. May, G. Cheney, & J. Roper (Eds.), *The debate over corporate social responsibility* (pp. 405–416). New York: Oxford University Press.

21.   Sorell, T. (1989). Beyond the fringe? The strange state of business ethics. In M. Parker (Ed.), *Ethics in organization* London: Sage, p. 17

22.   Vallance, E. (1995). *Business ethics.* Cambridge: Cambridge University Press.

23.   Baucus, M., & Baucus, D. (1997). Playing the piper: An empirical examination of longer-term financial consequences of illegal corporate behavior. *Academy of Management Journal, 40*(1), 129–151.

24.   Stark, A. (1993). What's wrong with business ethics? *Harvard Business Review, 71*, p. 43.

25.   Donaldson, T., & Freeman, R. E. (1994). *Business as a humanity.* New York: Oxford University Press.

26.   Boyes, M., & Walker, L. J. (1988). Implications of cultural diversity for the universality claim of Kohlberg's theory of moral reasoning. *Human Development, 31*, 44–59; Fraedrich, J. P., & Ferrell, O. C. (1992a). Cognitive consistency of marketing managers in ethical situations. *Journal of the Academy of Marketing Science, 20*, 245–252; Fraedrich, J. P., & Ferrell, O. C. (1992b). The impact of perceived risk and moral philosophy type on ethical decision making in business organization. *Journal of Business Research, 24*, 283–295; Gold, A. R., Christie, R., & Friedman, L. N. (1976). *Fists and flowers: A social psychological interpretation of student dissent.* New York: Academic Press; Harris, J. R., & Sutton, C. D. (1995). Unraveling the ethical decision-making process: Clues from an empirical study comparing Fortune

1000 executives and MBA students. *Journal of Business Ethics 14*, 805–817; Ma, H. K., & Cheung, C. K. (1996). A cross-cultural study of moral stage structure in Hong Kong Chinese, English, and Americans. *Journal of Cross-Cultural Psychology, 27*, 700–713; Reidenbach, R. E., & Robin, D. P. (1990). Toward the development of a multidimensional scales for improving evaluations of business ethics. *Journal of Business Ethics, 9*, 639–653; Rest, J., & Narvaez, D. (1991). The college experience and moral development. In W. M. Kurtines & J. L. Gewirtz (Eds.), *Handbook of moral behavior and development*, Vol. 2: Research, 229–245. Hillsdale, NJ: Lawrence Erlbaum.

27.   Some of the specific, organizational examples are taken from, or based on, May, S. (Ed.). (2006). *Case studies in organizational communication: Ethical perspectives and practices*. Thousand Oaks, CA: Sage.

28.   Hunt, S. D., Wood, V R., & Chonko, L. B. (1989). Corporate ethical values and organizational commitment in marketing. *Journal of Marketing, 53*, 79–90; Mael, F., & Ashforth B. E. (1992). Alumni and their alma mater: A partial test of the reformulated model of organizational identification. *Journal of Organizational Behavior, 13*, 103-123.

29.   Ashforth, B., & Mael, F. (1989). Social identity and the organization. *Academy of Management Review, 14*, 20-39; Mael, F. A., & Tetrick, L. E. (1992). Identifying organizational identification. *Educational and Psychological Measurement, 52*(4), 813–825.

30.   Pierce, J. L., Kostova, T., & Dirks, K. T. (2002). Towards a theory of psychological ownership in organizations. *Academy of Management Review, 26*, 298–310.

31.   Hunt, S. D., & Morgan, R. M. (1994). Organizational Commitment: One of Many Commitments or Key Mediating Construct? *Academy of Management Journal, 37*(6), 1568–1587.

32.   Mowday, R. T., Steers, R. M., & Porter, L. W. (1979). The measurement of organizational commitment. *Journal of Vocational Behavior, 14*, 224–247.

33.   Gregersen, H. B. (1993). Multiple commitments at work and extrarole behavior during three stages of organizational tenure. *Journal of Business Research, 26*, 31–47; Mathieu, R. C., & Zajac, D. M. (1990). A review and meta-analysis of the antecedents, correlates, and consequences of organizational commitment. *Psychological Bulletin, 108*, 171–198.

34.   Miller, V. D., Allen, M., Casey, M. K., & Johnson, J.R. (2000). Reconsidering the organizational identification questionnaire. *Management Communication Quarterly, 13*, 626–659.

35.   Smith, (1999). To thine own employer be true. *Parks & Recreation, 34*(12), 26–34.

36.   Korsgaard, M. A., Brodt, S. E., & Whitener, E. M. (2002). Trust in the face of conflict: Role of managerial trustworthy behavior and organizational context. *Journal of Applied Psychology, 87*, 312–319.

37.   Whitener, E. M., Brodt, S. E., Korsgaard, M. A., & Werner, J. M. (1998). Managers as initiators of trust: An exchange relationship framework for understanding managerial trustworthy behavior. *Academy of Management Review, 23*(3), 513–530.

38.   Lind, E. A., Kanfer, R., & Earley, P. C. (1990). Voice, control, procedural justice: Instrumental and noninstrumental concerns in fairness judgments. *Journal of Personality and Social Psychology, 59*(5), 952–959.

39.   Butler, J. K. (1991). Towards understanding and measuring conditions of trust: Evolution of a conditions of trust inventory. *Journal of Management, 17,* 643–663; Mayer, R. C., & Davis, J. H. (1999). The effect of the performance appraisal system on trust for management: A field quasi-experiment. *Journal of Applied Psychology, 84,* 123–136; Tyler , T. R., & Lind, E. A. (1992). A relational model of authority in groups. *Advances in Experimental Social Psychology, 25,* 115–191.

40.   Tyler, T. R. (1989). The psychology of procedural justice: A test of the group-value model. *Journal of Personality and Social Psychology, 57*(5), 830–838.

41.   Sitkin, S. B., Hernandez, M., & Long, C. P. (2007). *Cultivating trust in leaders: Are all leader behaviors equally influential?* Working paper, Duke University.

42.   Tetlock, P. E. (1998). Losing our religion: On the collapse of precise normative standards in complex accountability systems. In R. Kramer & M. Neale (Eds.), *Influence processes in organizations: Emerging themes in theory and research.* Thousand Oaks, CA: Sage.

43.   Kouzes, J., & Posner, B. (2002). *The leadership challenge* (3rd ed.). San Francisco: Josey-Bass.

44.   Dubin, R. (1982). Management: Meaning, methods and moxie. *Academy of Management Review, 7*(3), p. 378.

45.   Hernandez, M. (2007). Promoting stewardship behavior in organizations: A leadership model. *Journal of Business Ethics;* Worline, M. (2002). Courage and work: Breaking routines to improve performance. In R. Lord, R. Flimoski & R. Kanfer (Eds.), *Emotions in the workplace: Understanding the structure and role of emotions in organizational behavior* (pp. 295–330). San Francisco, CA: Jossey-Bass.

CHAPTER 6

BEYOND THE INVISIBLE HAND

Self-Interest, Profit Maximization, and the Social Good

William H. Shaw

Part 1 of this chapter explores the relationship between social good and the pursuit of self-interest in business, focusing on the limits of the invisible hand mechanism and their economic and ethical implications. Part 2 examines individual self-interest and the corporate good, focusing on the principal-agent problem and the fiduciary responsibilities of management and on the contrast with the invisible hand mechanism at the macro level. Part 3 explores the elusive ideal of profit maximization (e.g., Costco vs. Wal-Mart on low wages) and what this implies for the narrow view of corporate social responsibility. Part 4 concludes by exploring the paradox of self-interest at both the individual and corporate levels.

Self-interest stands in complex, tangled relation to the good and the right, and nowhere is this more evident than in the world of business. In this essay, I probe some of the complicated links between pursuing profit, on the one hand, and doing good and acting rightly, on the other. There would be few complications to probe if the pursuit of profit were

Doing Well And Good: The Human Face of the New Capitalism, pp. 113–129
Copyright © 2009 by Information Age Publishing
All rights of reproduction in any form reserved.

guaranteed to enhance the well-being of all as the invisible-hand doctrine proclaims. Accordingly, the first two sections of this essay examine that doctrine and discuss its economic and ethical limitations. However, even when they have abandoned the invisible-hand doctrine and the narrow view of corporate social responsibility that typically accompanies it, many economists and business theorists still believe that we cannot reasonably expect corporations to act other than in self-interested, profit-seeking ways. The final sections of the paper rebut this idea by inspecting the fiduciary responsibilities of management, the public's expectations of corporations, and the elusiveness of profit maximization. Doing so illustrates the sometimes subtle interconnections between self-interest and right action and supports the contention that corporations, and the people in them, have moral obligations that go beyond self-interest and maximizing profit.

THE INVISIBLE HAND

Although some earlier writers advanced closely related ideas,[1] we owe to Adam Smith the famous and fertile concept of the invisible hand, which encapsulates the thesis that in a free and competitive market system, by pursuing his or her self-interest, each individual acts to promote the economic well-being of society generally. Any discussion of self-interest and doing good in business must begin here.

Smith's own discussion begins with the observation that self-interest drives business, providing the motivating force that turns the wheels of commerce and industry. In the early pages of *The Wealth of Nations*, he puts this point memorably:

> Whoever offers to another a bargain of any kind, proposes to do this. Give me that which I want, and you shall have this which you want, is the meaning of every such offer; and it is in this manner that we obtain from one another the far greater part of those good offices which we stand in need of. It is not from the benevolence of the butcher, the brewer, or the baker, that we expect our dinner, but from their regard to their own interest. We address ourselves, not to their humanity but to their self love, and never talk to them of our own necessities but of their advantages.[2]

Businessmen and other worldly-wise people have long been skeptical of anyone claiming to do business on grounds other than self-interest. Smith joins them. "I have never known much good done by those who affected to trade for the public good," he writes. "It is an affectation, indeed, not very common among merchants, and very few words need to be employed in dissuading them from it."[3]

The goal of business and of individuals engaged in business is to turn a profit, and the desire for profit—the desire to make money—is a self-interested desire, if anything is. By definition, of course, if one is motivated by self-interest, then one is not motivated by anything else, for example, by the desire to do what is right or the desire to assist one's fellow men and women. It doesn't follow from this, however, that self-interested behavior, especially self-interested economic behavior, cannot produce results that are good for others. Indeed, the emergence of economics as a social science rests on the idea that the market channels the pursuit of self-interest in socially beneficial directions, an idea that we owe largely to Smith. The image of an invisible-hand, which he used to make this point, has become a permanent part of our intellectual culture:

> Every individual is continually exerting himself to find out the most advantageous employment for whatever capital he can command. It is his own advantage, indeed, and not that of the society, which he has in view. But the study of his own advantage naturally, or rather necessarily leads him to prefer that employment which is most advantageous to the society...By directing [his] industry in such a manner as its produce may be of the greatest value, he intends only his own gain, [but] he is in this, as in many other cases, led by an invisible hand to promote an end which was no part of his intention.... By pursuing his own interest he frequently promotes that of the society more effectually than when he really intends to promote it.[4]

Business people have always found the invisible-hand metaphor reassuring because it seems to guarantee that by enriching oneself one is maximizing social benefit. It thus ennobles the pursuit of self-interest, insulating it from moral criticism. I may be acting selfishly, but the world would be worse off if I acted in any other way. It's not surprising, then, that the invisible-hand defense of self-interested behavior is perennially popular and surfaces in so many areas. A variant of it emerges when potential recipients of tax cuts for the already well-to-do argue for them on the grounds that they will make society as a whole better off. We also catch more than a glimpse of the invisible-hand narrative in a recent writer's defense of international sweatshops.[5] He absolves corporate America of any wrongdoing in scouring the globe for the lowest paid workforce it can find on the grounds that those who get the sweatshop jobs would be worse off otherwise.

The invisible-hand defense also forms part of Milton Friedman's case for the thesis that the only social responsibility of a business corporation is to increase its profits.[6] No matter how well intentioned, any attempt to divert corporations from profit maximization will have seriously untoward consequences. In particular, it will reduce the efficiency and productivity of our economy and, thus, diminish overall well-being. Pursuit of profit is what makes our system go. Anything that dampens this incentive or inhibits its operation will weaken the ability of Smith's invisible hand to deliver the economic goods.

Friedman's thesis—which we can call the "narrow view of corporate social responsibility"[7]—does not destroy the idea of business ethics. A business is not permitted to do anything whatsoever to increase its profits. Business people are not gangsters, and it would be wrong for a company to steal from suppliers, defraud customers, or employ physical force against its competitors. Doing so would violate what Friedman calls "the rules of the game," that is, the rules that make possible a basically laissez-faire system of open and free economic competition. Even within a laissez-faire economic framework, business activity presupposes certain minimal norms without which it would be impossible. But aside from that, moral considerations should not intrude into business decision-making. Self-interest rules, and rightly so.

LIMITS TO THE INVISIBLE HAND

In the last passage I quoted from Smith, he describes the invisible hand as working "in this, *as in many other cases*." Working in many cases is not the same as working in all cases, and Smith was far from being a "market fundamentalist." He never maintained that markets are always the most efficient option[8] or that they necessarily maximize well-being.[9] He didn't believe that the market is the solution to all problems.[10] This is not to deny that Smith generally favored laissez-faire, an economic ideal that contemporary economic thought is widely believed to buttress. In particular, the First Fundamental Theorem of Welfare Economics establishes that any competitive market represents an efficient allocation of resources. Susceptible to rigorous mathematical proof, this theorem is an impressive, indeed foundational, disciplinary achievement, and it seems to support the invisible-hand argument for Friedman's narrow view of corporate responsibility (that is, that the only responsibility of business is to maximize profit). If we interfere with the profit mechanism or if corporations pursue other, non-profit-related goals, the economy will only become less efficient, to the detriment of us all.

However, it is easy to overlook how limited the theorem is. To begin with, the concept of efficiency it relies on is what economists call "Pareto efficiency." By definition, a result is Pareto efficient if it makes one or more persons better off without making anyone else worse off, and a situation is Pareto optimal if no one can be made better off without making someone else worse off. These are useful concepts, but they're obviously insufficient as moral goals or ethical guidelines. The efficiency of an exchange says nothing about the justice or otherwise of its starting point (in particular, about the justice or otherwise of the assets that the parties involved bring to the exchange). Likewise, the fact that an outcome is Pareto optimal doesn't imply that it maximizes utility, let alone that it is equitable or fair. For example, it would not be Pareto efficient to tax the rich some modest sum to ensure minimal health care for the children of the poor even if doing so enhanced social well-being or were required by considerations of justice or fairness. Economists are wont to put these concerns aside on the grounds that they represent non-economic ("equity") issues, outside their professional purview. Fair enough, one might think: leave equity to the philosophers. But if so, then the putative efficiency of the market falls far short of underwriting the narrow view of corporate social responsibility or, more generally, the invisible-hand defense of self-interested business conduct.

In the previous sentence I used the word *putative* when referring to the efficiency of the market. I did so for a reason. If, putting aside issues of equity, we focus purely on the economic, we find that the Fundamental Theorem rests on the staggeringly idealized presupposition that the market in question is perfectly competitive. This entails, among other things, that the participants have perfect knowledge of all goods, services, and costs, that they are perfectly rational, and that there are no externalities, no monopolistic distortions, and no transaction or enforcement costs. The unreality of these assumptions is obvious. To this point, however, votaries of the market typically respond in two first ways. They contend, first, that real-world markets can approximate these conditions closely enough to guarantee efficient results and, second, that in any case we should strive to move real-worlds markets as close as we can toward the laissez-faire ideal.

Both responses are problematic. Let us begin with the second, which faces a challenge from what is known as the theory of the second best.[11] This holds that, given an imperfect market, there is no guarantee that taking a step toward laissez faire, that is, toward more competitive market conditions, will improve efficiency. Increasing competition here or removing a government regulation there may only make matters worse. (The intuitive idea is that market imperfections can cancel each other out, so that removing one of them may have refractory results.) The first response, on the other hand, is undercut by the fact that in the past couple of decades work in economic theory has only underscored the Fundamental Theorem's limited applicability, so that one can no longer maintain that aside from a few delimited exceptions, competitive markets are efficient. In particular, whenever information is imperfect—in particular, whenever some individual knows something that others do not (which is almost always)—then the invisible hand cannot be counted on to deliver an efficient outcome.[12] Indeed, without appropriate government regulation and intervention, markets do not lead to economic efficiency.[13] As a result, it is misleading to insist that, despite certain imperfections, the market by itself tends to produce efficient result. It would be more accurate to see purely market-generated efficiency as the exception rather than the rule.

CORPORATIONS AS
NECESSARILY SELF-INTERESTED AND PROFIT MAXIMIZING

The two arguments of the previous section—that there is no guarantee that less-than-ideal markets, which are all that we find in the real world, even tend to produce Pareto efficient results and that Pareto efficiency is, in any case, a socially impoverished ideal—undermine use of the invisible hand as a moral defense of self-interested economic behavior. They destabilize the idea that by pursuing self-interest, agents act rightly because they contribute to the long-run good of all, and they weaken the case for Friedman's thesis that the only social responsibility of business is to make as much money as it can. If free, laissez-faire markets guarantee efficient results only in conditions that never obtain in the real world, and if efficient outcomes may be unfair or suboptimal (and if, contrariwise, fair or welfare- enhancing outcomes are almost certain to violate Pareto constraints), then pursuing profit within the minimal rules of the business game hardly guarantees that an individual is acting morally or that a company is acting in a socially desirable way.

An appreciation of the shortcomings of the invisible-hand has lead economists and other social theorists to stress the necessity of government regulation to, among other things, correct market failures, respond to externalities, address problems of imperfect knowledge, and attempt to protect workers, consumers, and others who are in a weak bargaining position vis à vis large firms. And, in fact, for these reasons the governments of all modern capitalist countries intervene extensively in their economies and impose various restrictions on business activity that are intended to boost overall social welfare. This is, I'm sure, all to the good. However, many economists and business theorists assume that it is morally sufficient for both companies and individual businesspeople to pursue their self-interest within the government-modified rules of the post-laissez-faire game. Although these theorists have abandoned invisible-hand pieties, something like the original argument recurs: In relentlessly pursuing profit, business people act rightly, and corporations act in a socially responsible way, as long as they act lawfully. Thus, former Secretary of Labor Robert Reich urges that we should "not blame corporations" for things like layoffs or urge them to acknowledge obligations beyond the bottom line. "They are behaving exactly as they are organized to behave." Rather, he continues, "if we want corporations to take more responsibility" for the economic well-being of Americans, then government "will have to provide the proper incentives."[14]

Reich's thinking probably represents the way most economists look at the matter. Corporations are essentially egoistic and self-seeking. If we want them to act in better, more socially beneficial ways, then we must constrain them to do so through regulation and either incentives or the threat of punishment. Although Reich and like-minded economists may dissent from the laissez-faire perspective of Friedman, they concur with him in holding that business is properly governed by self-interest alone. They do so not because they believe, as he does, that it would necessarily have bad results for business to have a sense of social responsibility that leads it to pursue goals other than profit. They do so because they believe that it is unrealistic to expect business corporations to act other than in the self-interested, profit-maximizing way they were designed to act. Because "ought implies can," if corporations cannot act otherwise, then they have no obligation to do so.

My own contrary view is that society cannot successfully rely on the law alone to regulate business conduct and steer it in socially beneficial directions and, thus, that it is important for companies and the people in them, not just to pursue profit, but also to act on moral principle and with a full appreciation of the moral implications and social consequences of their conduct. In pursuing their business goals, managers and firms need to have an internal moral compass, a broad sense of social responsibility, and a desire to do what is right even if it does not maximize profit. And, consistent with the principle that "ought implies can," I believe that it is possible for people in business to act in these ways. These are large contentions, and I cannot fully defend them here. However, in line with my theme of the interplay between self-interest, on the one hand, and doing good and acting rightly, on the other, I probe three topics—the fiduciary responsibilities of management, the role of public expectations, and the elusiveness of profit maximization—consideration of which, I believe, makes implausible the contention that self-interest alone either should, or inevitably must, govern business behavior.

MANAGEMENT'S FIDUCIARY RESPONSIBILITIES

Here it is helpful, if somewhat ironic, to turn to Friedman. His thesis that the only responsibility of business is to pursue profit draws support, not only from the invisible-hand doctrine that doing so benefits us all, but also from the fact that shareholders have invested in the corporation precisely on the understanding that it will endeavor to make as much money for them as it can. Within the rules of the game, a corporation acts rightly in pursuing self-interest to the exclusion of other considerations because it is morally obliged to endeavor to maximize shareholder wealth. One can criticize this argument in various ways,[15] but what is of interest here is that it presupposes, indeed insists upon, the idea that managers have fiduciary responsibilities to the company's shareholders. They are to subordinate their own interests to those of the stockholders, who own the company.

Since the 1930s, it has been evident to business observers that managerial control of the corporation had been decisively divorced from ownership.[16] But if managers run the company, what prevents them from running it for their own benefit, rather than for that of its nominal owners, the stockholders? This is sometimes called the principal-agent problem, and addressing it is a recurrent issue for contemporary American capitalism.[17] Business theorists have sought various ways to align the interests of managers with those of stockholders, to provide them incentives to act so as to protect and advance shareholder interests. The extravagant benefits and luxurious pay and retirement packages that corporate managers award themselves these days provide perhaps the most blatant evidence of a failure to find a mechanism that harmonizes the interests of managers and shareholders and prevents the former from enriching themselves at the latter's expense. That failure stems, at least in part, from the desire of economists and business theorists to devise a system for aligning managerial and ownership interests that relies only on providing material incentives for managers to act in the desired ways (for example, by awarding them stock options).

It is possible, however, for schools of business and for business culture in general to instill in managers a sense of moral obligation to the company and its shareholders, and to some extent they succeed in doing so. The law underscores this obligation since it speaks clearly of management's having a fiduciary duty to the firm and its shareholders. As with most other duties, legal or otherwise, this obliges managers to put aside their own interests in order to fulfill certain responsibilities to others. However, and this is the point I want to make, if managers can see themselves (as Friedman says they should) as stewards of the corporation, who have a duty to its shareholders, then there is no reason for thinking that they cannot also believe and act on the idea that proper stewardship involves more than merely making money for shareholders—that is to say, that it also involves recognizing and acting on the basis of responsibilities to employees, to vendors and customers, to the public at large, to the environment, and indeed to the corporation itself as an on-going collective entity. In other words, if managers are already assumed by Friedman to be moral agents, capable of acting for reasons other than self-interest, then there is no reason for artificially restricting the scope of the moral considerations that they need to take into account. Managers are not profit-directed automatons. Just as they can and should restrain their self-interest because of the demands placed on them by their fiduciary responsibility to the owners, similarly they can and should restrain the self-interest of the company because of the demands that morality and the social good place on it.

Assuming that corporations do have an obligation to try to increase shareholder wealth, this obligation has to be weighed against competing moral considerations. This does not imply that profit must always give way to other concerns. Creative ways can often be found to reconcile the company's search for profit with its other moral responsibilities. Intelligent, well-managed companies can do good and act rightly at the same time that they make money for their stockholders. And although there is no guarantee that acting rightly will always be profitable (just as there is no guarantee that individual virtue will always be rewarded), there is ample evidence that the most ethical American companies are also among the most profitable.[18] The main point here, however, is that the principal-agent problem at the heart of corporate management requires, not just ever more cleverly designed systems of material incentives, but also a management culture that embraces and guides itself by norms other than self-interest. This parallels the argument of earlier sections that no invisible hand guarantees that self-enriching behavior is either morally right or productive of the greater good. Just as individual managers must acknowledge the need sometimes to subordinate personal self-interest to fiduciary duty, so must they recognize that the corporations they direct must sometimes place other responsibilities ahead of profit.

PUBLIC EXPECTATIONS

The proposition that corporations should focus only on the bottom line—indeed, that they can't help doing so—is complicated by the fact that these days the public expects business to act in socially responsible ways. They want to buy from and do business with good companies,[19] and they want to be proud of the firms they work for.[20] In a era where consumer groups, the media, and public-interest lawyers are quick to seize on irresponsible corporate behavior, almost all companies seek to portray themselves as socially responsible citizens, concerned, among other things, to promote diversity, to enhance the well-being of their employees, to contribute positively to their local communities, to abstain from using sweatshop labor, and to play their part in protecting the environment. They view as a calumny the allegation that profit is their only, or even their chief, goal. True, this is sometimes empty posturing or public relations hype, and much of it may indeed be hypocritical. But the pressure to act, or at least to be perceived to act, in socially responsible ways is real and significantly affects corporate behavior today.[21]

Let us assume, then, that it is often in a company's self-interest to appear to be socially responsible, to appear to acknowledge other obligations beyond merely pursuing profit. Usually, the most reliable way to appear to be socially responsible is, in fact, to act in socially responsible ways. Thus, the pursuit of profit itself can dictate acting in ways that are not immediately profitable, and corporate self-interest can require it to act in non-self-interested ways. Doing so might seem to be only a matter of policy, not morality—enlightened, sophisticated policy, perhaps, but still policy. This assumption is inaccurate, however. A policy of acting in socially responsibly ways when and only when a firm cannot get away with acting otherwise is likely to backfire. A firm that acts in this way is unlikely to be as successful as a firm that genuinely acknowledges obligations other than profit maximization. Thus, it may be (and, I believe, generally is) in a company's interest, not just to pretend to be, but to actually become, an organization that pursues other goals in addition to profit and monitors its conduct, in part, on the basis of moral standards.

On this point, a parallel can be drawn between corporations and individual persons. Both ancient moralists and modern psychologists point out that people who are exclusively concerned with their own interests tend to live less happy and less satisfying lives than those whose desires extend beyond themselves. Self-interest thus instructs one to be less self-interested because those who care about only their own happiness generally end up less happy than those who care about the happiness of others. Similarly, it is, for many reasons, advantageous for us to be believed by others to be honest and morally upright. The easiest way to achieve this goal is to act in an honest and upright fashion, and the surest way to ensure that one acts honestly and in an upright way is to endeavor to become a person who actually is honest and upright. To be sure, Machiavelli counsels his prince to cultivate a reputation as an honorable man while never scrupling to do, behind closed doors, whatever is necessary to retain and aggrandize his power. But few are in a position to follow Machiavelli's advice successfully. For most people the strategy of counterfeiting virtue—of acting morally when and only when one is observed and of cutting moral corners whenever one can get away with it—is likely to prove more difficult and less successful than the alternative strategy of simply striving to be a more moral person. In this regard, corporations and individuals are analogous. It can be in the long-term interest of a company, just as it is of an individual, to become a company (or an individual) that genuinely cares about more than its own profits or its own self-interest.

In response to this line of argument, one might point out that it is difficult for selfish people to make themselves less selfish or for an amoral person to come to take moral concerns seriously. Reshaping one's own character is no simple matter. But however well taken this point is, it has less force when applied to corporations. Like universities and other large organizations, business firms are not monoliths; they are made up of divisions with different agendas and personnel with different goals. Suppose a company, for purely self-interested reasons, desires to enhance its reputation for social responsibility. It therefore proclaims itself to be an enlightened, socially responsible firm, one that stands by certain ethical principles and is motivated, not just by profit, but also by a concern for the social good. It knows, however, that merely asserting its virtue is unlikely to win it the reputation and the public trust it seeks. It therefore takes steps toward institutionalizing its public commitments. Perhaps it hires a corporate responsibility officer, or a vice-president in charge of diversity, or sets up an internal office whose task it is to monitor and improve the company's environmental performance or its relations with the local community. These people are likely to believe in what they are doing, to take their job descriptions seriously, and to pursue earnestly the agenda that the corporation, whatever its motivation, says it wants them to pursue. They will thus be a force inside the company advocating goals other than profit-maximization, a force pushing the firm to live up to its public affirmations of social responsibility. Indeed, because their remuneration and advancement inside the company are likely to hinge on their success in doing their jobs, it will also be in the self-interest of these individuals to guide, goad, and cajole the company to act on the basis of considerations other than immediate profitability.

THE ELUSIVE GOAL OF PROFIT MAXIMIZATION

The fact that companies that are genuinely socially responsible tend to be more profitable than companies that focus only on profit shows that the notion of profit maximization is far from representing the clear and unproblematic desideratum it is usually and uncritically taken to be. Other considerations further support this point, for even when it comes to apparently simple economic mechanisms, the real world rarely cooperates with popular economic theory or makes it easy to know what will and what won't be profitable. When the state of Washington raised its minimum wage to nearly $8 an hour, with guaranteed annual adjustments for inflation, business leaders predicted it would be a disaster for retailers, especially in towns near the Idaho border, where the minimum wage remained only $5.15 an hour. A reasonable prediction, one might think. But a decade later, small business owners near the Idaho border are prospering as never before.[22]

True, it is sometimes obvious that course A will be profitable and that course B will not, but these easy cases tend to be silly or uninteresting. (Suppose, for example, that course B differs from course A only in that it gives every employee a free car.) But imagine a more realistic scenario where the choice that a firm faces between course A and course B involves various factors and is far from obvious. Here it will be difficult to determine, not just whether A will be profitable, nor even whether it will be more profitable than B, but also whether it is the most profitable course of action open to the firm. Management success would be simple if determining how to maximize profits were easy. But the future is almost always hazy, and there are many factors and many unknown variables, including chance, which can affect the relative success of a business venture. Options that might have been even more profitable can go unnoticed and unconsidered. In ethical theory, act utilitarianism faces a similar challenge. Often it is manifest that a possible action (for example, giving a child an ice cream cone) will bring about some happiness and, moreover, that it will bring about more happiness than some alternative action (hitting the child with a stick). But is it the course of action that will bring about more happiness than anything else the agent could possibly have done? The answer to that question is elusive at best.

We can sometimes say of a business strategy that it has been shown to be profitable and that the firm that followed it is doing well, but we are rarely justified, even after the fact, in saying that the company chose the optimal or profit-maximizing course. Perhaps there was some other strategy that would have made the company more money or that would have been sustainable longer or that would have opened the door to further profit-making ventures. There are many possible corporate strategies and many roads to success. At best, one can say that a given strategy was one of several profit-making approaches that a firm might have elected.

Take Wal-Mart for example. Everyone agrees that part of its business success rests on its low-wage strategy, and in theory that strategy might seem impeccable: increase corporate profits by squeezing wages and benefits. On the other hand, Costco, a roughly comparable retailer, is even more profitable than Wal-Mart, and yet it pays significantly higher wages and provides more employee benefits than Wal-Mart does.[23] Could Costco increase its profits by following Wal-Mart? Experts think that the answer is no, that much of Costco's success stems from the dedication, low turnover, and high morale of its employees. Does that entail that if Wal-Mart were to pay its employees better, it would become even more profitable? Perhaps it would, but we have no compelling reason for thinking so. Different companies are built in different ways, inherit different challenges, enjoy different strengths, and operate in environments that are at least slightly different so that what works for Costco might or might not work for Wal-Mart and vice-versa.[24] To illustrate further the point that we can rarely, if ever, identify any single business strategy as the optimal or profit-maximizing one, consider the automobile industry. In 2007 it was reported that the Daimler-Chrysler Corporation—the product of the headline-making 1998 merger of Chrysler and Daimler-Benz—would be broken apart, that General Motors was selling off the stake in Fiat it had acquired a few years earlier, and that Ford Motor Company was moving to divest itself of Volvo, Jaguar, and Land Rover, all relatively recent acquisitions.[25] These three moves may or may not prove profitable, and looking back one may be able to determine how profitable or unprofitable the original mergers or acquisitions were. Things change, of course, and it is possible that both the original actions and their subsequent reversals were (or will be) not only wise moves at the time, but profitable ones, at least for a while. Were they profit-maximizing moves? I doubt whether anyone can say.

In an era when the popular business media tends to laud the CEOs of our largest corporations as business geniuses whatever they do (whether they are merging Chrysler and Daimler-Benz or splitting them apart), it is easy to forget that they are frequently flying by the seat of their pants because the factors that affect corporate success and profitability are so many and so varied that one can rarely, if ever, say that a given strategy is the profit-maximizing one. Indeed, the question "What is *the* profit maximizing strategy for this company in this situation?" may have no definite answer because answering it would involve knowing what the results or likely results of various alternative strategies would be in an environment that not only changes, but changes, often in unforeseeable ways, because of one's own decisions.[26] At best, a company may be presented with a number of apparently profitable options, without it being possible to say, either before or after the fact, whether one of them was better than the others, let alone that it was the single most profitable thing that the company could possibly have done.

If in the real world of business there is no one right or profit-maximizing answer, then management will almost always face a choice among several respectable options, among a number of alternatives, each of which appears viable from a business point of view. If so, then managers can, consistent with their duty to shareholders, choose the one that best fulfills the firm's other social and moral obligations. Appreciating the ineluctable elusiveness of profit maximization thus frees us from the moral tyranny of

Friedman and other economists, from the error of supposing there is a single profit-maximizing course to which all other considerations should, or at least inevitably will, give way. Profit maximization is an illusory ideal. Abandoning it allows us to recognize that there is ample room for the exercise of moral judgment in business and for creative action that greatly diminishes the likelihood of an irresolvable conflict between acting profitably, on the one hand, and acting rightly and doing good, on the other hand.

CONCLUSION

The doctrine of the invisible hand implies that business makes its greatest contribution to the public good simply by pursuing profit with all the vigor it can muster. We have seen, however, that both the moral and economic underpinnings of this doctrine are weak, and there is no reason to think that a firm, in seeking to maximize its own profits, thereby necessarily maximizes the social good. Still, even when the invisible-hand doctrine is abandoned, one might insist that business firms, being what they are, are incapable of pursuing any goal other than that of self-enrichment. Against this I have advanced three lines of argument. First is the contention that just as managers can acknowledge a fiduciary responsibility to the company and subordinate their personal interests to it, so they can acknowledge that the company has social responsibilities that go beyond making money and restrain its actions and redirect its choices accordingly. Second, the idea that companies can only pursue profit bumps up against the reality that the public expects corporations to care about more than profit and that it rewards those that do. Thus, the profit motive itself dictates that businesses be less obsessed with profit. Finally, the goal of profit maximization is inevitably indeterminate. As a result managers are likely always to be faced with a choice among a number of feasible business options, and this fact, in turn, opens space for moral choice.

NOTES

1. See, in particular, Bernard de Mandeville's *Fable of the Bees* (1714).
2. Adam Smith, *An Inquiry into the Nature and Causes of the Wealth of Nations*, ed. Richard F. Teichgraeber (New York: Modern Library, 1985), p. 16.
3. Ibid., p. 225.
4. Ibid., pp. 223, 225. See also pp. 305–306.
5. Ian Maitland, "The Great Non-Debate over International Sweatshops," *British Academy of Management Annual Conference Proceedings*, September 1997. Reprinted in William H. Shaw and Vincent Barry, *Moral Issues in Business*, 10th ed. (Belmont, Calif.: Wadsworth, 2007), pp. 198–205.

6. See Milton Friedman, *Capitalism and Freedom* (Chicago: University of Chicago Press, 1962) and "The Social Responsibility of Business Is to Increase Its Profits," *New York Times Magazine*, September 13, 1970.
7. Shaw and Barry, *Moral Issues in Business*, pp. 213–215.
8. For instance, Smith advocated a legally imposed maximum interest rate so that money would not be lent unproductive persons, who are likely to be the only ones willing to borrow at exorbitant rates. (Jeremy Bentham, interestingly enough, disagreed and wrote Smith to argue for leaving the market alone.) See Amaryta Sen, *Development as Freedom* (New Delhi: Oxford University Press, 2000), pp. 124–126.
9. Consider Smith's discussion of the need for caution in opening a previously protected domestic market to foreign competition based on an "equitable regard" for the interests of the domestic manufacturer (*Wealth of Nations*, pp. 241–242).
10. For example, Smith believed that toll roads should not be in private hands (*Wealth*, p. 391) and that industries important for national defense may have to be protected from foreign competition (p. 232). As a general matter, he unambiguously acknowledged that there are public institutions and public works that the market cannot provide (p. 388).
11. R. G. Lipsey and Kelvin Lancaster, "The General Theory of Second Best," *Review of Economic Studies*, Vol. 24, no. 1 (1956–57), pp. 11–32.
12. See Joseph E. Stiglitz's 2001 Nobel-Prize lecture, "Information and the Change in the Paradigm in Economics" (available at http://nobelprize.org/nobel-prizes/laureates/2001/stigliz-lecture.htm), especially, pp. 503–506. A standard example is the used-car market, where sellers typically have greater product knowledge than buyers. Unless the law forces used-car dealers to disclose defects or unless a code of ethics restrains them, the buyer is likely to purchase a product he doesn't want (at least not at that price) or, not trusting the dealer, to refrain from buying a product he needs. Either result is inefficient.
13. Joseph E. Stiglitz, *Making Globalization Work* (New York: Norton, 2006), p. xiv.
14. Robert B. Reich, "How to Avoid These Layoffs," *New York Times*, January 4, 1996, A13. See also Robert B. Reich, *Supercapitalism: The Transformation of Business, Democracy, and Everyday Life* (New York: Knopf, 2007), Chapter 5. In a similar vein, Teddy Roosevelt once proclaimed: "I believe in corporations. They are indispensable instruments of our modern civilization; but they should be so supervised and so regulated that they shall act for the interests of the community as a whole." Quoted by John Micklethwait and Adrian Wooldridge, *The Company* (New York: Modern Library, 2003), p. 182.
15. See Shaw and Barry, *Moral Issues in Business*, pp. 217–218.
16. For the classic statement of this thesis, see Adolf A. Berle, Jr., and Gardiner C. Means, *The Modern Corporation and Private Property* (New York: Macmillan, 1932).

17. For a good discussion of this, see John Cassidy, "The Greed Cycle," *New Yorker*, September 23, 2002. Reprinted in Shaw and Barry, *Moral Issues*, pp. 246–255.

18. James E. Post, Anne T. Lawrence, and James Weber, *Business and Society: Corporate Strategy, Public Policy, and Ethics*, 10th ed. (New York: McGraw-Hill, 2002), pp. 104-105; "Shares of Corporate Nice Guys Can Finish First," *New York Times*, April 27, 2005 (online); Marjorie Kelly, "Holy Grail Found," *Business Ethics*, Winter 2004; and Thomas Donaldson, "Defining the Value of Doing Good Business," *Financial Times* (supplement on "Mastering Corporate Governance"), June 3, 2005, 2. For more theoretical reflections, see Robert K. Frank, "Can Socially Responsible Firms Survive in a Competitive Environment?" in David M. Messick and Ann E. Tenbrunsel, eds., *Codes of Conduct: Behavioral Research into Business Ethics* (New York: Sage, 1996), pp. 86–103.

19. Among young Americans, 88% believe that companies have a responsibility to support social causes, and 86% say that they switch brands based on social issues. Almost three-quarters of all job seekers prefer to work for socially responsible companies. "The Corporate Givers," *Business Week*, November 29, 2004, pp. 102-103. See also O. C. Ferrell, John Fraedrich, and Linda Ferrell, *Business Ethics: Ethical Decision Making and Cases*, 7th ed. (Boston: Houghton Mifflin, 2008), pp. 20–21.

20. See Sue Shellenbarger, "Workers Leave If Firms Don't Stick to Values," *San Francisco Sunday Examiner & Chronicle*, June 27, 1999, CL31; Michael Skapinker, "Money Can't Make You Happy but Being in a Trusted Team Can," *Financial Times*, June 1, 2005, 8; and Linda K. Treviño and Katherine A. Nelson, *Managing Business Ethics: Straight Talk About How to Do It Right*, 4th ed. (Hoboken, N.J.: Wiley, 2007), p. 31. It's not surprising, then, that publicly traded firms on *Fortune*'s list of the 100 best companies to work for not only outperform the S&P 500, they (in the magazine's words) "wallop it." "The 100 Best Companies to Work For," *Fortune*, January 23, 2006, 100.

21. See the July 2007 reports for the UN Global Compact by Goldman Sachs and McKinsey and Company, available at www.unglobalcompact.org

22. "For $7.93 an Hour, Crossing the State Line Is Worth It," *New York Times*, January 11, 2007, A1. The article's anecdotes bear out its statistics: "We're paying the highest wage we've ever had to pay and our business is still up more than 11 percent over last year," reports the manager of a pizza parlor close to the state line. Another fast food proprietor says, "To tell you the truth, my business is fantastic. I've never done as much business in my life."

23. "The Costco Way," *Business Week*, April 12, 2004, pp. 76–77; "How Costco Became the Anti-Wal-Mart," *New York Times*, July 17, 2005, sec. 3, p. 1; and Wayne F. Cascio, "Decency Means More than 'Always Low Prices': A Comparison of Costco to Wal-Mart's Sam's Club," *Academy of Management Perspectives*, Vol. 20, no. 3 (August 2006), pp. 26–37.

24. By analogy, imagine a football league with many teams. One top team has built its success on defense, but its winning record is surpassed by a team with a distinctive, high scoring pass offense. Should the first team mimic what the second has done?

25.   "Ford Seeking a Future by Going Backward," *New York Times*, July 17, 2007, C1.

26.   This indeterminacy may be more than an epistemological problem; that is, it may be an indeterminacy, not in what we can know, but in the way things are. If determinism is false, then there is no absolute fact of the matter as to what would have happened had we done something other than what we did.

CHAPTER 7

BEYOND THE BOTTOM LINE

A Shifting Paradigm for Business?

Mark S. Schwartz

When it comes to major paradigm shifts in the business world over the last few years, a number of possible contenders come to mind. For example, some ideas that have recently come onto the business scene in a big way include: (1) corporate social responsibility; (2) business ethics; (3) stakeholder management; (4) sustainability; and (5) corporate citizenship. Many of these notions counter Milton Friedman's frequently-cited statement that the only responsibility of business "is to increase its profits within the rules of the game" Any of the above five frameworks could be considered to have shifted Milton Friedman's "profit maximization" paradigm of business in the direction of going "beyond the bottom line." Despite their differences, the five frameworks have certain elements in common, such as focusing business activities and practices not just on profits or shareholder value but on social impacts as well. Taken together, the five frameworks do appear to represent a paradigm shift for business, one which is based on: (1) generating net sustainable value for society (i.e., not just shareholder value); (2) balancing potentially conflicting stakeholder interests (i.e., beyond shareholders); (3) reflecting on important ethical standards; and (4) demonstrating sufficient accountability (e.g., through auditing and reporting). While each of the five frameworks currently permeates the business world, whether any one of the frameworks will take precedence in the long-term over the others remains to be seen.

Doing Well And Good: The Human Face of the New Capitalism, pp. 131–147
Copyright © 2009 by Information Age Publishing

131

When it comes to the proper role business should play in society, a range of possibilities exist. One of the more influential positions comes from Nobel prize winning economist Milton Friedman.[1] His oft-quoted statement from his 1970 *New York Times Magazine* article that the sole responsibility of business "is to increase its profits within the rules of the game"[2] continues to prevail within the business community[3] along with the support of many academic scholars.[4] Friedman's position, sometimes referred to as the "stockholder" or "shareholder" model, in many respects underlies the basis of the capitalistic market system. His view essentially suggests that managers of firms, as agents of their shareholders, should only focus on maximizing their firm's bottom line. The only constraints would consist of merely abiding by the law as well as "avoiding deception and fraud" while following "ethical custom." According to Friedman, the resolution of social problems is more properly the concern of governments, as opposed to business. While Friedman represents what many would consider to be one end of the spectrum in terms of the role that business should play in society,[5] as discussed below, others in both academia and business have suggested that Friedman's view may be too narrow. In this essay, five other business and society frameworks that have emerged over the years are discussed which counter or broaden Friedman's position and thus represent a possible paradigm shift for the business world. These frameworks include: (1) corporate social responsibility [CSR]; (2) business ethics [BE]; (3) stakeholder management [SM]; (4) sustainability [SUS]; and (5) corporate citizenship [CC]. After briefly discussing each of the five frameworks, a new model is proposed that attempts to tie together the core elements from each of these five frameworks, and thus propose a new role for business in society.

Corporate Social Responsibility: Today, many might suggest that CSR is now a dominant paradigm in the business world. CSR's original focus on reducing negative social impacts has appeared to shift over time to the more general notion of "doing good" for society. Archie Carroll, in his review of the evolution of corporate social responsibility, identifies its origins as taking place in the 1930s and 1940s.[6] He suggests, however, that it was Howard Bowen's work in 1953, *The Social Responsibilities of the Businessman* that really set the stage for the future development of CSR.[7] The CSR concept, while open to different interpretations, essentially suggests that companies possess not only economic and legal obligations, but ethical and philanthropic responsibilities as well.[8] While measures of CSR activities vary, many focus on what are considered to be socially responsible practices related to employees, customers, suppliers, communities, or the natural environment[9] In terms of its practical impact on the business community, many corporations now have CSR managers, engage in CSR auditing and reporting, or discuss their CSR activities on their Web sites or in their annual reports.[10] For example, in Toshiba's 2006 "Corporate Social Responsibility Report," President and CEO Atsutoshi Nishida states:

> Since I assumed the presidency of Toshiba a year ago, I have positioned the principles of CSR at the heart of management, *alongside sustained growth with profit*.... We strive to make CSR an integral part of daily business operations for each and eery business division and employee, and in doing so we hope to earn the trust of all our stakeholders and the business community.[11] [emphasis added]

Other business initiatives such as strategic philanthropy, venture philanthropy, and cause-related marketing have been linked to the CSR concept. CSR has also achieved prominence in the academic community in terms of journals and conferences.[12] Despite any possible deficiencies with CSR, according to Archie Carroll: "it appears that the CSR concept has a bright future because at its core, it addresses and captures the most important concerns of the public regarding business and society relationships."[13]

Business Ethics: A second possible paradigm shift is the BE movement. One could argue that the topic of business ethics has been around for quite some time: "Concern about ethical issues in business goes back as far as history itself; there has always been some form of mandate for people in commerce."[14] As an academic framework however, Richard De George might be considered the first to distinguish business ethics as a separate field of study. In discussing the past and future status of business ethics, De George identifies the 1970s as the period of time during which business ethics developed as a field. It wasn't until the mid-1980s however that business ethics became institutionalized: "By 1985 business ethics had become an academic field, albeit still in the process of definition."[15] There have been a number of important early contributors (among many others) to the field of business ethics over the years, primarily through their textbook publications.[16] Today, business ethics is firmly entrenched in academia through courses, conferences, and journals.[17]

Although the field of business ethics covers a broad range of topics, the core of the field is based in moral philosophy and its use of moral standards (i.e., values, principles, and theories) in order to engage in ethical assessments of business activity and to prescribe ethical courses of action. Such moral standards would clearly broaden the scope of what is ethically required of managers and firms according to Milton Friedman (i.e., beyond merely "avoiding deception and fraud" and abiding by "ethical custom"). Some of the more dominant moral theories include: utilitarianism; deontology (e.g., Kantianism); moral rights; justice; and moral virtue.[18] Recent corporate scandals further suggest that certain related core ethical values and practices such as transparency, accountability, honesty, integrity, and caring and are also critical to the field of business ethics.[19]

While originally discussing the morality of business in general, BE in both the academic and business communities appears to have become more focused recently on the notion of business and its agents "avoiding harm" to others due to major corporate scandals (e.g., Enron, WorldCom, etc.). Many important business ethics issues have been raised over the years, such as insider trading, aggressive accounting practices, product safety/recalls, deceptive marketing, discrimination, sexual harassment, privacy, gifts/bribery and corruption, child labor, operating in countries with repressive regimes, worker health and safety, whistle-blowing, downsizing, and outsourcing among others. In March 2002 U.S. President George Bush recognized the importance of business ethics when he stated that "corporate America must be made more accountable to employees and shareholders and held to the highest standards of conduct."[20] U.S. regulations like the 1991 *Federal Sentencing Guidelines for Organizations*[21] and the *Sarbanes-Oxley Act of 2002*[22] demonstrate the recent shift among government regulators towards more formal business ethics practices. Essentially, companies operating in the United States are required to implement and administer ethics programs, including such elements as ethics codes, ethics training, and ethics helplines or hotlines. Not only would the required ethical behavior as prescribed by most corporate codes of ethics go beyond that required by Friedman,[23] many ethics codes also include an explicit statement that profits should not trump ethical behavior. For example, Richard Waugh, CEO of Canada's Scotiabank, makes it clear in his introduction to his firm's "Guidelines for Business Conduct" that ethics must take priority to the bottom line when he states:

> Each of us must do what's right. This is always in the bank's best interests *even when doing the right thing seems to conflict with meeting sales or profit targets*. We do not compromise our ethics for the sake of other goal.[24] [emphasis added]

In addition to codes and training, many firms now possess their own ethics officer. There are now more than 1,200 members of the Ethics and Compliance Officers Association (ECOA) in the United States, who have the primary responsibility for their firm's ethics and compliance programs.[25]

Stakeholder Management: A third seemingly evident paradigm shift is *stakeholder management*. Over the past 20 years, stakeholder management has emerged as a dominant construct within management circles and a "mainstay of management theory."[26] In terms of its early history, "Evidence of stakeholder concepts can be traced as far back as Barnard (1938)"[27] Following the 1984 seminal publication of Edward Freeman's influential book, *Strategic Management: A Stakeholder Approach*,[28] the term stakeholder, became a mainstay of both academia and the business world. Freeman defined a "stakeholder" as an individual or group who affects or is affected by a firm's actions. Stakeholder management essentially shifted the focus from shareholders to the interests of non-shareholders. Today, virtually all firms and their managers now refer to their non-shareholder stakeholders including: employees, customers, suppliers, governments, communities, and even the natural environment. Many normative and instrumental arguments have been raised as to why (non-shareholder) stakeholders deserve managerial attention.[29] Scholars continue to debate however over the related issues of "who" should be considered to be a managerial stakeholder, and on "what basis" stakeholder interests should be prioritized.[30] Johnson & Johnson is an example of one company that makes it very clear however which stakeholders should take priority. The firm's corporate credo ("Our Credo") indicates: "We believe our first responsibility is to the doctors, nurses and patients, to mothers and fathers and all others who use our products and services.... Our final responsibility is to our stockholders."[31] Today, many firms practice "stakeholder engagement', in which they dialogue with their stakeholders and attempt to balance their potentially competing interests.[32] In addition, corporate governance legislation continues to evolve around the world to better take into account stakeholder (e.g., employees, creditors, minority shareholders, etc.) interests at the board of directors level.[33] Although not as extensive as a distinct area of academia as several of the other business and society frameworks, one can still find examples of stakeholder management in academia.[34]

Sustainability: A fourth contender for a paradigm shift away from Milton Friedman is the *sustainability* framework. The concept originated from the 1987 publication of *Our Common Future*, the report of the World Commission on Environment and Development, which defined sustainable development as meeting "the needs of the present without compromising the ability of future generations to meet their own needs."[35] More recently, sustainability has broadened its focus from the natural environment to also take into account additional social impacts. In 1994, John Elkington first introduced the business concept of a "triple bottom line" into management thinking, that is, the simultaneous pursuit of economic prosperity, environmental quality, and social equity.[36]

One proposed broad definition of sustainability links it to stakeholder management: "Corporate sustainability ... refers to a company's activities —voluntary by definition—demonstrating the inclusion of social and environmental concerns in business operations and in interactions with stakeholders."[37] Over the past decade, several authors have continued to develop the construct of sustainable development into a framework suitable for business applications.[38] Today, the triple bottom line concept has led to many firms producing environmental or sustainability reports. For example, Alcan's "Sustainability Report 2006": states:

> Building a successful, global and sustainable company involves *maximizing value for all our stakeholders*, especially by making a significant contribution— through the way we do business and the products we make—to the economic, social and environmental well-being of the communities in which we operate[39] [emphasis added]

Sustainability has also penetrated into the academic community.[40] According to Elkington, sustainability "is the emerging 21st century business paradigm."

Corporate Citizenship: The fifth and final contender for a new business paradigm shift is *corporate citizenship*. While originally focusing on corporate philanthropy and community involvement, corporate citizenship appears to have transformed into a broader business and society framework, and has significantly increased in popularity as a result.[41] For example, some suggest that: "the language of corporate citizenship (CC) appears to be replacing that of corporate social responsibility (CSR)"[42] Several definitions of CC have been suggested. Chris Marsden proposes a general definition for the concept: "Corporate citizenship is defined as a company's management of its influences on and relationships with the rest of society."[43] Sandra Waddock provides a more normative definition of CC:

> Good corporate citizens live up to clear constructive visions and core values. They treat well the entire range of stakeholders who risk capital in, have an interest in, or are linked to the firm through primary and secondary impacts through developing respectful, mutually beneficial operating practices and by working to maximize sustainability of the natural environment.[44]

While many equate corporate citizenship with corporate social responsibility, the notion of corporate citizenship differs by focusing on the rights and duties of corporations *as citizens* with respect to all of society. Today, the notion of corporate citizenship is often mentioned in many corporate Web sites and corporate citizenship reports.[45] HP indicates on its corporate Web site that corporate citizenship means going beyond profits:

> HP has a strong legacy of global citizenship. Our founders Bill Hewlett and Dave Packard recognized that a company *has a responsibility beyond making a profit* for its investors, including a commitment to enrich the businesses, lives and communities of its customers, partners and employees. For nearly 70 years, we have honored that responsibility by striving to be an economic, intellectual and social asset to each country and community in which we do business.[46] [emphasis added]

Corporate citizenship has also become an important part of the academic community.[47]

Table 7.1 summarizes the main dimensions for each of the five business and society frameworks.

When considered collectively, the ubiquity of the five frameworks in both the business and academic communities suggests that Milton Friedman's "profit maximization" paradigm has in fact shifted over the years towards a broader normative framework of going "beyond the bottom line." As further evidence of the shift beyond profits, one can now point to numerous examples of public firms that explicitly indicate that reasonable financial returns to shareholders might be sufficient. For example, rather than promise maximum returns, Johnson & Johnson states in referring to its Credo: "When we operate according to these principles, the stockholders should realize a fair return."[48] Such principles seem to have been applied during the immediate nationwide Tylenol recall in 1982 upon discovery of seven cyanide poisonings in the Chicago area.[49] Merck has also had a corporate motto for years that indicates that profits are not the superordinate goal of the firm. Their motto as indicated by George W. Merck is as follows:

> We try never to forget that medicine is for the people. It is not for the profits. The profits follow, and if we have remembered that, they have never failed to appear. The better we have remembered it, the larger they have been.[50]

This motto appears to have been lived up to when Merck spent tens of millions of dollars to produce a pill to help cure millions of people living in Africa and Latin America of river blindness, despite the fact that the users would not be able to pay for the drug.[51] Other firms indicating that reasonable returns are acceptable include Scotiabank (i.e., returns to shareholders must be "fair and reasonable"[52]), forestry firm Weyerhaeuser (i.e., returns must be "superior"[53]), and Australia's ANZ Bank (i.e., returns must be "sustainable"[54]).

Integrating the Five Frameworks—The "VBA Model": A closer analysis suggests that there may in fact be three core concepts which underlie, unify, and integrate the five frameworks together: *value*; *balance*; and *accountability* (i.e., the "VBA" model), representing a possible paradigm shift for business. The new paradigm is one that is based on: (1) generating net sustainable *value* for society (i.e., not just shareholder value); (2) *balancing* potentially conflicting stakeholder interests (i.e., beyond shareholders) while reflecting on important ethical standards; and (3) demonstrating sufficient *accountability* (e.g., through auditing and reporting). The portrayal of the three core concepts in a Venn diagram (see Figure 7.1) emphasizes the fact that abiding by only one or even two of the three

Table 7.1. Comparative Analysis of Dominant Business and Society Frameworks

Criteria/ Concept	Corporate Social Responsibility (CSR)	Business Ethics (BE)	Stakeholder Management (SM)	Sustainability (SUS)	Corporate Citizenship (CC)
History	1960s (and prior)	1970s	1980s	1990s	2000s
Origins	Social impact	Morality	Non-shareholders	Natural environment	Community/ philanthropy
Core definition	Do good	Avoid harm	Balance interests	Ensure future	Societal contribution
Focal entities	Organization	Managers, employees, and organization	Managers and organization	Organization	Organization
Narrow vs. Broad Versions	Economic/Legal vs. Ethical/ Discretionary	Law/ Compliance vs. Ethics/ Integrity/ Values	Narrow/Primary Stakeholders vs. Wide/ Broad/ Secondary stakeholders	Homocentric vs. Ecocentric	Philanthropy vs. Social
Theoretical offshoots	• Shareholder model • Corporate responsibility • Social issues in management • Corporate societal accountability/ responsiveness/performance	• Ethics-based management • Values-based management • Corporate governance and ethics • Moral leadership and ethics	• Stakeholder relations • Stakeholder engagement • Stakeholder corporation • Stakeholder capitalism	• Corporate environmentalism • Business and the environment • Sustainable capitalism	• Business citizenship

concepts is not only insufficient from a normative perspective but can eventually lead to either a firm's collapse or significant harm to society. For example, a company that fails to remain accountable (i.e., sufficiently disclose its activities), despite contributing to sustainable societal value while appropriately balancing the interests of stakeholders, will ultimately be challenged. According to John Elkington:

> Companies that have previously sought to justify no disclosure or low-disclosure policies will find that they...are increasingly operating in a global goldfish bowl ... the difficulties of keeping secrets will become immeasurably greater. Sooner or later, most things a company thinks or does will become public knowledge. Companies that fail to plan with this fact in mind must be prepared to pay the price.[55]

A firm that fails to act in a sustainable manner, despite balancing interests while demonstrating accountability, will also potentially face societal pressures, in addition to harming the world's ecosystem: "Many business

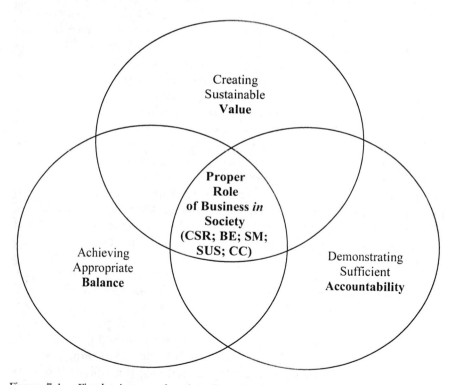

Figure 7.1.   Five business and society frameworks and their three core concepts [The "VBA Model"].

people will argue that it is not their business to save the world. But the expectation is growing around the world that business will deliver."[56] A firm that fails to appropriately balance competing interests despite generating sustainable value and demonstrating sufficient accountability, will also come under pressure. According to Archie Carroll and Anne Buchholtz: "whenever power and responsibility become substantially *out of balance*, forces will be generated [e.g., government, media, special interest groups] to bring them into closer balance"[57] [emphasis added]. Edward Freeman is even more explicit: "management must keep the relationships among stakeholders in balance. When these relationships *become imbalanced*, the survival of the firm is in jeopardy"[58] [emphasis added]. Any business that is judged as meeting all three core concepts can be said to be acting according to the primary concerns expressed by all five frameworks (i.e., CSR, BE, SM, SUS, and CC), and would be positioned in the middle of the Venn diagram. Figure one below portrays the five frameworks with respect to the three core concepts.

In terms of future research and teaching in the business and society field, the three core elements of *value*, *balance*, and *accountability* could be utilized to assess, analyze, or link together other fields such as strategic management or corporate governance, which over time have become more and more inter-connected with the various constructs of the business and society field. For example, research questions could be explored such as to what extent are a firm's strategies (i.e., corporate objectives or mission statements) directed towards generating sustainable societal value, appropriately balancing stakeholder interests, and/or demonstrating sufficient accountability? To what extent do boards of directors and managers act in ways that ensure value, balance, and accountability? To what extent do government regulators, stock exchanges, or industry associations require or encourage them to do so?

The core elements of value, balance, and accountability might also provide a more suitable means by which to evaluate or analyze corporate failures as well as successes. For example, Enron, prior to its collapse, appears to have failed to meet all three core elements: lack of providing sustainable societal value, inappropriate balance, and insufficient accountability. Enron did not act in a financially sustainable manner (e.g., destruction of share value), failed to ethically balance the interests of its stakeholders including its customers (e.g., manipulating energy markets in California), employees (e.g., pensions), and even paradoxically its shareholders (e.g., bankruptcy), and also demonstrated an utter lack of accountability by hiding its massive debt and shredding its own documents[59] Wal-Mart, while arguably generating net value for society through employment and more affordable consumer goods, continues to face criticism for not appropriately balancing competing stakeholder interests while insufficiently demonstrating accountability.[60] Other classic corporate examples taught in the business and society field such as the Exxon Valdez oil spill,[61] Union Carbide's poisonous leak from its pesticide plant in Bhopal India,[62] and the case of Ford's rollovers versus Firestone's tire blowouts,[63] could all be more fully examined or taught in relation to whether the core elements of the VBA model (i.e., value, balance, and accountability), were being realized.

Research could also be undertaken to examine the potential relationship between the three core elements of the model and long-term financial performance. For example, do companies that consistently generate sustainable societal value, appropriately balance stakeholder interests and/or moral standards, while demonstrating sufficient accountability, financially outperform or under perform those that do not in the long-term? Although more precise measurements for "net societal value," "appropriate balance," and "sufficient accountability" would necessarily have to be developed before such a study could be conducted, the three core elements suggests that an empirical focus beyond merely the relationship between corporate social performance and firm performance may be appropriate.[64] If research were in fact to demonstrate a positive relationship between firms that realize the three core elements and firm long-term financial performance, then Friedman's major concern over managers respecting the property rights of shareholders would necessarily be taken into account.[65]

In addition, the relationship between the three core elements could be more fully examined. For example, under what conditions is one element more necessary than the others? Which element should take precedence if any of the elements conflict with each other? Do greater accountability efforts (e.g., through social auditing and reporting) lead to a more appropriate balancing of stakeholder interests and/or generation of net societal value?

While Milton Friedman may have recently passed away, his theoretical legacy will certainly live on. While each of the five alternative business and society frameworks currently permeates the business world, and thus arguably have helped counter the predominance of Friedman, whether any the frameworks will continue to take precedence in the long-term remains to be seen.

NOTES

1.   Milton Friedman passed away at the age of 94 on November 16th, 2006.
2.   Friedman, M. (1970). The social responsibility of business is to increase its profits. *New York Times Magazine*, *33*, 122–126. This quote was originally

contained in his 1962 book *Capitalism and Freedom*. Chicago: University of Chicago Press.

3. See "The Good Company," in the *Economist*, January 20th, 2005.
4. For example, see Coelho, P. R. P., McClure, J. E., & Spry, J. A. (2003). The social responsibility of corporate management: A classical critique. *Mid-American Journal of Business*, *18*(1), 15–24.
5. A similar position is taken by Levitt, T. (1958). The dangers of social responsibility. *Harvard Business Review*, *36*(5), 41–50.
6. Carroll, A. B. (1999). Corporate social responsibility: Evolution of a definitional construct. *Business & Society*, *38*(3), 268–295.
7. Other important theoretical contributors include: Carroll, A. B. (1979). A three dimensional conceptual model of corporate social performance. *Academy of Management Review*, *4*, 497–505; Carroll, A. B. (1991). The pyramid of corporate social responsibility: Toward the moral management of organizational stakeholders. *Business Horizons*, *34*, 39–48; CED. (1971). Social responsibilities of business corporations. New York: Committee for Economic Development; Davis, K. (1960). Can business afford to ignore social responsibilities? *California Management Review*, *2*, 70–76; Davis, K. (1973). The case for and against business assumption of social responsibilities. *Academy of Management Journal*, *1*, 312–322; Davis, K. & Blomstrom, R. L. (1966). *Business and its environment*. New York: McGraw Hill; Drucker, P. F. (1984). The new meaning of corporate social responsibility. *California Management Review*, *26*, 53-63; Epstein, E. M. (1987). The corporate social policy process: Beyond business ethics, corporate social responsibility and corporate responsiveness. *California Management Review*, *29*(3), 99–114; Frederick, W. C. (1960). The growing concern over business responsibility. *California Management Review*, *2*, 54–61; Jones, T. M. (1980). Corporate social responsibility revisited, redefined. *California Management Review*, Spring, 59–67; McGuire, J. W. (1963). Business and society. New York: McGraw-Hill; Preston, L. E. & Post, J. E. (1975). Private management and public policy: The principle of public responsibility. Englewood Cliffs, NJ: Prentice Hall; Sethi, S. P. (1975). Dimensions of corporate social performance: An analytic framework. *California Management Review*, *17*, 58–64; Steiner, G. A. (1971). *Business and society*. New York: Random House; Swanson, D. L. (1995). Addressing a theoretical problem by reorienting the corporate social performance model. *Academy of Management Review*, *20*, 43–64; Walton, C. C. (1967). *Corporate social responsibilities*. Belmont, CA: Wadsworth; Wartick, S. L. & Cochran, P. L. (1985). The evolution of the corporate social performance model. *Academy of Management Review*, *10*, 758–765; Wood, D. (1991). Corporate social performance revisited. *Academy of Management Review*, *16*(4), 691–718.
8. For example, in 1963 McGuire states: "The idea of social responsibilities supposes that the corporation has not only economic and legal obligations, but also certain responsibilities to society which extend beyond these obligations." McGuire, J. W. (1963). *Business and society*. New York: McGraw-Hill, p.144. See also Carroll, A. B. (1991). The pyramid of corporate social responsibility: Toward the moral management of organizational

stakeholders. *Business Horizons, 34,* 39–48. For a reformulation of Carroll's "Pyramid of CSR", see Schwartz, M. S. & Carroll, A. B. (2003). Corporate social responsibility: A three domain approach. *Business Ethics Quarterly, 13*(4), 503–530.

9.   For example, see Social Accountability 8000 [http://www.sa-intl.org/index.cfm?fuseaction=document.showDocumentByID&nodeID=1&DocumentID=136] or the Global Reporting Initiative [http://www.globalreporting.org/Home].

10. In London, Britain one can attend the "CSR Academy" which specifically teaches CSR skills. See: http://www.csracademy.org.uk/about.htm

11. See p. 4 of Toshiba's "Corporate Social Responsibility Report, at: http://www.toshiba.co.jp/csr/en/report/index.htm

12. For example, there are CSR courses (e.g., Stanford); concentrations (e.g., Nottingham); journals (e.g., *Business & Society*; *Business and Society Review*); conferences (e.g., International Association of Business For Society; Social Issues in Management); centers (e.g., Berkeley); and Chairs (e.g., Columbia).

13. Carroll, A. B. (1999). Corporate social responsibility: Evolution of a definitional construct. *Business & Society, 38*(3), p. 292.

14. McMahon, T. M. (1997). History of business ethics. In P. H. J. Werhane, & R. E. Freeman (Eds.), *Blackwell Encyclopedic Dictionary of Business Ethics*, 317–320. Cambridge, MA: Blackwell, p. 317.

15. De George, R. T. (1987). The status of business ethics: Past and future. *Journal of Business Ethics, 6,* 201–211, See p. 203.

16. For example, Beauchamp T. L. & Bowie N. E. (1979). *Ethical theory and business.* Upper Saddle River, N.J.: Prentice-Hall; Donaldson, T. & Werhane, P. H. (1979). *Ethical issues in business: A philosophical approach.* Englewood Cliffs, N.J.: Prentice Hall; De George, R. T. (1982). *Business ethics.* New York: Macmillan Publishing Company; Velasquez, M. G. (1982). *Business ethics: Concepts and cases.* Upper Saddle River, N.J.: Prentice Hall; Hoffman, W. M. & Moore, J. M. (1984). *Business ethics: Readings and cases in corporate morality.* New York: McGraw Hill; and Boatright, J. R. (1993). *Ethics and the conduct of business.* Englewood Cliffs, NJ: Prentice Hall.

17. For example, one can find business ethics in courses (e.g., U. of Michigan); concentrations (e.g., Bentley College); journals (e.g., *Journal of Business Ethics*; *Business Ethics Quarterly*; *Business Ethics: A European Review*; *Business and Professional Ethics Journal*); conferences (e.g., Society for Business Ethics, European Business Ethics Network); and centers (e.g., Wharton); Chairs (e.g., U. Detroit)

18. A literature review indicates that five moral standards have been applied in the field of business ethics to a greater extent and with greater consistency than others. Two moral theories are particularly dominant in the business ethics literature: utilitarianism and deontology [Brady, F. N. (1985). A janus-headed model of ethical theory: Looking two ways at business/society issues. *Academy of Management Review, 10*(3), 568–576; Klein, S. (1985). Two views of business ethics: A popular philosophical approach and a value based interdisciplinary one. *Journal of Business Ethics, 4,* 71–79; Lewis, P. V.

& Speck, H. E. (1990). Ethical orientations for understanding business ethics. *The Journal of Business Communication, 27*(3), 213–232]. Utilitarianism, often expressed as a teleological or consequentialist framework, is primarily based on the writings of Jeremy Bentham and John Stuart Mill. Deontology (i.e., duty-based obligations) is often expressed in terms of "Kantianism" (or more specifically as the principle of the "categorical imperative"), being primarily based on the writings of Immanuel Kant. In addition to utilitarianism and deontology, two other moral theories (typically considered deontological in nature) have been used extensively in the business ethics field: moral rights; and justice (e.g., procedural and distributive) [Cohen, J. (2001). Appreciating, understanding and applying universal moral principles. *The Journal of Consumer Marketing, 18*(7), 578–594; Fritzche, D. J. & Becker, H. (1984). Linking management behavior to ethical philosophy: An empirical investigation. *Academy of Management Journal, 27*(1), 166-175]. The fifth moral theory receiving attention appears to be moral virtue, being primarily based on the writings of Aristotle (Macdonald, J. E. & Beck-Dudley, C. L. (1994). Are deontology and teleology mutually exclusive? *Journal of Business Ethics, 13*, 615–623; Solomon, R. C. (1992). Corporate roles, personal virtues: An Aristotelean approach to business ethics. *Business Ethics Quarterly, 2*(3), 317–339. The predominant use by business ethicists of these moral theories points towards their importance in the field. Other important moral standards that are also utilized (albeit to a somewhat lesser extent) in the field of business ethics include: moral relativism and ethical egoism (both of which underlie Milton Friedman's position) as well as religious doctrine.

19. See Schwartz, M. S. (2005). Universal moral values for corporate codes of ethics. *Journal of Business Ethics, 59*(1-2), 27–44.

20. CNN. (2002, Mar. 7). In wake of Enron debacle, Bush pushes rules for corporations. Web site: http://edition.cnn.com/2002/ALLPOLITICS/03/07/bush.corporations/

21. U.S. Federal Sentencing Guidelines for Organizations, Ch. 8, 1991 [http://www.ussc.gov/2005guid/tabconchapt8.htm].

22. U.S. *Sarbanes-Oxley Act of 2002* [http://fl1.findlaw.com/news.findlaw.com/hdocs/docs/gwbush/sarbanesoxley072302.pdf].

23. For example, see the survey conducted by Berenbeim, R.E. (1999). *Global corporate ethics practices: A developing consensus*, New York: The Conference Board.

24. See "A Message from the President" in Scotiabank's "Guidelines for Business Conduct," [http://www.scotiabank.com/images/en/filesaboutscotia/8598.pdf].

25. See Ethics & Compliance Officers Association (ECOA) Web site [http://www.theecoa.org/].

26. See p. 483 in Harrison, J. S. & Freeman R. E. (1999). Stakeholders, social responsibility, and performance: Empirical evidence and theoretical perspectives. *Academy of Management Journal, 42*(5), 479–485.

27. Rowley, T. (1997). Moving beyond dyadic ties: A network theory of stakeholder influences. *Academy of Management Review, 22*(4), 887–910. See p. 888).

28. Freeman, R. E. (1984). *Strategic management: A stakeholder approach.* Boston: Pitman.

29. Mitchell, R. K., Agle, B. R., & Wood, D. J. (1997). Toward a theory of stakeholder identification and salience: Defining the principle of who and what really counts. *Academy of Management Review, 22*(4), 853–886.

30. See Johnson and Johnson's "Our Credo" [http://www.jnj.com/our_company/our_credo/].

31. See Johnson & Johnson's "Our Credo" [http://www.jnj.com/our_company/our_credo/].

32. For example, see Future 500 [http://www.future500.org/custom/16/] or Business for Social Responsibility [http://www.bsr.org/CSRResourcesIssueBriefDetail.cfm?DocumentID=48813].

33. For example, see B. H. McDonnell, "Corporate Constituency Statutes and Employee Governance," *William Mitchell Law Review, 30*(4), 1227–1259.

34. For example, there are stakeholder management courses (e.g., IMD International); and special issues on stakeholder management in journals).

35. The report is more formally known as the "Brundtland Report." See: Brundtland, G. (Ed.). (1987). *Our common future: The world commission on environment and development.* Oxford: Oxford University Press.

36. See "Triple Bottom Line." [http://en.wikipedia.org/wiki/Triple_bottom_line].

37. Marrewijk, M. V., & Werre, M. (2003). Multiple levels of corporate sustainability. *Journal of Business Ethics, 44*(2/3), 107–119. See p. 107.

38. Some of the major contributors include: Schmidheiny, S. (1992). *Changing course.* Cambridge, MA: The MIT Press; Hawken, P. (1993). *The ecology of commerce: A declaration of sustainability.* New York: HarperBusiness; Elkington, J. (1999). *Cannibals with forks.* Gabriola Island, British Columbia, New Society Publications; Elkington, J. (2001). *The chrysalis economy.* Oxford, UK: Capstone Publishing Ltd.; Hart, S. L. (1995). A natural resource-based view of the firm. *The Academy of Management Review, 20*(4), 986–1014; Hart, S. L. (1997). Beyond greening: Strategies for a sustainable world. *Harvard Business Review, 75*(1), 66–77; Hart, S. L. (1998). From heresy to dogma: An institutional history of corporate environmentalism. *Academy of Management Review, 23*(2), 354–358; Hawken, P., Lovins, A. & Hunter Lovins, L. (1999). *Natural capitalism.* Boston, MA: Little, Brown and Company; Nattrass, B. & Altomare, M. (1999). *The natural step for business.* Gabriola Island, British Columbia: New Society Publishers; Freeman, R. E., Pierce, J. & Dodd, R. H. (2000). *Environmentalism and the new logic of business.* New York: Oxford University Press; Zadek, S. (2001). *The civil corporation.* London, UK: Earthscan Publications; and Willard, B. (2002). *The sustainability advantage: Seven business case benefits of a triple bottom line.* Gabriola Island, British Columbia, New Society Publishers.

39. For example, see p. 4 of Alcan's "Sustainability Report 2006" [http://www.publications.alcan.com/sustainability/2006/en/pages/index.html].

40.   For example, sustainability can be found as a distinct course (e.g., Cornell); as a concentrations (York U.); journals (e.g., *International Journal of Sustainable Development*; *Sustainable Development*); centers (e.g., Erasmus); and Chairs (e.g., INSEAD).

41.   For example, some of the major contributors to the notion of corporate citizenship include Carroll, A. B. (1998). The four faces of corporate citizenship. *Business and Society Review, 100*(1), 1–7; Waddock. S. (2002). *Leading corporate citizens*. Boston, MA: McGraw Hill; McIntosh, M., Leipziger, D., Jones, K., & Coleman, G. (1998). *Corporate citizenship: Successful strategies for responsible companies*. London: Financial Times—Pitman Publishing; and McIntosh, M., Thomas, R., Leipziger, D., & Coleman, G. (2003). *Living corporate citizenship: Strategic routes to socially responsible business*. London: Financial Times & Pearson.

42.   Logsdon, J., & Wood, D. J. (2002). Business citizenship: From domestic to global level of analysis. *Business Ethics Quarterly, 12*(2), 155–187. See p. 155.

43.   Marsden, C. (2000). The new corporate citizenship of big business: Part of the solution to sustainability? *Business and Society Review, 105*(1), 9–26. See p.11.

44.   Waddock. S. (2002). *Leading corporate citizens*. Boston, MA: McGraw Hill. See p. 5.

45.   For example, see Exxon Mobil's corporate citizenship report [http://www.exxonmobil.com/Corporate/Citizenship/citizenship.asp].

46.   See "Global Citizenship at HP" [http://www.hp.com/hpinfo/globalcitizenship/gcreport/globalcitizen.html].

47.   For example, corporate citizenship can be found in courses (e.g., ESADE Business School); concentrations (e.g., Warwick); journals; (e.g., *The Journal of Corporate Citizenship*); centers (e.g., Boston College); and Chairs (e.g., Indiana U.)

48.   See Johnson & Johnson's "Our Credo" [http://www.jnj.com/our_company/our_credo/].

49.   See: 1982 Chicago Tylenol murders. [http://en.wikipedia.org/wiki/Tylenol_scare].

50.   See Merck's Web site [http://www.merck.com/newsroom/executive_speeches/120150.html].

51.   See: Merck's Web site [http://www.merck.com/about/feature_story/05192004_mectizan.html]. Note however the recent Vioxx incident whereby Merck delayed its decision to recall its arthritis drug Vioxx despite apparent knowledge of numerous deaths caused by the drug which seems to suggest otherwise. See Berenson, A. (2006, Apr. 12). Merck jury adds $9 million in damages. *The New York Times* [http://www.nytimes.com/2006/04/12/business/12vioxx.html]

52.   See "A Message from the President" in Scotiabank's "Guidelines for Business Conduct," [http://www.scotiabank.com/images/en/filesaboutscotia/8598.pdf].

53.   See Weyerhaeuser's Mission statement which states: "Produce superior returns for our shareholders by focusing on our customers and safely growing and harvesting trees, manufacturing and selling forest products, and

building and selling homes." [http://www.weyerhaeuser.com/aboutus/ourvision/default.asp].

54. See ANZ's "Employee Code of Conduct" at p.1 [http://www.anz.com/australia/aboutanz/corporateinformation/corpgovpolicy/default].

55. Elkington, J. (1999). *Cannibals with forks*. Gabriola Island, British Columbia, New Society Publications. See p. 8.

56. Elkington, J. (1999). *Cannibals with forks*. Gabriola Island, British Columbia, New Society Publications. See p. 20.

57. Carroll, A. B., & Buchholtz, A. K. (2003). *Business and society: Ethics and stakeholder management* (5th ed.). Mason, Ohio: Thomson South-Western. See p. 19.

58. Freeman, R. E. (2004). A stakeholder theory of the modern corporation. In T. L. Beauchamp and M. E. Bowie (Eds.), *Ethical Theory and Business* (7th ed.), 55–64. Upper Saddle River, N.J.: Pearson Prentice Hall. See pp. 60–61.

59. For example, see McLean, B. and Elkind, P. (2003). *The Smartest Guys in the Room*. New York, Penguin Group.

60. Frazier, M. (2005). Academia chimes in on debate over retailing behemoth. *Advertising Age*, 76(46), 10; Johnson, B. (2005). Wal-Mart is the best! No, wait, it's the worst! *Advertising Age*, June 13, 14.

61. See: Exxon Valdez. U.S. Environmental Protection Agency's Web site [http://www.epa.gov/oilspill/exxon.htm].

62. See: Bhopal information center. [http://www.bhopal.com/].

63. See Ackman, D. Tire trouble: The Ford-Firestone blowout. Forbes.com, June 20, 2001 [http://www.forbes.com/2001/06/20/tireindex.html].

64. For example, see: Building the business case for ethics. Margolis, J., Walsh, J., and Krehmeyer, D. (2006). Business Roundtable Institute for Corporate Ethics   [http://www.darden.edu/corporate-ethics/pdf/business_case.pdf]; Orlitsky, M., Schmidt, F. L., & Rynes, S. L. 2003. Corporate. social and financial performance: A meta-analysis. *Organization Studies, 24*, 403–442.

65. If empirical research were to establish that shareholders do not merely prefer share value maximization, but also have concerns over the firms in which they have invested generating sustainable societal value, appropriately balancing stakeholder concerns and ethical principles, while demonstrating sufficient accountability, then Friedman's concerns over acting in the best "interests" of the shareholders would also be addressed by the VBA Model.

PART III

MAKING THE CHANGE HAPPEN:
VOLUNTARY AND REGULATORY EXAMPLES

CHAPTER 8

THE INTEGRITY DIVIDEND AND "DOING GOOD"

Tony Simons

This chapter discusses research on behavioral integrity—the perceived pattern of a person's word-action alignment – in light of the overarching theme of this volume. I argue that behavioral integrity is a critical pillar of any effective leadership, and is also a key challenge. A study of employee perceptions and company operational and financial performance at 76 Holiday Inn hotels suggests that managers' behavioral integrity is a very potent driver of customer satisfaction, employee turnover and hotel profitability. Behavioral integrity is not all it takes to lead; nor is it all it takes to be good —but it is a pivotal challenge that warrants the sustained attention and effort of leaders and aspiring leaders. You cannot lead without it—and it seems likely that you cannot be good without it either.

The integrity dividend is the measurable bottom-line-benefit of having employees see that their bosses live by their word. Does that boss consistently keep promises? And does she demonstrate the values she espouses for others? I call this perception behavioral integrity (Simons, 2002) and it is not the same as doing good, or being ethical, or even being a good leader. It is, though, a central ingredient of all of them. These other ideas are important, and I value them deeply. But they are not the topic of this essay. This essay focuses simply on the perception of word-deed alignment or behavioral integrity. Excellent behavioral integrity is extremely challenging to maintain, and it has profound, measurable performance consequences. It is a necessary prerequisite for any excellent leadership, and any aspiring manager does well to devote considerable attention and effort to developing and maintaining this quality.

First, it is appropriate to describe the relationship between behavioral integrity and the guiding principle of this book, which is "doing well by doing good," or acting ethically. In the language of logic, behavioral integrity is a *necessary but not sufficient* condition for ethical action. By that I mean that other things equal, failure to live by one's word is almost always unethical, but aligning one's actions to one's words is only an ethical choice where the original words described an ethical act. It is difficult or impossible to act ethically without word-action alignment, but having it does not suffice to render an action ethically acceptable. Nor does *actual* word-action alignment guarantee that the alignment will be *perceived* as alignment. Behavioral integrity is a critical element of any defensible ethical standard, but it is not complete in and of itself.

This chapter will further clarify what behavioral integrity is and is not. It will describe how it affects people. It will lay out a demonstration of the integrity dividend—the concrete payoff of perceived alignment. Finally, it will describe a few of the many reasons why this alignment is relatively rare and why managers find it difficult.

WHAT BEHAVIORAL INTEGRITY IS AND IS NOT

The Random House College Dictionary (Random House, 1975) defines integrity as "adherence to moral and ethical principles," which is another way of saying, "doing good," in whatever way those principles define that good. The concept of behavioral integrity, though, draws on a secondary definition of integrity: seamlessness, as in the integrity of a boat hull. Watertight—no gaps. Words and actions aligned. Promises kept. Espoused values enacted. Formally speaking, "Behavioral integrity (BI) is the perceived pattern of alignment between an actor's words and deeds. It entails both the perceived fit between espoused and enacted values, and perceived promise-keeping" (Simons, 2002). Behavioral integrity is an ascribed trait, and is subjectively determined.

I am not an ethicist or an ethical philosopher, but I suspect that many would say that behaviors that are poorly aligned, and so show low behavioral integrity, are generally unethical, as they might constitute intentional deceit—as when a promise was made with no intention of follow-through.

The ethics of misalignment becomes more murky when the misalignment is due to circumstance, to miscommunication, or to limited self-knowledge.

From a practical standpoint, though, the consequence of the misalignment—the broken promise or the apparent hypocrisy—follows regardless of intent. People tend to trust others who they see as living by their word, and they mistrust those who do not. Excuses or explanations are limited in their mitigating impact. And being trusted makes any manager more effective, because a trusted manager inspires greater loyalty, greater honesty, and greater effort from those they manage. There are similar payoffs for any trusted salesman, customer, service provider, spouse, or friend. At a larger scale, the same is true for any trusted brand or company. It serves self-interest to maintain a reputation for impeccable integrity. Even where ethics might let one off the hook for an unintended breach, or one where the broken promise exists only in the mind of the self-identified victim. It is simply good business to minimize others' perception of promises broken. It is not enough to merely keep promises; there is an additional element that is proactive.

Behavioral integrity is not about the particular content of values a person espouses or enacts—it is about the consistency with which that value is applied. I might judge someone to be unethical due to the content of their values, but that is separate from the question of their behavioral integrity. For example—I knew a former colleague during a time when he was deeply wounded and embittered about life in general and the workplace in particular. He once sat in a department meeting and declared that he did not care what was good for the department or what was good for the school: his decisions henceforth would be driven by pure self-interest. I did not like the man's position at that time. I did not trust him and I do not personally consider that he was behaving ethically. But I must give him credit for accurately representing his guiding values, and so demonstrating behavioral integrity. I suppose that because of that consistency, he was being more trustworthy than someone who is behaving in the more common pattern of self-interest cloaked in avowals of altruistic motives. He could, perhaps, only afford to be so honest because he was tenured at the university, and thus practically unfireable. Behavioral integrity is about the alignment of words and actions; in principle, this applies even when those words and actions are ignoble. An avowed racist might be another example of someone who is not behaving in line with most ethical principles, but would, if he is consistent about practicing what he preaches, be acting with behavioral integrity.

Behavioral integrity, in sum, is closely related to doing good and behaving ethically, but the overlap is not complete. On one hand, effectively managing behavioral integrity entails taking responsibility for miscommunications and unforeseen circumstances for which no ethical obligation exists. On the other hand, ethically unacceptable values can be held with strong behavioral integrity, as long as the holder both espouses and enacts the value consistently.

WHY BEHAVIORAL INTEGRITY HAS IMPACT

A leader's behavioral integrity, or its lack, profoundly affects the work of the people around him. Michael Kay, former president and CEO of LSG SkyChefs, described the impact well:

> It's all about results time. It ain't about feeling good. It ain't about being a nice place to come to work. It's that heightened levels of trust produce heightened levels of results. Because people feel better, work better, *are* better, in a trusting setting and environment than they are in one where distrust saps their energy. (personnal communication, April 2005)

Excellent leadership is about engaging people's hearts, so that they give of their soul to benefit their company. Workers' discretionary behaviors, called "organizational citizenship behaviors" are a key driver of any company's financial success. Workers go an extra mile in a thousand small and large ways, going beyond their formal job descriptions, and this flexibility and extra effort propels and lubricates the great machine of the company. Many studies have shown this pattern to hold (for a review, see (Podsakoff & MacKenzie, 1997). If you doubt it, consider the impact when nurses or other workers stage a protest in the form of "work-to-rule," wherein the participants do only the work required by their legal contract. Everything grinds to a halt when that happens.

To get employees to go that extra mile that is so critical for company performance, an excellent leader must reach workers deeply, and so must touch their hearts—to engage them. The workers won't let you close to their hearts if they do not trust you. And they will not trust you if they cannot believe what they say.

It is not a black-or-white issue. I am not talking about the few heinous deceivers as opposed to everyone else. It is a matter of degree. How many of the bosses you have had in your life have been absolutely impeccable in their promise-keeping and their consistent demonstrations of espoused values? Unless you are very lucky, you probably cannot list more than a handful. A lot of them are pretty good. There is a big gap between "pretty good" and "impeccable." That gap shows up in the commitment that it stirs in the hearts of followers. It is not easy to bridge that gap, to be sure, but there is a lot of power hiding there.

The second way in which behavioral integrity operates is simply through clarity of communication. When you send a consistent and clear message with your words and actions, people know better what you are after, so they are better equipped to deliver it. Michael Kay says,

> When it's easy for the people who work for you to figure *you* out, when you're clear about who *you* are, it is easier for the people who work for you to decide how most effectively to work with you.

Behavioral integrity leads to credibility. As a leader, you erect many signposts for others to follow: What do we value here? What is forbidden? But the signs only work if people believe them. Frank Guidara is the president and CEO of UNO's Chicago Grill chain of restaurants. He says,

> The laying out of consequences, good and bad, is fundamental to leadership. When, as a leader, you say you're going to do something and you don't do it, it's not going to destroy your leadership status, but each time there will be a little bit more erosion, and a little more, until finally you really can't lead any longer.

Credibility, people's ability to rely on what you say as a predictor of consequences and as a signpost, determines your ability to direct traffic and ultimately to guide your people. This second mechanism is not about getting people to go the extra mile—it is about getting people to drive the first mile in the right direction.

A DEMONSTRATION OF THE INTEGRITY DIVIDEND

Several years ago, I was able to survey all the employees for a large hotel company. The company trusted me enough to share operational and financial numbers for each of their hotels—on condition that I not tell their competitors exactly how profitable they were, how high their employee turnover, how happy their guests were, and so on. This level of access allowed me to ask workers about the behavioral integrity they saw in their department managers, and to track the impact of that perception through worker attitudes and behaviors, to the customers, and finally to the financial bottom line.

Typical employee surveys ask fairly safe questions like, "please rate your satisfaction with your pay," "with your coworkers," and perhaps most dangerously, "with your supervision." They might ask about how well service is supported or incented. My survey was edgier. I asked questions like, "How much do you agree or disagree with the statement, 'My department manager keeps his promises,' 'My manager practices what he preaches,' or 'I would be willing to let my manager have complete control over my future in this company?' " The first two questions are examples from the behavioral integrity scale, and the third is from the trust scale.

Working with a colleague, Judi McLean Parks of Washington University, we ran focus groups to determine the words employees use to describe behavioral integrity. We used those words to form the survey questions. We translated the survey into five different languages, and pilot-tested the different versions with a few hotels. We then asked all the company's employees to complete the survey. Participation was voluntary. Employees were permitted to complete the surveys anonymously, on paid company time, with a raffle for small prizes as a participation incentive. Most employees filled out paper surveys, but we set up "read-aloud" tables for the roughly 7% of hotel employees with limited literacy.[1] At each hotel, we surveyed line employees, supervisors, department managers, and the general manager.

We also measured organizational commitment using an established question set (Mowday, Steers, & Powter, 1979), perceived fairness (Niehoff & Moorman, 1993), satisfaction with different job attributes (Hackman & Oldham, 1975), discretionary service behavior (Blancero & Dyer, 1996) frequent traveler satisfaction, employee turnover, gross revenues, and net profits (earnings before depreciation, amortization, and taxes).

Each attitude or perception, whether on the part of the employee or the customer, was measured with a set of three or more related questions that were averaged to triangulate on the underlying concept. This process, widely practiced among scientific investigators of attitudes and perceptions, filters out the "noise" or measurement error that emerges from idiosyncratic interpretations of a single question.

Roughly 80 employees responded from each hotel, and they were spread over six to eight departments. The biggest departments by far were typically housekeeping and front office. Two-thirds of all hotel employees completed our surveys. We set up feedback reports for every manager with four or more employees, describing their relationships with him or her, and then set about analyzing the results in greater depth. In the months after the survey, for each hotel we collected employee turnover information, the results of independently conducted customer satisfaction surveys, and financial performance information.

We averaged employee perceptions at each hotel, and applied path analysis to evaluate all the links in a chain of impact at the same time. We expected to find a chain that runs from employee perceptions of their managers' behavioral integrity, to employee trust in their managers, to their commitment to the company, which would in turn drive both employee turnover and discretionary service behavior. Discretionary service behavior should drive customer satisfaction, and profit should be affected by both employee turnover and customer satisfaction. Figure 8.1 shows the expected chain of impact.

The results of the study were striking. As Figure 8.2 shows, the average employee perception of how much the employee's manager kept promises and lived stated values was a closer correlate of hotel profitability than the five other attitudes measured by the survey. It seems that behavioral integrity may be a more potent performance driver than worker satisfaction or even commitment. It is more important that workers know their bosses live by their word than it is for those workers to be happy or even to feel emotionally connected to the company. Those other issues are important—but the word comes first. Everything else follows from that.

In our surveys, we asked employees to respond to statements with a number from 1 = "strongy disagree" to 5 = "strongly agree." To measure each attitude or perception, we averaged each worker's answers to several related questions. To estimate a score for each hotel, we averaged scores for all the participating workers at that hotel. Our research showed that one-eighth of a point difference in the average employee behavioral integrity ratings between two hotels on this scale points to a difference in profits of around 2½% of revenues. It raised the portion of each dollar of revenue that the company got to keep as profit by two-and-a-half cents. Given that typical revenue streams for that size and tier of hotel run around $10 million annually, *that difference in behavioral integrity raised profit by an average $250,000 per hotel per year.* We had detected the Integrity Dividend.

Figure 8.3 shows what came out when we applied path analysis to test the full chain of impact that we hypothesized in Figure 8.1. Recall we had theorized the following causal chain:

- Where employees feel their managers keep promises and live by the values they describe, those employees will trust their managers more.

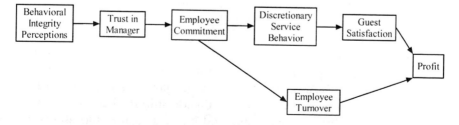

Figure 8.1.   Expected chain of impact for behavioral integrity.

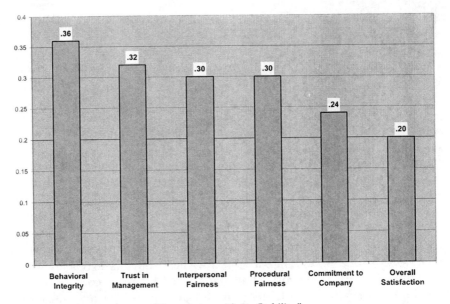

Note: Vertical axis represents "Correlation with Profitability."

Figure 8.1.   Strength of association between business profitability and different employee attitudes

- Where they trust their managers more, they come to care more deeply about the mission of the company, and to take pride in working for it.
- Where they feel that way about their company, they are more willing to go beyond their formal job descriptions to serve and satisfy customers.
- They are also less likely to quit their job.
- Customers who experience discretionary service from hotel employees like it.
- Happy customers translate to repeat business, which boosts profits.
- Employee turnover is costly, and reducing it also boosts profits.

In other words, behavioral integrity allows a leader to engage workers *hearts*, and engaging workers' hearts makes for a more efficient and productive company. And, of course, it also makes for happier workers. Isn't engaging hearts toward a goal what leadership is all about?

In Figure 8.3, the number attached to each arrow represents the strength of the chain link, which can range from 0 (no link, as between,

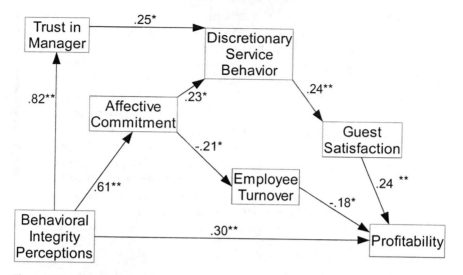

Figure 8.3.   Results of path analysis of hotel survey and operational information.

say, height and IQ among adults) to plus or minus 1.0 (absolute identity, as between, say, height in centimeters and height in inches). Positive numbers mean that the two go up together, and negative numbers mean that one going up drives the other down. The single-starred numbers mean that the specified link is asserted with 95% confidence, and the double-starred ones are made with 99% confidence. When links appear in sequence as part of a chain, you can assess the total link from beginning to end by multiplying the numbers on each link. That means, of course, that multi-link chains will tend to predict less strongly than short chains, because measurement at each stage includes some imprecision. The straight link along the bottom of the model—between behavioral integrity and profitability—says that the multi-link chains above describe only a small fraction of the total profit consequence of leaders being seen as living by their word.

The links that resulted from the analysis matched our predictions, with two exceptions [Are they really "exceptions" or just additional nuances and additional information?]:

1.   The impact of behavioral integrity does not emerge only through attitudes toward managers: It emerges also through an effect on attitudes toward the company ("Affective Commitment"). This point is shown by the two upwards arrows emerging from behavioral integrity perceptions. Both Affective Commitment and Trust

in Manager affect employees' willingness to expend special effort to provide excellent service. Employees hold the company accountable for the integrity of their managers. When employees see their managers as *not* living by their word, it does not just cause them to mistrust those managers: it causes them to be less committed to the company as a whole.

2. The chain that runs through employee turnover and customer satisfaction explains only about 20% of the strong link between behavioral integrity and business unit profitability: The remaining .30 link is driven by other mechanisms that I had not measured. It is likely, for example, that managers' behavioral integrity not only raises trust but also simplifies communication because there is no need for guessing about what the manager really means or wants: Employees know he means what he says—which makes it easier to get the job done.

Behavioral integrity exerts its affect in more ways than I was able to measure in this one survey. Also, while integrity drives performance, performance might also drive integrity—in concrete terms, managers at unprofitable hotels may well be more likely to renege on promised promotions or performance reviews. The direct link from behavioral integrity to profitability—the one along the bottom of the diagram—probably captures both additional forms of impact and reverse causality. In sum, I measured behavioral integrity and found it to be a strong driver of profitability. I was able to measure only some of the mechanisms through which it exerts this influence.

The survey of over 6,000 employees at 76 Holiday Inn Hotels demonstrated the impact of perceived managerial integrity on profits. A mere 1/8 point difference on the 5-point scale means roughly $250K profit per year for each individual hotel—or a difference of 2.5% of gross revenues. Many of the hotels, with high management integrity, converted over 10 cents more of each revenue dollar into profits than others. This association holds true whether it is analyzed in isolation—as a simple bivariate correlation or a linear regression—or when behavioral integrity is entered as a predictor of profitability after already statistically controlling for employee commitment, satisfaction, and perceptions of procedural and interpersonal justice.[2] Does behavioral integrity make a difference to the bottom line? My evidence clearly says yes.

This study took place in a single industry—the hotel business. Is there evidence of similar impact in other industries? Informal conversations with managers and professionals in wide-ranging businesses provide another emphatic yes—but further empirical study is warranted. As a framework for systematic studies, the notion of behavioral integrity is new

—even if the essential idea has long been discussed as an element of good leadership. Coming years will see an increasing number of such demonstrations in other industries, as more scholars join in studying this critical issue. The hotel business is unique in some ways, but there is strong evidence that the effect carries over into other businesses as well. The hotel business is a service industry that sells positive guest experiences, and employees' emotional response to their work affects the service product in a way that may be more profound than it would a manufactured product. It may be that the integrity dividend is smaller in other industries—but even if it were to drop by half, it would still represent a huge financial return.

WHAT MAKES BEHAVIORAL INTEGRITY DIFFICULT?

Given the apparent common sense appeal of the preceding arguments, you might expect managers of impeccable word to be the norm. To the contrary, most people I have talked to about it—and the number grows large—can point to only a few such managers, if any. They are more the exception than the rule. Why should that be the case? In my experience, managers are like anyone else—they are generally intelligent, especially at higher ranks, and generally benevolent. What gives?

It turns out that it is very hard work keeping full integrity, and there are circumstances and other forces that combine to make it especially difficult. Those forces can be grouped into aspects of the business environment, the company, the manager herself, and the observer.

The business environment. A few aspects of the business environment present challenges to behavioral integrity. One is the increasing pace and volatility of business in general, termed by D'Aveni (1994), "hypercompetition." Technology has changed, and will continue to change, the competitive environment in ways that many do not foresee. There are global changes in the resource base. Governments rise and fall and change. As the larger environment changes in unpredicted ways, it sometimes becomes more difficult for managers to keep yesterday's promises. Large-scale shifts might change the customer base and so force a plant closing. Global opportunities might demand the implementation of practices that were not considered acceptable within the local context—such as bribery or the outsourcing of local production. Uncertainty in the larger environment can shift the ground upon which prior commitments were made, and so undermine the keeping of those commitments.

A second source of environmental challenge to behavioral integrity emerges from the fashion-like aspect of management ideas like this one. With increasing frequency and rapidity, new management ideas have been widely adopted and then discarded by the business community. Abrahamson (1996) and others document how business media, consultants, management gurus and business schools vie for prominence and race to sense emergent preferences and to "get out in front" of them—thus increasing the momentum assigned to them. As management ideas become "fashionable," many companies and managers, swept up in an enthusiastic demonstration of the latest cutting edge, implement them in partial and unskilled ways. Such haphazard change implementations often result in inconsistencies between policies and across time that undermine workers' sense of their managers' behavioral integrity.

The company. Factors within the company also challenge behavioral integrity. Organizational change by its very nature challenges behavioral integrity, as the authority relationships and the policies under which a manager's commitment was made are sometimes up for grabs, and may be out of the committing manager's purview. If I, as a middle manager, promise a performance review or a promotion to an employee, and a relevant policy change gets passed down from the top office, it is my word that is broken. Even if I intentionally left myself an escape clause—such as a promise that "I will try"—it is entirely likely that the promise's recipient will consider my word to be less credible after the event.

Another element of the company that challenges behavioral integrity is something I term, "the middle manager's dilemma." Executives I interviewed were unfamiliar with it, but lower managers recognized it instantly: Managers are often asked to implement—and to sell—policies with which they disagree. Middle managers' subordinates often know them well enough to notice when a middle manager does not believe in the policy he is implementing or selling, and doing so undermines their perceptions of his integrity. Yet the middle manager's distancing himself from the unliked policy is generally unacceptable to the superiors and may undermine the middle manager's credibility further. Hence the dilemma. There are ways to manage the dilemma from both executive's side and from the middle manager's side—but it is an aspect of organizational life wherein the management of integrity becomes crucial.

The manager. Attributes of the manager herself contribute to her ability to maintain an impeccable word. Some managers are, by nature, more emotionally volatile than others (Goldberg, 1990), and these managers might well face greater challenges in maintaining a record of high consistency. The personality dimension of conscientiousness (Goldberg, 1990) describes attention to follow-through, and so would affect the ease with which a person keeps track of and fulfills commitments. Some managers are higher "self-monitors" than others (Anderson, 1991), meaning that they tend to base their conduct on external cues more than internal states or abiding principles. Higher self-monitors might face greater difficulty in maintaining the behavioral consistency that supports behavioral integrity perceptions. Several aspects of personality are likely to challenge or support managers' maintenance of the consistency that affects workers' integrity perceptions.

The level of a manager's self-knowledge affects their ability to maintain consistency. As human beings, we navigate through a sea of conflicting values, priorities, and desires. Most of us are unaware of those profound ambivalences to some degree—but they still affect our behavior. Where a manager can recognize the full spectrum of often conflicting values, she becomes better able to make only those commitments with which one is fully (internally) aligned, and so to deliver consistently on them. Some of us are better able to predict our reactions to future events than others. To the extent that self-knowledge enables us to better predict and to regulate our behavior, it makes us better able to tell others what to expect from us —and so to enhance behavioral integrity.

Personal discipline is a quality that I increasingly recognize as a key antecedent to behavioral integrity. It takes discipline to monitor and modify one's language to reduce easily misinterpreted phrases and social niceties that risk leading to a perception of a broken promise—think, for example, about the bland assertion, "we should do lunch sometime!" It takes discipline to maintain one's perspective and to refrain from impulsive commitments in the face of others' distress or demands—and to refrain from making commitments until one is certain that one is fully inclined and able to guarantee their fulfillment. And it takes discipline to religiously keep track of one's outstanding promises as they accumulate through life. Having this quality—and/or developing it—dramatically facilitates behavioral integrity.

The perceiver. A fourth source of behavioral integrity challenge is perhaps one of the biggest. It stems from the fact that behavioral integrity must be subjectively assessed and ascribed in order to exert any impact. There is a necessary distinction between a manager's *actual* word-action alignment and that which is perceived. Different observers experience different slices of any given manager's language and action. One might interpret an action as a violation of espoused value A and so evince poor behavioral integrity. Another observer might see the same action as well-aligned with espoused value B and so evince high behavioral integrity. A dependent observer might be expected to monitor words and actions more closely than one who does not depend as much on the target. A cynical or previously wounded observer might be expected to bias their perceptions toward low behavioral integrity, so as to confirm expectations. People to whom an espoused value is especially important can be expected to notice actions that are inconsistent with that value and to respond especially harshly to them. A recent study (Simons, Friedman,

Liu, & McLean Parks, 2007) found evidence of heightened sensitivity to behavioral integrity on the part of Black employees than other employees. The fact that behavioral integrity is subjectively determined calls for substantial extra effort on the part of leaders to communicate clearly and to take account of different constituencies' expected biases. It makes managing and maintaining behavioral integrity far more difficult than "simply" managing one's own word-action consistency.

CONCLUSION

Behavioral integrity is not the same as doing good. It does not require adherence to accepted moral or ethical principles—only that one enact the principles one espouses. However noble or vile they might be. It also requires keeping promises—which most moral codes endorse. Behavioral integrity seems thus to comprise an element of good moral conduct, but not the totality of the concept. Likewise, behavioral integrity is a necessary ingredient for effective leadership, but not the whole formula. It is not even the whole formula for trustworthiness—but again, it seems to be a necessary but not sufficient condition. I would argue that positive values tend to be associated with behavioral integrity, if for no other reason than executives' tendency to voice socially acceptable or even noble values in their efforts to stir loyalty. More executives probably bespeak noble values while failing to live up to them—effectively overpromising—than bespeak ignoble values while enacting noble ones. However, I have witnessed both forms of inconsistency. While I (and probably most people) prefer an underpromise to an overpromise, a consistent pattern of match is preferable.

Behavioral integrity is critical for effective leadership for two reasons: by enhancing trust, it enables a leader to gain access to workers' passion, and so to stimulate them to go beyond formal duties to better serve the company. The second source of impact seems more mundane: by enhancing credibility, in gives a leaders' words greater power to guide workers' behavior. It tightens the linkages between the steering wheel and the tires.

Managers' behavioral integrity has demonstrated substantial bottom-line impact for companies. A study of employees at 76 Holiday Inn Hotels showed a correlation of $r = .36$ between workers' assessments of their managers' behavioral integrity and the profitability of the hotels. So strong was this link that one-eighth point difference on a 5-point scale translated to an expected annual profit difference of $250,000. This difference is the integrity dividend.

Though the argument may seem like common sense, very high levels of behavioral integrity seem to be more the exception than the rule. The reason for this rarity is simple: For a variety of reasons, several enumerated here, it is really difficult to manage.

This difficulty, coupled with the extraordinary measurable benefits associated with behavioral integrity, suggest that aspiring leaders and managers would do well to dedicate considerable attention and effort to increasing their ability to effectively manage behavioral integrity.

NOTES

1. If I were to run the survey again, I would engage illiterate employees through use of use voice-recognition telephone technology, which has advanced considerably in recent years. The read-aloud tables tended create ate a social atmosphere, wasted time, and yielded many incomplete surveys.

2. At this level of analysis, behavioral integrity was closely correlated with trust in management, so entering both into a regression resulted in both coefficients becoming nonsignificant.

REFERENCES

Abrahamson, E. (1996). Management fashion. *Academy of Management Review, 21*(1), 254–285.

Anderson, L. R. (1991). Test-retest reliability of the revised self-monitoring scale over a two-year period. *Psychological Reports, 68,* 1057–1058.

Blancero, D., & Dyer, L. (1996). Due process for Non-Union Employees: The Influence of System Characteristics on Fairness Perceptions. *Human Resource Management, 35*(3), 343–359.

D'Aveni, R. A. (1994). *Hypercompetition: Managing the Dynamics of Strategic Maneuvering.* New York: Free Press.

Goldberg, L. R. (1990). An alternative description of personality: The big five factor structure. *Journal of Personality and Social Psychology, 59*(6), 1216–1229.

Hackman, J. R., & G. R. Oldham (1975). Develoment of the job diagnostic survey. *Journal of Applied Psychology, 60*(2), 159–170.

Mowday, R. T., R. M. Steers, Powter L W. (1979). The measurement of organizational commitment. *Journal of Vocational Behavior, 14,* 224–247.

Niehoff, B. P., & R. H. Moorman (1993). Justice as a mediator between methods of monitoring and organizational citizenship behavior. *Academy of Management Journal, 36*(3), 527–556.

Podsakoff, P. M., & S. B. MacKenzie (1997). Impact of organizational citizenship behavior on organizational performance: A review and suggestions for future research. *Human Performance, 10*(2), 133–151.

Random House. (1975). *Random House College Dictionary* (Revised ed.). New York: Author.

Simons, T. (2002). Behavioral integrity—The perceived alignment between managers' words and deeds as a research focus. *Organization Science, 13*(1), 18–35.

Simons, T. L., R. Friedman, Liu L. A., & McLean Parks J. (2007). Racial differences in sensitivity to behavioral integrity: Attitudinal consequences, in-group effects, and "trickle down" among Black and non-Black employees. *Journal of Applied Psychology, 92*(3), 650–665.

CHAPTER 9

DETERMINING A JOB CANDIDATE'S ETHICS PROFILE

Integrity, Personality, and Moral Reasoning Level Tests

Denis Collins

When an employer hires someone, the new employee's ethics, as well as job skills and expertise, are brought to work. This chapter reviews current research on a variety of personality tests to screen job candidates for their ethics. The strongest predictors of ethical and unethical behaviors include integrity tests and surveys that measure conscientiousness, organizational citizenship behavior, and social dominance orientation. The Myers-Briggs Type Indicator, mental disabilities tests, and values orientation surveys do not provide meaningful information about a job candidate's ethics. Using level of moral reasoning scales for job screening purposes remains a promising, though highly underdeveloped, area.

Doing Well And Good: The Human Face of the New Capitalism, pp. 167–185
Copyright © 2009 by Information Age Publishing
All rights of reproduction in any form reserved.

INTRODUCTION

Sometimes, after dismissing an employee for an ethical breach, a manager might wonder—How did that person get through the hiring process?

Efforts to maximize ethical behavior at work, and minimize unethical behavior, must begin during the hiring process. Yet, most companies focus on screening job candidates for technical skills, not ethical skills. A new employee with great skills but questionable ethics can significantly alter an organization's culture and lead a work unit down a destructive path. Including ethics as part of the job screening process is essential to an organization's success given the tremendous damage an unethical person can cause an organization.

Hiring individuals of high integrity has obvious economic benefits. The biggest source of retail industry theft is employees, not customers. According to the 2006 National Retail Security Survey, employees accounted for $17.8 billion of the $37.4 billion worth of theft in the industry, exceeding the $12 billion attributed to shoplifting.[1] The United States Chamber of Commerce attributes one-third of annual business failures to employee theft and other personnel crimes.[2] The Association of Certified Fraud Examiners report that a typical business organization loses six percent annually to fraud. This is particularly problematic for small businesses, which tend to have less ability to absorb such losses.[3]

Theft can occur at all levels of an organization. Dennis "Deal-A-Month" Kozlowski, one of the highest paid CEOs in the world, and other Tyco executives defrauded shareholders of more than $600 million. Other employee behaviors detrimental to a company's economic performance include lying about work quality, verbal abuse that can contribute to high employee turnover, and alcohol and drug use. Organizations incur an economic risk by hiring an individual with violent or criminal tendencies. Companies can be sued for "negligent hiring" if the lives of other employees, customers, or the general public are put at risk.[4]

Employers have a variety of job screening tools at their disposal, including surveys, reference checks, and background checks. Approximately 30 percent of U.S. companies perform psychological testing as part of the job selection process.[5] This chapter summarizes and evaluates different types of surveys that can be administered to develop an ethical profile of a job candidate—integrity tests, personality tests, moral reasoning level tests, and values orientation.

INTEGRITY TESTS

Integrity tests, sometimes referred to as honesty tests, ask job candidates about their behaviors and attitudes regarding unethical workplace activities, such as theft. Three popular integrity tests are portions of the Reid Report, Stanton Survey, and Personnel Selection Inventory (PSI).[6] These tests ask to what extent (from "Strongly Agree" to "Strongly Disagree") a statement describes a job candidate's behaviors or attitude.

Integrity tests may take any of the following four approaches:[7]

1. Direct admission of performing an illegal or questionable activity: "I stole money from my previous employer."
2. Opinions regarding illegal or questionable behavior: "It is okay for people to steal from employers."
3. Personality traits related to dishonesty: "I constantly think about stealing from my employer."
4. Reaction to a hypothetical situation featuring dishonest behavior: "If I saw an employee steal money, I would ignore the situation and wait for the boss to find out."

Integrity tests have been used as a pre-employment assessment tool since the late 1940s. Their popularity grew in 1988 when Congress passed the Employee Polygraph Protection Act, which significantly restricted non-government organizations from using lie detector machines as part of the job hiring process. In 1990, with more than 5,000 businesses using integrity tests, the federal government's Office of Technology Assessment (OTA) published a report summarizing research on the tests' validity (did the tests really measure integrity or something other than integrity?) and reliability (would the same person taking the test twice receive similar scores?).[8]

The OTA found that many of the research studies had been conducted by businesses marketing the test and lacked appropriate scientific rigor, suggesting potential biases in the design of their research studies. Among the research studies that applied appropriate scientific methods, 94 to 99% of the individuals who passed the integrity test (and thus classified as honest) did not later steal from their employer. Depending on the study, however, 73 to 97% of the individuals who were hired despite being classified by test results as dishonest, also did not steal. In other words, the determined difference between the two groups—those classified as honest and those as dishonest—did not really exist.

This large group of "false positives" raised troubling questions about the tests' validity. Another company could have denied employment to those classified as dishonest. These false positive applicants, who later turned out to be honest, would have been jobless for the wrong reason.

When presented with these findings, integrity test providers countered that the false positive applicants could still steal in the future, might have stolen but were not caught, or might have engaged in a dishonest behavior other than stealing. Civil libertarians pointed out that this reasoning, in which individuals are being assumed guilty (they will steal) until proven innocent, is contrary to constitutional law. The OTA report concluded that research had neither proved nor disproved whether these types of integrity tests measured an individual's propensity to steal.

New, and more rigorous, scientific research studies with larger databases and better control for competing hypotheses, however, support the predictability of integrity tests. Researchers have found that individuals with low integrity test scores at the time of employment, compared to those with higher scores, are more likely to later engage in theft, have high absenteeism, break rules, cheat, and become disciplinary problems.[9] One company used integrity tests to screen job candidates in 600 of its 1,900 stores and then compared inventory theft and employee turnover between the two groups of stores. The outcome differences were dramatic. After one year, the group of stores using integrity tests as a job screening tool experienced a 35% *decline* in inventory loss and 13% *decline* in employee turnover, while the stores not using integrity tests experienced a 10% *increase* in theft and a 14% *increase* in turnover.[10]

Despite these impressive findings, using self-report integrity tests may deny companies the services of some honest individuals. Researchers point out that integrity tests have a social desirability bias and the answers are easy to fake.[11] Tutorials and coaches are available to help individuals score high on integrity tests. The "best" integrity test answer is often obvious and, as a result, dishonest individuals who lie can score higher than honest individuals. For example, a common integrity test statement is: "I am a trustworthy person." A dishonest person wanting the job would lie by choosing "Strongly Agree." Or, a criminal might perceive him/herself as trustworthy within a network of criminals. Meanwhile, an individual of high integrity, remembering a few untrustworthy past behaviors, might choose "Agree" to honestly note personal imperfections, thus resulting in a lower score.

Including integrity tests as part of the job screening process can have very positive impacts on reducing theft and employee turnover. They also signal to job applicants that integrity does matter and dishonest individuals may decide not to continue pursuing employment. But given the false positives and social desirability concerns, integrity tests should not be the sole determining factor of a person's ethics. Specific test statements with relatively lower scores should be corroborated with other ethics measures, such as reference checks, or discussed during the personal interview process.

PERSONALITY TESTS

Integrity tests are primarily concerned about an individual's experience and attitudes about theft and other unethical activities. Personality tests offer a much broader psychological understanding of the job candidate and identify characteristics that might be associated with ethical or unethical behaviors. There are literally hundreds of personality factors that can be measured. Personality measures that may provide the most insight into a job applicant's ethics are reviewed in this section.

Big Five Personality Profile Model

Over the course of several decades, personality theorists and researchers have reached a general consensus on a broad personality profile called the "Big Five Model." The five personality factors are listed in Table 9.1.[12]

Researchers report that scores on three of the Big Five personality factors—agreeableness, conscientiousness, and emotional stability—correspond to integrity test scores.[13] Of these three, conscientiousness is the strongest predictor of ethical behavior.[14] Individuals who behave ethically also happen to be responsible, dependable, and hard-working. This is particularly noteworthy because conscientiousness is also a strong predictor of job performance.[15] Ethical behavior is not related to being extroverted or introverted, nor is it related to being imaginative or pragmatic.

Table 9.2 below lists survey statements used to measure conscientiousness.[16] Survey respondents self-report to what extent each item describes

Table 9.1. Big Five Personality Profile Model

Personality Factor	Descriptors
Extraversion	talkative, assertive, energetic
Agreeableness	empathetic, cooperative, trustful
Conscientiousness	responsible, dependable, hard-working
Emotional stability	calm as opposed to anxious, insecure or bad-tempered
Openness to experience	independent-minded, imaginative

Table 9.2.   Survey Items Measuring "Conscientiousness"

Positively Stated Items	Negatively Stated Items
Am always prepared	Leave my belongings around
Pay attention to details	Make a mess of things
Get chores done right away	Often forget to put things back in their proper place
Like order	Shirk my duties
Follow a schedule	Neglect my duties
Am exacting in my work	Waste my time
Do things according to a plan	Do things in a half-way manner
Continue until everything is perfect	Find it difficult to get down to work
Make plans and stick to them	Leave a mess in my room
Like to tidy up	

their behaviors. As with integrity tests, personality tests can be prone to eliciting socially desirable answers because the character trait being measured is somewhat obvious. For example, individuals may report that they get chores done right away when that is not the case.[17] This can be verified later when a reference check is conducted.

Organizational Citizenship Behavior

Organizational Citizenship Behavior (OCB) is another measure that can help managers better understand the ethics of job candidates.[18] OCB refers to voluntary helping behaviors that go beyond normal job requirements, such as aiding others with their job-related problems. OCB is most often measured using five factors: altruism, courtesy, civic virtue, conscientiousness, and sportsmanship.[19] Researchers report that individuals who score high on OCB also score high for task effectiveness and performance.[20]

Social Dominance and Bullies

Managers should also consider using the "Social Dominance Orientation" (SDO) scale for determining a job candidate's ethics. Ethics demands sincere, open-minded conversations about alternative actions under consideration. SDO is the belief that an individual's group (defined in terms of race, gender, religion, or ethnicity) is superior to other groups. Individuals with high SDO scores believe that their superior group must bully and control the inferior group to achieve desired goals. SDO survey items include: "To get ahead in life, it is sometimes necessary to step on other groups" and "Inferior groups should stay in their place."[21]

In a survey of U.S. workers, approximately 30 percent reported being bullied by a boss or co-worker.[22] Being "bullied" was defined as experiencing at least two negative acts weekly for at least six months. The three most common forms of bullying were having information held that affected job performance, being exposed to an unmanageable workload, and being ordered to do work below one's level of competency. A predisposition to bullying others has been associated with racial and gender discrimination.[23]

Even an ethical bully is something to be concerned about. Ethics requires that everyone's opinion be expressed and respected, though not necessarily agreed with or followed. An ethical person with dictatorial tendencies can be just as belligerent as an unethical bully, and be just as damaging to workplace morale.

Myers-Briggs Type Indicator

Is there anything about an individual's ethics that a company can learn from one of the most popular personality assessment tools, the Myers-Briggs Type Indicator (MBTI)? Annually, more than 2 million job candidates and employees take MBTI,[24] which provides individuals with a better understanding of their personal preferences. As with zodiac signs, none of the 16 MBTI profiles are meant to imply that one person is more ethical than another. Rather, each MBTI profile has different strengths and weaknesses in terms of leadership style, working with others, and conflict resolution.

Questions are continually raised about MBTI's validity and reliability. MBTI proponents, on the one hand, provide a list of studies that support scientific claims.[25] But more independent researchers dispute these research studies.[26]

MBTI does not provide any useful information about an individual's ethics and would be an inappropriate ethics screening tool.

Other popular personality survey instruments include the California Psychological Inventory, Personnel Reaction Blank, PDI Employment Inventory, and Reliability Scale of the Hogan Personality Series. Many of these scales, along with the Big Five, are available on the Internet.[27]

Mental Health Tests

Tests that measure general personality attributes must be differentiated from those that diagnose personality disorders or mental disabilities, such as the Minnesota Multiphasic Personality Inventory (MMPI), for legal reasons.[28] MMPI, the most frequently used instrument for diagnosing personality disorders, includes scales for hysteria, paranoia, schizophrenia, and depression.[29] Both physical and mental disabilities have "protected class" status under the Americans with Disabilities Act. It is illegal to administer mental health and other medical tests until after a bona fide job offer has been made. If these tests reveal a physical or mental disability, the company must provide accommodations unless doing so is burdensome.

An individual diagnosed with manic-depression, for instance, cannot be screened out of the candidate pool solely for having a mental disability, just as a woman cannot be screened out solely because of her gender. With proper medication, the disability may not negatively impact job performance. A person with manic-depression or bi-polar disorder, for instance, can only be denied a job if the mental disability directly affects job performance or puts the public at risk.

Mental health tests are recommended, and at times mandated by law, for jobs involving high levels of stress, personal risk, and responsibility. Customers and the general public have a strong interest in not wanting individuals with a mental illness to obtain jobs such as nuclear power plant operators, armed security guards, or air traffic controllers.[30]

Mental health tests like the MMPI are not a valid way to determine an individual's ethics. A person with a manic-depression disorder who takes the appropriate medication is no more, or less, ethical than the general population.

MORAL REASONING LEVEL

Several methods are available to assess a job candidate's level of moral reasoning or stage of moral development. Employees experience many situations on a daily basis in which rules are ambiguous, unknown, or not applicable; at these times they must rely on their moral judgment to determine what action should be taken. Complex issues require a sophisticated degree of moral reasoning.

Moral Judgment Interview

Psychologist Lawrence Kohlberg and his colleagues, influenced by the writings of developmental psychologist Jean Piaget, studied the reactions of children and adults to moral dilemmas and concluded that there are three levels of moral reasoning, each consisting of two stages.[31] The first level (pre-conventional) of moral reasoning is based on self-interest, the second level (conventional) is based on conformity to social norms and expectations of family and peers, and the third level (post-conventional) is based on universal ethical principles centered on the concept of "justice." Individuals advance through these stages sequentially, with universal ethical principles, the sixth stage, characterized by the most complex ethical analysis. Progress might stop at any stage.

Kohlberg and his colleagues developed a "Moral Judgment Interview" (MJI) instrument, a 45-minute semi-structured interview that involves coding responses to an individual's verbal response to three hypothetical ethical dilemmas. A major virtue of MJI is that respondents express their own moral reasons for justifying a particular action. MJI, however, is not practical for an HR Department because of the complicated, and time consuming, 24-step coding procedure. Kohlberg's scoring manual numbers more than 800 pages.[32]

The Defining Issues Test

James Rest, a Professor of Educational Psychology, simplified the scoring process tremendously by developing the Defining Issues Test (DIT), a multiple choice moral reasoning survey instrument, consisting of six one-paragraph hypothetical ethical dilemmas that can be group administered and computer scored.[33] The respondent chooses a preferred behavior and then evaluates a list of already articulated reasons for justifying such action.[34] Multiple ethical dilemmas are provided to determine consistency or trends in the individual's reasoning process. The ethical dilemmas use a third person format (John or Sue is faced with this situation) to reduce social desirability bias.

The DIT is a well-validated and reliable instrument and has been used in thousands of research studies.[35] DIT-2, an updated version of DIT, consists of five dilemmas on general topics, some of which are related to a business situation.[36] The dilemma contexts have been revised for a contemporary audience.

At the conclusion of the dilemma the respondent is asked whether he or she agrees with a particular action the decision maker could take. Next, the respondent is given a list of reasons the decision maker might consider (i.e., "Shouldn't the community's laws be upheld?") and rates each reason on a 5-point Likert scale ranging from "Great Importance" to "No Importance." Each reason represents a unique stage of moral reasoning. A respondent might report that every issue listed is of great importance (meaning all ethical theories are of equal value), or demonstrate a preference for one level of moral reasoning. Last, the respondent rank orders the four most important reasons the decision maker should consider. This forces the respondent to choose one stage of moral reasoning as being the most important for this particular situation. See Appendix A for an example.

A "P-Score" and "N2-Score" are calculated, each of which ranges from 0 to 95. The P-Score, meaning "Principled Judgment," is the percentage of times the respondent uses the highest levels of moral reasoning, Kohlberg's post-conventional stages 5 and 6. The N2-Score modifies the P2-Score by taking into consideration the respondent's rejection of self-centered reasons (Kohlberg's stages 1 and 2). The higher the P and N2 scores, the more sophisticated an individual's moral reasoning and the higher the stage of moral development.

The "N2-Score" is considered more useful because it takes into consideration both post-conventional and pre-conventional responses.[37] Almost all research using DIT or DIT-2, however, report only P-Scores. In studies comparing different groups of people, moral philosophers and theologians had average P-Scores of 65.2, whereas graduate business students and college students scored 42.8 and 42.3 respectively, prison inmates 23.5, and junior high school students 21.9.[38]

Developers of the DIT have improved the instrument's utility in response to critics.[39] For instance, the DIT had been criticized for a political bias—political "liberals," compared to "conservatives," were more likely to choose the highest principled reasons. The bias has been significantly reduced in DIT-2.[40]

Thinking in morally sophisticated ways, however, does not necessarily mean that the person will choose the most moral action. As dramatized in an infinite number of novels, movies, and biographies, individuals may know what is "right," and then do what is "wrong." Researchers have explored the relationship between reasoning and actual behavior. They report only moderate relationships between stage of moral reasoning and action variables such as helping behaviors, job performance, cheating, and stealing.[41]

The copyrighted DIT-2 dilemmas and scoring system are available through The Center for the Study of Ethical Development.[42] DIT-2 type ethical dilemmas related to specific job functions (such as accounting, marketing, finance, etc.), and available for public use, can be found in many business textbooks. Unfortunately, these dilemmas do not include a list of responses representative of different stages of moral development, or an accompanying scoring system.

Other Moral Reasoning Orientation Surveys

Several other survey instruments measure a person's level of moral reasoning, and some of these provide dilemmas that emphasize business situations. William Boyce and Larry Jensen developed a Moral Content Test

(MCT) based on Kohlberg's ethical dilemmas.[43] Their questionnaire consists of six dilemmas, including whether Heinz should steal an expensive drug for his dying spouse, followed by ten reasons justifying the action. Each reason is rated on a 1–5 scale in terms of importance and then the four most important reasons are ranked. The reasons represent egoism, utilitarianism or deontology. The ranking of each ethical theory is inserted into a chart and then the totals are accumulated for the six ethical dilemmas to determine a pattern in moral reasoning.[44]

Linda Thorne tested four dilemmas that are very relevant for auditors: being instructed to modify negative client information, assisting a client to recruit a CFO, disclosing relevant client information to another client, and disclosing a substantial management fee in a related party transaction.[45] Thorne provides a list of 12 moral concerns for each dilemma. See Appendix B for a dilemma example.

Greg Loviscky, Linda Trevino and Rick Jacobs have created a Managerial Moral Judgment Test (MMJT) designed specifically for use by Human Resources personnel, though it requires additional scholarly testing for validity and reliability.[46] The MMJT consists of six business related ethical dilemmas: misuse of sick days, funding employee training, providing substandard product quality in order to meet an important deadline, providing negative feedback to an abrasive employee, reporting a budget mistake, and a promotion decision. A list of responses for each dilemma is provided, and a scoring sheet is available from the authors upon request.

Another DIT-2 type survey under development is the Moral Reasoning Inventory (MRI).[47] The MRI consists of two ethical dilemmas, each about responding to an unethical boss, followed by eight justifications for either obeying or not obeying the boss.

All of these measures require further testing for validity and reliability.

VALUES ORIENTATION

Knowing a job candidate's value orientation might also provide useful information about the person's ethics. Value systems help clarify an individual's basic convictions about what is right or wrong.

The seminal work on value orientation was performed by Milton Rokeach.[48] He maintained that individuals possessed a hierarchy of values that were relatively stable and enduring. Rokeach differentiated between two types of values—terminal values and instrumental values. Terminal values are end-states that individuals hope to achieve. The terminal value list includes a comfortable life, an exciting life, a sense of accomplishment, a world of peace, and equality. Instrumental values are those values that are a means to achieving terminal values. This list includes being ambitious, broad-minded, honest, obedient, and responsible. Survey respondents are asked to rank order these values in terms of their importance.

Researchers have found minimal differences between social groups and their value preferences, which calls into question the utility of this survey instrument. For instance, one would expect corporate managers to possess a uniquely different set of values than either union members or community activists. But that is not the case. The top three terminal values for corporate executives—self-respect, family security, and freedom —were among the top four values for union members and the top five values for community activists.[49] The executives' top three instrumental values—honest, responsible, and capable—were within the top five for both union members and community activists, with honesty being the top value for both the executives and community activists, and second for the union members. Knowing a job candidate's rank ordering of instrumental and terminal values is not a useful way to determine differences in ethical behavior.

CONCLUDING COMMENTS

Administering ethics-based surveys during the job screening process sends a strong message to both job candidates and current employees that ethics matter. This chapter reviewed a wide range of survey methods that could help companies determine a job candidate's ethics profile.

Integrity tests ask job candidates about unethical behaviors, such as having stolen money or property from previous employers. This information accurately predicts future theft, absenteeism, and disciplinary problems.

Of the hundreds of possible personality measures, "conscientiousness" —which measures responsibility, dependability, and work ethic—is the best predictor of ethics and job performance. Social dominance orientation and bullying measures predict a propensity for racial and gender discrimination, and can result in hostile work environments. Organizational Citizenship Behavior measures an individual's propensity to help others. Social desirability biases must be taken into consideration when interpreting the results of these useful survey instruments. "Moral Reasoning Level" is an underused and underdeveloped survey instrument, but can be very helpful. The higher the score the more sophisticated a person's ethical analysis.

The Myers-Briggs Type Indicator, mental health surveys, and values orientation surveys do not provide useful information about an individual's ethics. There is no evidence that one particular MBTI profile, or one particular set of instrumental or terminal values, is any more ethical than the others. Eliminating a job candidate, prior to a job offer, based solely on a mental health score violates the American Disabilities Act because the survey instrument measures mental disabilities, not personality.

APPENDIX A: DIT-2 Sample Story—The Famine[50]

The small village in northern India has experienced shortages of food before, but this year's famine is worse than ever. Some families are even trying to feed themselves by making soup from tree bark. Mustaq Singh's family is near starvation. He has heard that a rich man in his village has supplies of food stored away and is hoarding food while its price goes higher so that he can sell the food later at a huge profit. Mustaq is desperate and thinks about stealing some food from the rich man's warehouse. The small amount of food that he needs for his family probably wouldn't even be missed.

What should Mustaq Singh do? Do you favor the action of taking the food? (*Check one*)

Strongly Favor: 1 ___

Favor: 2 ___

Slightly Favor: 3 ___

Neutral: 4 ___

Slightly Disfavor: 5 ___

Disfavor: 6 ___

Strongly Disfavor: 7 ___

Rate the following **12 ISSUES** in terms of importance (1 = great, 2 = much, 3 = some, 4 = little, 5 = no). Please put a number from 1 to 5 after each of the 12 issues.

1. Is Mustaq Singh courageous enough to risk getting caught for stealing? ____
2. Isn't it only natural for a loving father to care so much for his family that he would steal? ___
3. Shouldn't the community's laws be upheld? ____
4. Does Mustaq Singh know a good recipe for preparing soup from tree bark? ____
5. Does the rich man have any legal right to store food when other people are starving? ____
6. Is the motive of Mustaq Singh to steal for himself or to steal for his family? ____
7. What values are going to be the basis for social cooperation? ____
8. Is the epitome of eating reconcilable with the culpability of stealing? ____
9. Does the rich man deserve to be robbed for being so greedy? ____
10. Isn't private property an institution to enable the rich to exploit the poor? ____
11. Would stealing bring about more total good for everybody concerned or not? ____
12. Are laws getting in the way of the most basic claim of any member of a society? ____
13. Which of the 12 issues above is the 1st most important? (write the number of the item) ____

a. Which of these 12 issues is the 2nd most important? ____
b. Which of these 12 issues is the 3rd most important? ____
c. Which of these 12 issues is the 4th most important? ____

APPENDIX B: Accounting Ethical Dilemma[51]

Alice and the ABC Company

Alice is a senior auditor and a Certified Accountant for a national Certified Accounting firm that provides auditing, tax, and consulting services. The firm has developed a package called the ACME Accounting System which is sold to the general public as well as the firm's clients. Alice is the auditor in charge of the field work on the ABC Company, Inc. audit. During the course of this audit assignment, Alice is asked to evaluate the quality control of the accounting system which happens to be the ACME package. Alice uncovers several severe control weaknesses in the ACME system. Before rendering the management letter to ABC management, Alice is told by her boss to modify the negative comments regarding the ACME package.

Ideally, should Alice amend the management letter? (*Check one*)

Alice should amend it ____   I can't decide ____   Alice should not amend it ____

In the process of advising Alice whether she should amend the management letter, many issues need to be considered. Rate the following 12 ISSUES in terms of importance (1 = great, 2 = much, 3 = some, 4 = little, 5 = no). Please put a number from 1 to 5 after each of the 12 issues.

1. Whether the weaknesses in the ACME system may be easily remedied by compensating controls. ____

2. Would a good employee defer to her superior's judgment? ____

3. Whether Alice's job may be threatened by her refusal to revise the letter. ____

4. Whether fair deliberation on the client's financial position can predict professional reputation. ____

5. What is best for Alice's firm? ____

6. Whether Alice has a duty to ensure the management letter is accurate. ____

7. What is the potential value of an independent audit in lieu of society's current perspective on an enterprise's net worth? ____

8. How is society best served? ____

9. Whether clients really care about internal control or if all they ever really want is a clean audit opinion. ____

10. Would amending the management letter be consistent with what Alice thinks is right? ____

11. What action would Alice's peers in the audit firm expect her to make? ____

12. What factors are relevant in determining Alice's professional responsibility? ____

From the list above, rank the four issues of greatest importance to an "ideal" response.

Most Important ____   3rd Most Important ____

2nd Most Important ____   4th Most Important ____

Scoring System

Alice Accounting Dilemma

Step #1: The M ("validity check") issues are answers 4 and 7.

Step #2: If the "Most Important" issue is 4 or 7, person gets 4 "M" points

Step #3: If the "2nd Most Important" issue is 4 or 7, person gets 3 "M" points

Step #4: If the "3rd Most Important" issue is 4 or 7, person gets 2 "M" points

Step #5: If the "4th Most Important" issue is 4 or 7, person gets 1 "M" points

Step #6: Add up these points for the person's total "M" score

Step #7: If the "M" score is 6 or greater, then the instrument is invalid

Step #8: The P ("principled") issues are answers 8, 10, and 12.

Step #9: If the "Most Important" issue is 8, 10 or 12, person gets 4 "P" points

Step #10: If the "2nd Most Important" issue is 8, 10 or 12, person gets 3 "P" points

Step #11: If the "3rd Most Important" issue is 8, 10 or 12, person gets 2 "P" points

Step #12: If the "4th Most Important" issue is 8, 10 or 12, person gets 1 "P" points

Step #13: Add up these points for the person's total "P" score

Step #14: If "P" score is

- 2 or less—Pre-conventional stage of moral reasoning
- 3 or 4—Conventional stage of moral reasoning
- 5 or higher—Post-conventional Principled stage of moral reasoning

NOTES

1. http://www.geninfo.com/backgroundreporter/june2006/nrs_page2.htm
2. Walczyk, J.J., Schwartz, J.P., Clifton, R., Adams, B., Wei, M., & Zha, P. (2005). Lying person-to-person about life events: A cognitive framework for lie detection, *Personnel Psychology, 58,* 141–170.
3. Whitaker, B. (2005, February 22). Employee theft can do you in. *New York Times,* p. 2.
4. Falcone, P. (2002). *The hiring and firing question and answer book.* New York: Amacom, (American Management Association), p. 15.
5. Krohe, J., Jr. (2006). Are workplace tests worth taking? *Across the Board, 43*(4), 16–23.
6. Noe, R. A., Hollenbeck, J. R., Gerhart, B., & Wright, P. M. (2006). *Human resource management* (5th ed.). New York: McGraw-Hill Irwin.
7. Murphy, K. R. (1993). *Honesty in the workplace.* Pacific Grove, CA: Brooks/Cole.
8. U.S. Congress, Office of Technology Assessment. (1990). *The use of integrity tests for pre-employment screening,* Washington, DC: U.S. Government Printing Office.
9. Bernardin, H. J., & Cooke, D. K. (1993). Validity of an honesty test in predicting theft among convenience store employees. *Academy of Management Journal, 36*(5), 1097–1108; Berry, C. M., Sackett, P. R., & Wiemann, S. (2007). A review of recent developments in integrity test research. *Personnel Psychology, 60*(2), 271–301; Ones, D. S., Viswesvaran, C., & Schmidt, F. L.

(1993). Comprehensive meta-analysis of integrity test validities: Findings and implications for personnel selection and theories of job performance. *Journal of Applied Psychology, 78*(4), 679–703.

10.   Krohe, J., Jr. (2006). Are workplace tests worth taking? *Across the Board, 43*(4), 16–23.

11.   Alliger, G. M., & Dwight, S. A. (2000). A meta-analytic investigation of the susceptibility of integrity tests to faking and coaching. *Educational and Psychological Measurement, 60*(1), 59–72; Berry, C. M., Sackett, P. R., & Wiemann, S. (2007). A review of recent developments in integrity test research. *Personnel Psychology, 60*(2), 271–301; Cunningham, M. R., Wong, D. T., & Barbee, A. P. (1994). Self-presentation dynamics on overt integrity tests: Experimental studies of the Reid report. *Journal of Applied Psychology, 79*(5), 643–658.

12.   John, O. P., & Srivastava, S. (1999). The big-five trait taxonomy: History, measurement, and theoretical perspectives. In L. A. Pervin & O. P. John (Eds.), *Handbook of personality: Theory and research* (2nd ed.) (pp. 102–138). New York: Guilford Press; Robbins, S.P., & Judge, T.A. (2008). *Essentials of organizational behavior* (9th ed.). Upper Saddle River, NJ: Pearson Prentice Hall; Big 5 Scales: http://ipip.ori.org/newBigFive5broadKey.htm# Conscientiousness

13.   Berry, C. M., Sackett, P. R., & Wiemann, S. (2007). A review of recent developments in integrity test research. *Personnel Psychology, 60*(2), 271–301.

14.   Mount, M., Ilies, R., & Johnson, E. (2006). Relationship of personality traits and counterproductive work behaviors: The mediating effects of job satisfaction. *Personnel Psychology, 59*(3), 591–622.

15.   Robbins, S. P., & Judge, T. A. (2008). *Essentials of organizational behavior* (9th ed.). Upper Saddle River, NJ: Pearson Prentice Hall.

16.   http://ipip.ori.org/newBigFive5broadKey.htm#Conscientiousness

17.   Hurtz, G. M., & Alliger, G. M. (2002). Influence of coaching on integrity test performance and unlikely virtues scale scores. *Human Performance, 15*(3), 255–273.

18.   Organ, D. W., Podsakoff, P. M., & MacKenzie, S. B. (2005). *Organizational citizenship behavior: Its nature, antecedents, and consequences.* Thousand Oaks, CA: Sage Publications.

19.   Organ, D.W. (1988). *Organizational citizenship behavior—The good soldier syndrome.* Lexington, MA: D. C. Heath and Company.

20.   Podsakoff, P. M., MacKenzie, S. B., Paine, J. B., & Bachrach, D. (2000). Organizational citizenship behaviors: A critical review of the theoretical and empirical literature and suggestions for future research. *Journal of Management, 26*(3), 513–563.

21.   Sidanius, J., & Pratto, F. (2001). *Social dominance: An intergroup theory of social hierarchy and oppression.* Cambridge: Cambridge University Press.

22.   Lutgen-Sandvik, P., Tracy, S. J., & Alberts, J. K. (2007). Burned by b8llying in the American workplace: Prevalence, perception, degree and impact. *Journal of Management Studies, 44*(6), 837–862. See also Bassman, E. (1992). *Abuse in the workplace.* New York: Quorum Books.

23. Parkins, I. S., Fishbein, H. D., & Ritchey, P. N. (2006). The influence of personality on workplace bullying and discrimination. *Journal of Applied Social Psychology, 36*(10), 2554–2577.

24. www.myersbriggs.org; Krohe Jr., J. (2006). Are workplace tests worth taking? *Across the Board, 43*(4), 16–23.

25. Myers I. B., & McCaullet M. H. (1998). *Manual: A guide to the development and use of the Myers-Briggs type indicator.* Palo Alto, CA: Consulting Psychologists Press.

26. Murphy Paul, A. (2004). *The Cult of Personality,* New York: Free Press.

27. Web sites with personality scales: 204 Scales Web site: http://ipip.ori.org/newIndexofScaleLabels.htm; Values in Action Survey Items: http://ipip.ori.org/newVIAKey.htm#Integrity_Honesty; Big 5 and other Scales: http://ipip.ori.org/newNEOKey.htm#Altruism; Big 5 Scales: http://ipip.ori.org/newBigFive5broadKey.htm#Conscientiousness; California Psychological Inventory: http://ipip.ori.org/newCPIKey.htm#Dominance; HEX: http://ipip.ori.org/newHEXACO_PI_key.htm#Greed_Avoidance; Personal Attributes Survey (PAS): http://ipip.ori.org/newPASKey.htm#Locus-of-Control; Jackson Personality Inventory: http://ipip.ori.org/newJPI-RKey.htm#Machiavellianism

28. Murphy Paul, A. (2004). *The Cult of Personality,* New York: Free Press.

29. http://www.falseallegations.com/mmpi-bw.htm

30. Arnold, D. W., & Jones, J. W. (2002). Who the devil's applying now? *Security Management, 46*, 85+.

31. Kohlberg, L. (1981). *The philosophy of moral development.* New York: Harper Collins.

32. Colby, A., & Kohlberg, L. (1987). *The measurement of moral judgment.* New York: Cambridge University Press.

33. Rest, J. (1979). *Development in judging moral issues,* Minneapolis, MN: University of Minnesota Press; Rest, J.R., & Narvaez, D. (1994). *Moral development in the professions,* Hillsdale, NJ: Lawrence Erlbaum Associates; Rest, J. R., Narvaez, D., Bebeau, M., & Thoma, S. (1999). *Postconventional moral thinking: A neo-Kohlbergian approach.* Mahwah, NJ: Lawrence Erlbaum Associates.

34. See the appendix for the Heinz dilemma, which is available on the Center for the Study of Ethical Development's Web site: http://www.centerforthestudyofethicaldevelopment.net/DIT%20--Sample%20Dilemma.htm

35. Bebeau, M. J. (2002). The defining issues test and the four component model: Contributions to professional education. *Journal of Moral Education, 31*(3), 271–295; Rest, J., Navarez, D., Bebeau, M., and Thoma, S. J. (1999). A NeoKohlbergian Approach: The DIT and Schema Theory. *Educational Psychology Review, 11*(4), 1999, 291–324; Thoma, S. (2006). Research on the Defining Issues Test. In M. Killan & J.G. Smetana (Eds.) *Handbook of Moral Development.* Mahwah, New Jersey: Lawrence Erbaum Associates.

36. http://www.centerforthestudyofethicaldevelopment.net/DIT2.htm; The five dilemmas of DIT-2 are: (a) a father contemplates stealing food for his starving family from the warehouse of a rich man hoarding food; (b) a newspaper reporter must decide whether to report a damaging story about

a political candidate; (c) a school board chair must decide whether to hold a contentious and dangerous open meeting; (d) a doctor must decide whether to give an overdose of pain-killer to a suffering but frail patient; (e) college students demonstrate against U.S. foreign policy.

37.   Walker, L. J. (2002). The model and the measure: An appraisal of the Minnesota approach to moral development. *Journal of Moral Education, 31*(3), 353–367.

38.   Rest, J. R., & Narvaez, D. (1994). *Moral development in the professions*, Hillsdale, NJ: Lawrence Erlbaum Associates.

39.   Rest, J. R., Narvaez, D., Thoma, S.J ., & Bebeau, M. J. (1999). DIT2: Devising and testing a revised instrument of moral judgment. *Journal of Educational Psychology, 91*(4), 644–659; Rest, J., Edwards, L., & Thoma, S. (1997). Designing and validating a measure of moral judgment: Stage preference and stage consistency approaches. *Journal of Educational Psychology, 89*(1), 5–28; Thoma, S.J., Narvaez, D., Rest, J., & Derryberry, P. (1999). Does moral judgment development reduce to political attitudes or verbal ability? Evidence using the defining issues test. *Educational Psychology Review, 11*(4), 325–341.

40.   Bailey, C. D., Phillips, T. J., & Scofield, S. B., (2005). Does 'political bias' in the DIT or DIT-2 threaten validity in studies of CPAs? *Behavioral Research in Accounting, 17*, 23–45; Fisher, D.G, & Sweeney, J.T. (1998). The relationship between political attitudes and moral judgment: Examining the validity of the defining issues test. *Journal of Business Ethics, 17*, 905–916.

41.   Loviscky, G. E., Trevino, L. K., & Jacobs, R. R., (2007). Assessing managers' ethical decision-making: An objective measure of managerial moral judgment. *Journal of Business Ethics, 73*, 263–285; Thoma, S. (1994). Moral judgments and moral actions. In J. R. Rest & D. Narvaez, (Eds.), *Moral development in the professions*, Hillsdale, NJ: Lawrence Erlbaum Associates.

42.   http://www.centerforthestudyofethicaldevelopment.net/index.html

43.   Boyce, William D., & Larry Cyril Jensen, 1978, *Moral Reasoning: A Psychological-Philosophical Integration*, Lincoln, Nebraska: University of Nebraska Press.

44.   For a scoring example, see Appendix, pp. 262-267, in Boyce, William D., & Larry Cyril Jensen, 1978, *Moral Reasoning: A Psychological-Philosophical Integration*, Lincoln, Nebraska: University of Nebraska Press.

45.   Thorne, L. (2000). The development of two measures to assess accountants' prescriptive and deliberative moral reasoning. *Behavioral Research in Accounting, 12*, 139–169.

46.   Loviscky, G. E., Trevino, L. K., & Jacobs, R. R., (2007). Assessing managers' ethical decision-making: An objective measure of managerial moral judgment. *Journal of Business Ethics, 73*, 263–285. The six dilemmas appear in their appendix.

47.   Weber, J., & McGivern, E. (2007). *The moral reasoning inventory: A new methodological approach for studying moral reasoning in business settings*. Working Paper.

48.   Rokeach, M. (1973). *The nature of human values*. New York: Free Press.

49.   Frederick, W. C., & Weber, J. (1990). The values of corporate managers and their critics: An empirical description and normative implications. In W. C. Frederick & L. E. Preston (Eds.) *Business ethics: Research issues and empirical studies.* Greenwich, CT: JAI Press.

50.   Rest, J. R., Narvaez, D., Thoma, S. J., & Bebeau, M. J. (1999). DIT2: Devising and testing a revised instrument of moral judgment. *Journal of Educational Psychology, 91*(4), 644–659. Instructions for scoring this dilemma is available from the Center for the Study of Ethical Development at the following Web site: http://www.centerforthestudyofethicaldevelopment.net/DIT%20--Sample%20Dilemma.htm; format slightly modified.

51.   Thorne, L. (2000). The development of two measures to assess accountants' prescriptive and deliberative moral reasoning. *Behavioral Research in Accounting, 12,* 139–169; format slightly modified.

CHAPTER 10

MULTINATIONAL CORPORATIONS AND BASIC HEALTH SERVICES

Duane Windsor

The following chapter presents theoretical argument for how and why it may be profitable for multinational corporations to participate in provision of certain basic health services in developing countries where they operate. The chapter examines the pros and cons of such participation from both strategic and citizenship perspectives. Diseases are endemic in tropical countries: for example, HIV, malaria, dysentery, river blindness, and so forth. A couple of examples are Merck's river blindness program and the recent announcement that Marathon Oil (headquartered in Houston) is addressing malaria in West Africa. I attempt to identify various examples reported in the literature and press. A consideration in this analysis is that relatively low expenditures can have marked benefits for the affected population while building moral capital for the company. A potential difficulty is whether corporate programs might run afoul of collusion with pharmaceutical companies seeking non-informed patient testing programs. The recent Hollywood film *The Constant Gardener* focuses on such an alleged activity. I examine what (if any) evidence exists on this matter. If there is such evidence, the chapter will discuss ways of avoiding such collusion.

Doing Well And Good: The Human Face of the New Capitalism, pp. 187–214
Copyright © 2009 by Information Age Publishing
All rights of reproduction in any form reserved.

This volume's theme concerns the ethics of businesses doing well and doing good simultaneously. (An alternative expression is good deals and good deeds.) This chapter isolates a particular instance of this theme focused on provision of basic health services in host developing countries by multinational corporations (MNCs). There are instances of such provision. This chapter examines how and why it may be sound business strategy for MNCs to participate in provision of certain basic health services in developing countries where they operate. The chapter assesses the pros and cons of such participation from both strategic and citizenship perspectives. The author identifies various examples of such participation reported in the literature and press. The examples identified do not constitute a systematic survey. A key consideration in this assessment is that relatively low corporate expenditures can have marked benefits for an affected population while building moral capital (i.e., reputation) for the company. A potential difficulty is whether corporate programs might run afoul of collusion with pharmaceutical companies seeking non-informed patient testing programs. The recent book and film *The Constant Gardener* focused on such an alleged activity. The chapter examines what (if any) evidence exists on this matter. The chapter discusses ways of avoiding or safeguarding against such collusion. At this stage of inquiry, advice must be cautionary and fairly general.

The explicit assumption of the "old capitalism" was that corporate financial performance on behalf of shareholders is reduced improperly by any discretionary corporate social responsibility (CSR) activities beyond mandatory compliance with legal requirements. However, Friedman[1] relaxed his defense of this strict tradeoff between profitability and CSR somewhat by (a) viewing customary ethics as equally binding as legal requirements, and (b) permitting what can be regarded as a prudent altruism aimed at forestalling even more costly legal requirements by satisfying politically influential stakeholders.[2]

This chapter focuses narrowly on MNCs and basic health services in developing countries. It does not seek to develop a more general justification of CSR. One basis for MNCs going beyond Friedman's stance to address social issues such as basic health services in certain countries and circumstances is moral obligation. MNC top management may decide that the firm has some moral responsibility, as a good corporate citizen, to assist developing countries in which it operates in particular ways. This notion of moral obligation extends beyond Friedman's view of customary ethics. This sense of moral obligation does not depend on, but may be strengthened by, any arguments that basic health services should be fundamental human rights everywhere in the world. Moral obligation arguments—which go beyond customary ethics—leave vague whether

CSR is necessarily at the expense of corporate financial performance, as argued by Friedman.

The fundamental conception of a proposed "new capitalism" is that businesses can have a human face of corporate social contribution while meeting investor and management requirements for corporate financial performance. This conception does not eliminate moral obligation. Rather, the conception argues that one can often specify a reasonable business case for doing some defined good on behalf of people with some unfulfilled need. This need occurs beyond effective market demand for goods and services. Unless there is some business case, doing such good might become pure altruism, in the form of corporate philanthropy, as argued by Friedman.[3] A business case might be strictly short term, in the sense of direct and immediate contribution to the corporate bottom line. A business case might be more loosely long term, in the sense of relatively more distant contribution to the corporate bottom line through investment in future stakeholder support or building of moral capital (i.e., reputation).

Independently of management, customers, employees and investors may feel there is some moral responsibility in such regard. This notion of stakeholder interest extends beyond Friedman's view of prudent altruism. Customers may prefer responsible companies; and employees may prefer to work for and be more motivated at responsible companies. This stakeholder interest may prove particularly strong for pharmaceutical companies selling products in developing countries. Employees may be demoralized and customers disaffected by a purely profit oriented management in the context of AIDS, malaria, and other health problems. While moral obligation might be regarded as ultimately subjective, stakeholder influence is as objective as market forces.

Corporations formulate and implement commercial strategy, which can have a reasonably broad scope and a reasonably distant time horizon in terms of building a sustainable business. Commercial sustainability involves non-market as well as market dimensions of strategizing. Nevertheless, a business case is distinct from a voluntary sense of moral obligation or a socially mandatory compliance with laws and public policies.[4] In some way, either CSR is immediately profitable or in the longer term stakeholder support of the firm increases as a result of CSR.

Margolis and Walsh suggest that there are ample opportunities for this mutually beneficial combination of corporate financial performance and corporate social contribution.[5] They identified some 95 studies over roughly three decades (1972–2000) bearing on the question.[6] The bulk of the studies (80) treated corporate social performance as an independent variable and explored the effects on corporate financial performance.[7] Margolis and Walsh report that 53% of the 80 studies found a positive relationship, 24% no relationship, 4% a negative relationship, and 19% a mixed relationship. If these results are reliable, then firms can sometimes do well by doing good. This conclusion supports the concept of "new capitalism." A small proportion of the studies (19) treated corporate social performance as a dependent variable and explored the effects of corporate financial performance.[8] Margolis and Walsh report that 68% of the 19 studies found a positive relationship, 16% no relationship, and 16% a mixed relationship. They reported no study finding a negative relationship. If these results are reliable, then firms can afford to do good when they are doing well. This conclusion corresponds to altruism, whether prudent or pure. Evaluation is fraught with scientific difficulties due to considerable heterogeneity of measures and data sources.[9] Orlitzky, Schmidt, and Rynes report stronger results from a meta-analysis of 52 studies.[10] Other authors, such as Doane[11] and Vogel,[12] argue that the likely business worth of CSR is strictly limited. However, even a limited advantage is not a zero advantage. This chapter argues that provision of basic health services in developing host countries is a reasonable business strategy.

Margolis, Walsh, and Kreymeyer emphasize that the question "Does Ethics Pay?" (which they answer positively) is merely the beginning and not the end of business ethics and CSR. Evaluating ethical performance solely in terms of financial impact ignores social benefits and other beneficiaries (i.e., stakeholders). There may be compelling circumstances in which businesses absolutely must face negative financial impacts in order to do the right thing. These circumstances define moral obligation, strictly speaking. Furthermore, businesses must prepare to meet rising social, stakeholder and legal expectations concerning both financial and ethical performance. Margolis, Walsh, and Kreymeyer stress the "organization's mission, principles, and values" as justifying ethical performance and determining how to assess unavoidable tradeoffs.[13] Merck's free distribution of river blindness medication, discussed later, is an example. Chenault, in his commentary attached to Margolis, Walsh, and Kreymeyer, emphasizes the "social compact" in which society permits the corporation to exist because it contributes to the "common good."[14] This social compact is now going global. Chenault distinguishes among doing well (financially), doing right (ethically), and doing good (benefiting stakeholders).[15] Where these conditions can be fulfilled simultaneously, there is "new capitalism;" where they cannot be fulfilled simultaneously, moral obligation is overriding—especially in the instance of fundamental human rights. This chapter applies these considerations to the relationship between MNCs and basic human services in developing countries.

The remainder of this chapter is organized as follows. The second section following this introduction explains why basic health services in developing countries are a critically important social issue area for MNCs. The third section addresses the matter of whether basic health services are a fundamental human right, or if not presently will become so in the future. The section includes some illustrative information concerning diseases in developing countries. The third section assesses the relationship of CSR to the common good in the basic health context. The fourth section discusses funding and governance of global (or international) public goods, of which basic health services are examples. The purpose is an examination of the likely roles of MNCs. The fifth section concludes the chapter as follows. The section first examines the risks that may arise with business involvement in basic health service delivery in developing countries. Two potential risks concern the Libya experience and *The Constant Gardener* warning. The section then marshals the case for MNC involvement in basic health service delivery, in particular circumstances in developing countries, despite those potential risks.

BASIC HEALTH SERVICES IN DEVELOPING COUNTRIES

Basic health services are a critically important social issue in developing countries and thus for MNCs operating in those countries. Host countries and MNC stakeholders have significant concerns. On September 18, 2000, the UN General Assembly adopted a Millennium Declaration. The essence of the resolution was that by 2015 there should be specific measurable progress on eight Millennium Development Goals (MDGs). These eight goals are progress toward (1) eradicating extreme poverty and hunger, (2) achieving universal primary education, (3) promoting gender equality and empowerment of women, (4) reducing child mortality, (5) improving maternal health, (6) combating diseases such as HIV/AIDS and malaria, (7) ensuring environmental sustainability, and (8) developing a global partnership for development. Global development assistance will have to be doubled. The goals concerning child mortality, maternal health, and combating diseases are directly relevant to this chapter.

In light of the relevant MDGs, there are six specific reasons for focusing corporate attention on basic health services. First, the UN Global Compact does not include directly any specific principles addressing basic health services. This circumstance suggests a voluntary initiative opportunity for MNCs. The Global Compact, initiated by UN Secretary-General Kofi Annan, is a voluntary association of corporations and other organizations. The Compact asks businesses to adhere to ten principles or core values in the four areas of human rights, labor standards, environmental protection, and anti-corruption.[16] Labor standards (Principles 3–6) and environmental protection (Principles 7–9) are not directly relevant to this chapter.[17] Basic health services have not reached the status of a globally recognized, fundamental human right. Nevertheless, it should be emphasized that the two human rights principles are subject to interpretation and change over time.[18] Principle 1 states: "Businesses should support and respect the protection of internationally proclaimed human rights." Principle 2 states: businesses should "make sure that they are not complicit in human rights abuses." Bales (1999) estimated that there are at least 27 million held in conditions definable as slavery.[19] The human rights principles rest on the 1948 Universal Declaration of Human Rights. That declaration concerns equality, life and security (i.e., freedom from governmental abuse), personal freedom (privacy and movement), and economic, social, and cultural freedoms. The anti-corruption, tenth, principle is relevant, because official and commercial corruption is reportedly high in many developing countries where MNCs often operate. This principle, added in June 2004, rests on the United Nations Convention Against Corruption.

Second, as noted above, lack of basic health services is not yet plainly a human rights violation. Such provision is generally regarded as a governmental function. Moreover, the UN does have a health arm. The World Health Organization (WHO), a UN agency formed in 1948, has presently a 6-point agenda. It seeks to promote development by focusing on the poor, the underserved, and the vulnerable. It attempts to foster health security, especially against epidemics. It seeks to strengthen global health systems. It provides research, information, and evidence. It engages in partnerships, with public and private organizations. It attempts to improve performance efficiency and effectiveness. Nevertheless, basic health services are moving over time toward broader acceptance as a fundamental human right.

Third, the very nature of basic health services in developing countries is that they are widely non-existent or at best highly deficient at the "bottom of the pyramid."[20] Prahalad uses this term to define the roughly four billion people in the world who subsist on less than $2 a day. He argues that markets rather than charity can enable dignity and choices for poor populations. Nevertheless, basic health services might be handled by markets, despite governmental incapacity. For example, the Aravind Eye Hospital in Southeastern India has been financially self-sufficient and expanding its services for cataract surgery to multiple hospitals. From 1991–92 to 1998–99, expenditures ranged between 38% and 51% of income annually. In 1999, Aravind treated nearly 1.3 million patients. In 1992, Aravind established Aurolab to produce its own intraocular lenses (IOLs) for implanting and exports such lenses to over 80 countries largely to non-profit institutions. By 2000, Aurolab had diversified into pharmaceuticals and micro-sutures. Aravind has had since 1992 a 500 rupee fee for surgery, the fee being waived for patients unable to afford payment. With support of the Lions Clubs International Foundation, Aravind set up the Lions Aravind Institute of Community Ophthalmology (LAICO) to provide assistance to India's other eye hospitals. Dr. Govindapaa Venkataswamy (born 1918) founded the hospital in 1976 as a 20-bed facility. By 1992, the hospital expanded to 1,224 beds.[21]

Fourth, health improvements are likely to be highly cost-effective. This circumstance makes MNC action particularly attractive. There are relatively low MNC costs and very high social payoffs. The human capital and economic growth effects in developing countries can be powerful. The health improvements can be quite simple, including for example dietary supplements and control of parasitic diseases.[22] A study based on data from India indicates that the long-term effects of malaria eradication should be very substantially positive. A nationwide eradication program occurred there in the 1950s. The data suggest that gains of about 12 percentage points in literacy and primary school completion rates were due to eradication, explaining about half of the gains in those rates in areas (all non-urban) where malaria had been prevalent. There were gains in such rates for men, women, and so-called scheduled (i.e., disadvantaged) castes and tribes.[23]

Fifth, global warming and global development are likely spreading diseases. Unless targeted for quick and decisive action, problems may get worse. The time for action is now; and it is a matter of "all hands on deck" including MNCs operating in developing countries. Malaria is spreading into the highlands of Kenya, where export coffee is grown. Malaria-bearing mosquitoes have been detected at 6,243 feet above sea level. Malaria parasite requires temperatures above 64 degrees for development.[24] Although once nearly eradicated in Peru during the 1950s and 1960s, malaria is coming back in that country's Amazon rain forest as a result of development and in-migration.[25] Dengue fever, both common "bonebreak fever" with very severe flu-like symptoms and the deadly hemorrhagic form characterized in addition by internal and external bleeding, is likely to increase greatly in Latin America. While there is no drug treatment for hemorrhagic dengue, proper care can reduce the death rate to 1%. Dengue can spread across international borders through travelers and into the mosquito population.[26] In signing the Kyoto protocol, advanced countries have accepted responsibility for global warming, which is one of the factors promoting tropical diseases.

Sixth, there is a common good (or global public good) dimension to global basic health services, as noted above with dengue fever. Quick and decisive action at particular points can have widespread benefits. In Latin

America, an estimated 10–12 million people are infected with Chagas parasite; and perhaps one million of them will die unless there are improvements in treatment. Blood banks in the United States now must screen for this parasite; and organ donor screening may have to follow. The American Red Cross reported that in Los Angeles (where there is a high rate of travel to/from Latin America) the infection rate in blood donors has risen from 1 in 9,850 in 1996 to 1 in 3,800 in 2006. The problem affects the U.S. presently when blood and organ donors have traveled to Latin America and been infected by a blood-sucking insect looking like a striped cockroach. When the infection is caught early, the parasite can be controlled or sometimes eliminated by anti-protozoal drugs. Later in the infection cycle, pacemakers, heart drugs, and even heart transplants may be involved.[27]

Extensively drug-resistant tuberculosis (the health issue in *The Constant Gardener*) is becoming a greater danger. The strain XDR-TB has been identified in 28 countries. TB spreads through coughing or sneezing. It can be extremely deadly and untreatable. Typically, the strain attacks AIDS patients, but it does affect HIV-negative patients as well. In March 2007, billionaire George Soros donated $3 million to a nonprofit coalition in Lesotho to support prevention and research. The WHO estimates that South Africa alone will require $650 million annually for prevention and research. It is reported that a single outbreak of tuberculosis in New York in the 1980s and 1990s cost $1 billion to contain.[28] TB travels in the wake of AIDS—to India, Russia, and China for example.[29]

These six considerations constitute the essential case for MNC involvement in basic health services in developing countries. The case is one of voluntary action at relatively low MNC costs for relatively high social benefits. The case is relatively stronger for some industries (e.g., pharmaceuticals and resource extraction) than for others. The case is relatively stronger in some places (e.g., tropical countries) and for some conditions (e.g., AIDS, dengue, and malaria) than others. A key consideration is that quick action now will be more effective globally. At one level, the case is one of moral obligation. Who can act, in a particular situation, is the one responsible for action. Employees at the point of operation may be particularly affected. At another level, the case becomes a broader instance of "new capitalism": stakeholder support can be improved and new profit opportunities may develop over time. While this case is not airtight (basic health services is not yet a fundamental human right broadly accepted as such), arguing a contrary position that MNCs should ignore basic health issues around them in developing countries does not seem defensible.

BASIC HEALTH SERVICES AS A FUTURE HUMAN RIGHT

Although basic health services are not yet a fundamental human right, as gauged by the UN Global Compact for example, these important social issues are heading in that direction. Moreover, where human rights can be fulfilled on a cost-effective basis arguments for not doing so seem particularly weak. Former U.S. President Jimmy Carter and The Carter Center seek to broaden the understanding of human rights from political and civil to include a human right, for children at least, to live. For example, Carter has been working to eradicate Guinea worm disease, which may after some two decades of effort be eradicated within the next 5 years. The Guinea worm is a two-foot-long parasite that feeds inside the body and eventually comes out very painfully.[30] While basic health services are not yet plainly a human right, various initiatives are working in that direction. Corporations can be early into this development.

The Global Fund to Fight AIDS, Tuberculosis, and Malaria targets those three named diseases. The William J. Clinton Foundation addresses AIDS worldwide. There are, of course, many other diseases and health problems, especially in tropical developing countries. Millions of children in developing countries have cleft lip and palate, which can be readily fixed by widespread provision of free cleft surgery. The SmileTrain, which funds such surgeries through donations, reports a donation cost of $250 per surgery, with overhead covered by funding supporters, and more than 265,000 surgeries provided since March 2000.[31] Globally, diarrhea from contaminated water kills an estimated two million people, mostly young children. Charcoal and chlorine water filters cost about $35. PATH, a nonprofit headquartered in Ballard, Washington, has a $17 million grant from the Bill and Melinda Gates Foundation to tackle water quality. It is concentrating on helping companies develop a range of low-cost filters and other water treatment products. One example is development of a water purification powder that for a cost of 8 cents will treat almost three gallons of water.[32] For MNCs to stand aside from this global battle seems unconscionable and thus over the longer run likely to cause disaffection in key stakeholder groups such as customers and employees, as well as attention from human rights activists. While some risks may be attendant on MNC involvement in health issues, both strategic and citizenship considerations argue in favor of such involvement.

WHO / UNICEF data (2002) suggest that maternal and neonatal tetanus (MNT) kills annually almost 180,000 infants and 30,000 mothers in 51 developing countries. The daily death rate is (by computation) about 575. Vaccination can prevent tetanus. BD, a medical technology company, committed $15 million in the form of 135 million auto-disable injection devices (BD Uniject™) and more than $3 million in funds to the U.S. Fund for Unicef.[33]

One widely-repeated estimate reports that 35 million people are HIV infected, with about 95% residing in sub-Saharan Africa.[34] In a single country, however, India has the largest living HIV/AID population at 5.7 million, followed by South Africa. Distribution in India of even free anti-retroviral drugs is a difficulty. While available in the cities, where barbers work as education agents to provide condoms and informational comic books to men, people in rural areas must travel to the cities at relatively high cost in money, distance, and time.[35] Baylor College of Medicine's Pediatric AIDS Corps program expects to have 40,000 children in care in Africa by the end of 2007.[36]

A key consideration is the cost-effectiveness and widespread benefits of addressing basic health services. Malaria can be prevented and palliated. It is conceivable that it might be eradicated. There may be various ways for tackling the disease. At least 300 million people are malaria sick annually.[37] It is reported that some 3,000 people daily die of malaria (or about 1.1 million annually by computation).[38] Most of the victims are children in sub-Saharan Africa; and the count there alone may be as much as 3,000 children daily.[39] Nearly 20% of children in Zambia do not reach the fifth birthday.[40] Malaria mostly affects the poor.[41] While there are four species of malaria parasites, one (*Plasmodium falciparum*) causes about half of all infections and 95% of deaths. This particular parasite can attack the brain and kill within a day.[42] Since malaria-carrying mosquitoes bite at night, one useful defense is mosquito netting for sleeping. Insecticide-treated netting can reduce infections by 50% and child deaths by 33%.[43] HIV/AIDS interacts with and accelerates malaria.[44] If so, then one method of halting AIDS is to eliminate malaria.[45] Since netting is quite inexpensive by advanced country standards, widespread free distribution and careful use would be an effective approach. Malaria is concentrated in sub-Saharan Africa but occurs elsewhere, especially in Southeast Asia and Latin America.

Not only humans are at risk. An Ebola virus outbreak has reportedly killed an estimated 3,500 to 5,000 gorillas in the Western Republic of the Congo. One proposal is to inoculate surviving gorillas with an Ebola vaccine that has proven effective.[46] Gorillas and common chimpanzees are largely concentrated now in Gabon and Western Congo.

CORPORATE SOCIAL RESPONSIBILITY AND THE COMMON GOOD

Summarizing the key findings so far, basic health services in host developing countries are desperately needed and can be cost-effective with widespread benefits. Basic health services are not yet plainly a basic human right even for children, but various initiatives are working in that direction. Some host governments are incapable of effectively handling the problem. MNCs operating in host developing countries thus face a choice defining CSR in a particular dimension. The choice is not theoretical, but practical and compelling. MNCs are geographically positioned in developing countries for markets, resources and production. A relatively simple principle can be stated: where one can help, and in this instance at reasonably low cost, one should help. Such help may improve a company's moral capital. Whether additional profitable opportunities may open over time is difficult to assess, but Merck had good success historically in both Japan and China in this regard. It seems the better strategic and citizenship path to do what one can.

The European Commission (EC) provides the following working definition:

> Corporate social responsibility (CSR) is a concept whereby companies integrate social and environmental concerns in their business operations and in their interaction with their stakeholders on a voluntary basis. It is about corporations deciding to go beyond minimum legal requirements and obligations stemming from collective agreements in order to address societal needs.[47]

The EC communication introduced a voluntary European Alliance on CSR to encourage business participation in accomplishing a number of societal objectives. The communication states that, "CSR practices are not a panacea and can not on their own be expected to deliver these [specific] outcomes. They are not a substitute for public policy, but they can contribute to a number of public policy objectives" such as labor market and social inclusion of disadvantaged groups, investment in employable skills development, innovation through interaction with external stakeholders, and the principles of human rights, environmental protection and labor standards (in other words, the UN Global Compact principles). More closely relevant to this chapter's concern are the public policy objectives of (a) "improvements in public health" through "marketing and labelling of food and non-toxic chemicals," (b) "a more positive image of business and entrepreneurs in society" in order to enhance entrepreneurship, and (c) "poverty reduction and progress towards the Millennium Development Goals."[48] The MDGs include some health dimensions.

There are continuing theoretical, empirical, and political controversies over corporate social responsibility (CSR) and corporate social performance (CSP). The theoretical controversy concerns whether voluntary assumption of a CSR orientation is potentially profitable business strategy or a costly moral and political obligation assumed by business executives.

Profitable CSR activity is simply business at work.[49] A costly obligation, on the other hand, might reflect moral values of executives (they can have them) or errors in judgment (they do make them) or responsiveness to increasing stakeholder activism (they may regard voluntary CSR as the lowest-cost solution to external pressures). The empirical controversy, summarized at the outset of the chapter, concerns what the set of studies about the linkage between CSP and corporate financial performance (CSF) demonstrate reliably, if anything, about whether CSR is profitable or not—and under what conditions. The political controversy concerns the relationship between business and society with respect to the broad scope of CSR as distinct from strict legal compliance.

The European Commission (EC) has been promoting within the European Union (EU) a process of CSR consultation including businesses and stakeholders. The UN has initiated a voluntary Global Compact addressing human rights, labor rights, and environmental sustainability.[50] The International Organization for Standards (ISO) is working on CSR "guidance" (ISO 26000), as distinct from "standards," scheduled to be issued in late 2008. The OECD Guidelines for Multinational Enterprises were revised in 2000.[51] Generally such standards and guidelines do not address basic health services.

There is a widespread understanding today that MNCs are well-advised to behave as if good corporate citizens and good neighbors. One dimension of this understanding is that such corporations suffer from the "liability of foreignness" in host countries and should attempt to satisfy host country governments and other host country stakeholders.[52] Another dimension of this understanding is that corporate reputation in the company's home country and in other advanced countries and with global nongovernmental organizations (NGOs) is important. These two dimensions affect all multinationals more or less equally. There are in addition definable duties of rescue and justice.[53] These duties may interact with a firm's unique competencies[54] as well as its geographic location. Pharmaceutical companies have special duties due to competencies. Other companies may have insecticides or netting capabilities. MNCs operating in host developing countries have special duties due to such positioning. Additionally, the governments of developing countries are often corrupt[55] and incapable of adequate public service delivery.[56] There are competing arguments that MNCs contribute to host country corruption and are not capable of solutions to developmental problems.[57]

One report concludes that CSR has evolved from philanthropic activity to an integration of responsible business principles into core business activities. In this regard, European companies tend to be ahead of North American companies; and Japanese companies tend to be strong on environmental performance. Large companies tend to be more active than smaller companies. Progress is not as good on human rights approaches.[58] There are two motives at work. One motive is business-like: companies have strong strategic interest in stakeholder and societal support.[59] Another motive is responsibility. "Even as business organizations may be instruments for creating wealth, they also may be the entities of last resort for achieving social objectives of all stripes," Joshua Margolis says. "Manifest human misery and undeniable corporate ingenuity should remind us that our central challenge may lie in blending the two."[60]

There are already various examples of corporate involvement in basic health services in host developing countries. The classic instance of corporate commitment is the decision of Merck to address river blindness and then elephantiasis through a medication donation program.[61] In the 1980s, Merck researchers discovered that an antibiotic Mectizan® (ivermectin) being developed to combat parasites in animal could palliate river blindness (onochocerciasis) in humans. Black flies breeding near rivers and streams spread small parasitic worms by their bite. After 7 years of clinical trials, Merck made the decision in October 1987 to fund free distribution itself in a partnership with the WHO and other organizations through the Mectizan® Donation Program. The decision rested on the commitment of Merck Chairman and CEO P. Roy Vagelos.[62] By 2004, Merck was providing such treatment to more than 40 million people annually in 34 countries (in Africa, Latin America, and Yemen). In 1998, Merck extended this program to use Mectizan against elephantiasis (lymphatic filariasis) in eight African countries where it coexists with river blindness. By 2003, it was treated more than 20 million individuals in those countries for elephantiasis. It is estimated that there may be as many as 120 million carriers and 44 million sufferers.[63] The financially expensive decision to begin the donation program was ultimately made by the board of directors. The value orientation of the company tilted strongly in the direction of a positive decision. George W. Merck, founder, had stated: "We try never to forget that medicine is for the people. It is not for the profits. The profits follow, and if we have remembered that, they have never failed to appear."[64]

A way of assessing the Merck combination of strategy and citizenship is to consider the effects of deciding to do nothing. The corporate financial performance has not been, over the long run, adversely affected to a significant degree. Some customers and certainly human rights and health activists and media would be disaffected with Merck. Employees, particularly those involved in Merck research and development activities, would be seriously demoralized. Merck's behavior would be highly inconsistent with its culture and its stated values. On the positive side, Merck has accumulated some valuable reputation. In recent years, Merck has suffered from the Vioxx settlement and a settlement of U.S. health care fraud charges. No company is perfect. But stakeholders may feel better about Merck than they would otherwise in the wake of these scandals—both because of its citizenship activities and its quite robust financial performance (in spite of recent financial settlements).

Merck has had some difficulties in recent years with its image.[65] For example, Merck undertook a lobbying campaign to promote its vaccine (Gardasil) against cervical cancer, to gain an advantage over GlaxoSmithKline, also developing such a vaccine. The vaccine (a three-dose series at about $400) is nearly 100% effective against two strains of the HPV virus. Cervical cancer is the second-leading cancer killer of women in the world. Some 9,700 Americans are diagnosed and 3,700 die annually. Nineteen states of the U.S. introduced legislation for mandatory vaccination of school girls. Governor Rick Perry of Texas tried an executive order; and his former chief of staff had become a lobbyist for Merck.[66] In the wake of the resulting outcry, Merck abandoned its lobbying efforts.[67]

In November 2007, Merck announced a $4.85 billion settlement of all claims arising from its arthritis painkiller Vioxx (rofecoxib).[68] Dr. Eric J. Topol raised questions about both Vioxx and Celebrex (celecoxib), co-marketed by Pfizer and Pharmacia.[69] Merck stopped selling Vioxx in September 2004 when a clinical trial suggested risk of heart attacks and strokes.[70] Merck then battled each resulting lawsuit individually, winning most of them. Upon announcement of the settlement, Merck stock rose 2.5%, because the settlement was viewed as low-cost relative to potential risk. The settlement amounted to nine months' of Merck profits. While Merck had received FDA approval in 1999, cardiovascular risk reportedly had not been appropriately tested at the time; only after more than 80 million patients and over $2.5 billion in annual sales was a review of that risk undertaken.[71] In December 2006, FDA approved marketing of Pfizer's Celebrex to children with a severe form of arthritis.[72]

In 2003, Pfizer committed to donate $500 million worth of the antibiotic Zithromax (whose patent would expire in 2 years), 135 million doses, in order to help eliminate trachoma by 2020. Pfizer had donated 8 million doses over the preceding 5 years and decided to increase its commitment. Trachoma results from a parasite chlamydia found in poverty areas of Africa, Asia, and Latin America in poor sanitation conditions. Infection leads to turned-in eyelashes which scratch and scar the cornea into blindness. Trachoma can be transmitted by person or flies. The estimated number of blinded persons is 6 million. An annual dose of Zithromax substitutes for the previous treatment of ointment applied twice daily for six weeks.[73]

Marathon Oil Corp. and Noble Energy Corp., both headquartered in Houston (Texas), operate in Equatorial Guinea, West Africa, to develop natural gas fields.[74] The country also has oil reserves. Malaria is rampant.

On Bioko Island, in the Gulf of Guinea, where offshore energy development operations are located, families always prepared tiny graves for children. Marathon, in partnership with the country's natural gas company and two Japanese companies, is building a liquified natural gas facility on Bioko. On that island, Marathon and Noble are spearheading a five-year, $12.8 million campaign to eradicate malaria. About 250,000 people, half the population of the country, live on the island. After 3 years, the program in 2007 reported a 95% reduction in malaria mosquitoes. The campaign brought in a reluctant consortium led by nonprofit Medical Care Development International (headquartered in Maine), which focuses on health conditions in developing countries. The reluctance had to do both with working with international oil companies and working with the government, which ranks as very corrupt in Transparency International corruption perception index (CPI) data and is suspected of human rights abuses.[75] Anti-mosquito insecticide spraying operations involve various practical difficulties. Mosquitoes need a vertical surface on which to rest and digest blood. The campaign undertook to spray the walls of some 100,000 buildings annually. When the mosquitoes developed immunity, the campaign changed insecticide and sprayed twice a year. The campaign involves annual health surveys, drug therapies, and other activities. Marathon later decided to help move the campaign to the country's mainland at additional cost.[76]

Exxon Mobil has spent at least $30 million in a campaign to develop better malaria therapies for children, provide bed netting, and increase the time netting retains insecticide coating. Chevron Corp. in Angola sends nurses to employees' homes to provide information on mosquito elimination, home screening, and bed netting.[77]

FUNDING AND GOVERNANCE OF GLOBAL PUBLIC GOODS

There is a broader context for assessing CSR in this dimension of development. Basic health services are one aspect of what has been termed global (or international) public goods necessary or desirable to the common good.[78] Instances are vaccine and agriculture research, health, and education, where in developing countries there is both market failure and governmental incapacity. Poverty (i.e., wealth distribution) may be harder to tackle than economic growth stimulation (i.e., wealth generation).[79] This circumstance raises particular issues concerning funding and governance. Those issues mean opportunities for businesses to forge working partnerships with governments and nongovernmental organizations (NGOs).

In 2005, President George W. Bush announced a $1.2 billion U.S. funding over 5 years for the global malaria campaign in 15 sub-Saharan African countries.[80] The nonprofit Nothing But Nets (NothingBut-Nets.net/Houston) provides bed nets in malaria areas. These pesticide-impregnated nets cost $10 to make and deliver. The Bill and Melinda Gates Foundation pledged to match each individual donation of a $10 net with another net. As of November 2007, the nonprofit had raised $16 million.[81]

President Hugo Chavez of Venezuela recently proposed publicly that members of the Organization of Petroleum Exporting Countries (OPEC) should, above a price of $100 a barrel, develop a plan to assist poor populations in poor countries cope with energy costs. The centerpiece of his general philosophy is a redistribution of wealth from developed to developing countries by using controlled price of oil as a transfer tax.[82] He stated, "I always say it would be marvelous if we sold oil to the rich countries at $200 a barrel and to the poor countries at $5 a barrel." Venezuela already provides preferential credit terms to countries in Latin America and the Caribbean.[83]

Oil exporting countries are building up large reserves of free cash. Saudi Arabia, Russia, and Norway are in that order the world's three largest oil exporters. The per capita income in Norway is $65,509 second in the world only to tiny Luxembourg. Norway has placed more than $350 billion in North Sea oil revenues into an investment fund (originally the Petroleum Fund, from 2005 the Government Pension Fund). Norway provides the highest per capita donations to other countries. With oil at about $96 a barrel, Norway receives about $1.8 billion weekly. The Saudi royal family receives most of Saudi Arabia's wealth. Nigeria and Venezuela have high corruption. China established a $200 billion fund (from export sales) in 2007. In October 2007, Libya established a $40 billion fund.[84]

Pricing of drugs remains a disputed matter.[85] A number of developing countries have negotiated reduced prices with Western drug companies. Brazil recently issued a "compulsory license" bypassing Merck's U.S. patent on the AIDS drug efavirenz. The action permits Brazil to buy or produce an expensive generic version. Brazil rejected Merck's offer of a 30 percent discount, reducing price to $1.10 from $1.57 per pill. The country has asked for 65 cents, the price obtained by Thailand.[86] In 2003, Abbott Laboratories withdrew its applications for registration of new drugs in Thailand when the government decided on "compulsory licensing" for the company's AIDS medication. There was an effort to organize a global boycott of Abbott products.[87] By contrast, Microsoft will provide a stripped-down version of its software for $3 to people in developing countries and to low-income populations in the bottom 15% of the developed countries (defined at about $15,000 annual household income) through a new program called Microsoft Unlimited Potential. Microsoft had earlier offered discounted versions of Windows selectively to some countries such as Malaysia and Thailand at $30 or less.[88]

There are increasing prospects for reducing tropical diseases in developing countries. The Measles Initiative, started in 2001, has cut mortality from 757,000 in 2000 to 242,000 in 2006. The 1990 mortality was 1.06 million. The largest mortality and the largest mortality decrease are in Africa.[89] The Global Polio Eradication Initiative is also progressing. An experimental malaria vaccine (RTS,S/AS02A or Mosquirix, developed by GlaxoSmith-Kline Biologicals) tested in Mozambique through a clinical trial of three injections protected 65% of more than 2,000 infants (ages 1–4). This initial trial suggests the possibility of a vaccine approach to malaria, available as early as 2012. The PATH Malaria Vaccine Initiative sponsored the trial with funding by the Bill and Melinda Gates Foundation.[90] Gene manipulation may result in new breeds of mosquitoes that are resistant to malaria parasites and can outbreed natural mosquitoes.[91]

THE CASE FOR MNC INVOLVEMENT IN BASIC HEALTH SERVICES IN DEVELOPING COUNTRIES

There are at least two potential exposures or risks attached to corporate involvement in basic health services. These risks should be recognized and assessed. One risk is that any negative effects on patients might create legal, reputation, and political problems for companies. The author labels this potential problem the Libya risk after the recent notorious HIV prosecution of foreign doctors and nurses in that country. Another risk is that corporate programs might run afoul of collusion, or accusation or perception of such collusion, with pharmaceutical companies seeking non-informed patient testing programs. The author labels this potential problem *The Constant Gardener* risk after the recent book and film of that title, which focused on such an alleged (i.e., fictional) activity.

The term Libya risk is adopted from the ordeal of six foreign medical workers at the hands of Muammar Gadhafi's government.[92] Libya convicted five Bulgarian nurses and a Palestinian doctor of deliberating infecting hundreds of children with HIV virus and imprisoned them for more than 8 years from 1999. By December 2006, more than 50 children had died.[93] The six received death sentences by firing squad, which were commuted to life imprisonment in July 2007 by Libya's highest court. The commutation followed a commitment that each of 460 families of infected children would receive $1 million compensation in exchange for dropping their pressure for the death sentences. There was a report that the medical workers suffered torture to obtain confessions. The Libyan allegation was variously that there was a medical experiment gone wrong or that the medical workers had acted to undermine the regime on orders of American and Israeli intelligence services. The French government, acting through President Sarkozy's wife, and the European Union finally secured the release of the six in July 2007 after 3 years of diplomatic efforts and payment of compensation. In 2002, Libya accepted responsibility for the bombing of the Pan Am 103 aircraft in 1988 over Lockerbie, Scotland. In 2003, Libya formally announced ending nuclear, chemical, and biological weapons development programs. The families reportedly asked for $10 million per child, which amount happens to be the same that Libya agreed to pay for each of the 270 people killed in the Lockerbie bombing.[94] A foundation headed by Gadhafi's son handled the negotiations with the families. It was reported, but not confirmed, at the time that a number of countries (in Eastern Europe) had forgiven or were considering forgiving Libyan debt. Given that the charges are widely viewed as false and absurd, the Libya risk indicates what a rogue government can do to foreign nationals engaged in delivery of health services in the host country. Following the release of the imprisoned individuals, Baylor College of Medicine (in Houston, Texas) announced that its International-Pediatric AIDS Initiative would proceed with plans to send several doctors to help treat 400 HIV infected children in fall 2007 in a specialty government hospital in Benghazi, Libya.[95] Baylor College of Medicine operates HIV/AIDS clinics for children in several locations, particularly in sub-Saharan Africa.

There was an outbreak of polio in Nigeria due to a mutated polio vaccine. In Northern Nigeria, which is heavily Muslim, polio vaccination ceased in 2003 for nearly a year due to rumors that that vaccination sterilized girls or contained AIDS virus. WHO reported that about 70 of the last 1,300 polio cases in Nigeria resulted from a mutated vaccine virus. Such mutation is rare but not impossible.[96]

A variation of the Libya risk is the alleged sexual and physical abuse scandal at the Oprah Winfrey school in South Africa.[97] Winfrey, a billionaire, spent $47 million to build a luxury academy campus for girls who would be future leaders. The management process apparently failed, and it was some time before alleged abuse was reported. There is reportedly a high rate of rape and assault in South Africa: a quarter of teens are assaulted in school.

A French charity, l'Arche de Zoe (Zoe's Ark), attempted in October 2007 to remove 103 African children by air from Chad to France.[98] A number of individuals were arrested in Chad on charges of attempted kidnapping and fraud. The charges could result in 20 years imprisonment. Arrested were six members of Zoe's Ark, three journalists accompanying the group, and seven air crew personnel. Nine of these individuals are French citizens. Zoe's Ark was placing the children on a Boeing 757 near the Chad border with Sudan. There were allegations that many of the children were not refugees from Sudan (Darfur), as claimed, but rather Chadians. Zoe's Ark reportedly did not have proper Chad government permission.

In 2001, the well-known British spy novelist John le Carré published a novel *The Constant Gardener*.[99] The book was the basis for a 2005 movie directed by Fernando Meirelles and starring Ralph Fiennes and Rachel Weisz. The latter won several best supporting actress awards (including Golden Globe, Screen Actors Guild, and Academy of Motion Picture Arts and Sciences). The movie won a number of British prizes for best film and various other awards and nominations. Filming occurred on location in Kenya, in a small town on the shore of Lake Turkana and in the slums of Nairobi. In le Carré's novel, the activist wife of a British diplomat stationed in Nairobi, is killed in a remote area. He is informed that his wife was raped and murdered by a doctor with whom she was traveling. The diplomat's inquiry reveals that his wife had discovered corporate misconduct. A major pharmaceutical company had used the camouflage of AIDS treatment testing to evaluate a tuberculosis drug which turned out to have severe side effects. The company concealed the side effects and continued development of the drug. (The fictional purpose was to prepare for multi-resistant tuberculosis.) The diplomat conducts an undercover investigation world-wide. He unravels a conspiracy that includes not only the drug company and his wife's murder but also a German pharmawatch, an African assistance station, and ultimately corruption in the British Foreign and Commonwealth Office. The fictional situation is not so far fetched as to be strictly impossible.[100] In 2004, soon after completion of filming, *the Constant Gardener* trust was established to help the areas in which filming occurred. Fiennes, le Carré, Meirelles, and Weisz were reportedly patrons of the Trust.

Drug companies do conduct clinical trials in developing countries.[101] A suspicion is that host country regulations are weaker.[102] In 1996, Pfizer conducted clinical trials in Nigeria of an experimental antibiotic Trovan. There was a severe outbreak at that time of cerebrospinal meningitis in Kano, the Northern state of Nigeria. Reportedly 190 infected children took part in the trials, which compared Trovan to the approved treatment ceftriaxone. The reported survival rate with treatment was 94% compared to 60% survival rate without treatment. Trovan was slightly better than ceftriaxone. The state of Kano and the Nigerian federal government filed criminal and civil actions on claims that Pfizer had not obtained proper advance approvals and written consent of participants. A Kano doctor testified that he received $20,000 from Pfizer as principal investigator and had prepared and post-dated approval by a non-existent local ethics committee. The federal government subsequently filed a $7 billion civil lawsuit alleging fraud in addition to failure to obtain proper family consent.[103]

There are tradeoffs in drug use. For example, the antibiotic Ketek (produced by Sanofi-Aventis) is linked to rare reports (13 through September 2006) of liver failure including a few deaths, as well as to blurry vision.[104] More than 5.6 million prescriptions have been issued in the United States since 2004 FDA approval. An expert panel advised FDA in a nonbinding recommendation that it modify approval to exclude riskier treatment for pneumonia while continuing less risky treatment for less serious bacterial infections (e.g., bronchitis and sinusitis).

These examples of the Libya risk and *The Constant Gardener* risk suggest caution and due diligence in provision of basic health services in any form by MNCs in host developing countries. MNCs must recognize that host governments are often corrupt. It is advantageous to partner with NGOs and UN agencies where possible. MNCs must address action in this sphere just like risk management in other spheres. However, there are examples of successful and low-risk intervention identified in this chapter. MNCs should find it useful to study the lessons of both good and bad examples.

Despite these potential risks, the case for MNC involvement in basic health services in developing countries is a strong (although not air-tight) one. No MNC can expect its employees to operate in developing countries while ignoring the health disasters around them. Marathon and Noble faced this reality in Africa. Merck faced this reality when its research and development personnel discovered a palliative for river blindness, which other institutions could not or would not fund. Merck discovered that it must address distribution as well as provision. Stakeholders and managers will discover unavoidable moral obligations in health conditions in developing countries. Moreover, these health conditions require global public goods for addressing and have common good effects of ultimately global reach. This chapter does not attempt to develop a general theory of CSR for all firms in all countries. Rather, the chapter argues that the circumstances of basic health services are practical and compelling for MNCs that operate in developing countries. Assessing Merck's choice concerning river blindness must consider the effects of declining to be involved (at relatively low cost over the long run for relatively high and ultimately global benefits) on strategy and reputation among affected stakeholders. Customers, employees and investors are not strictly financial in their orientations. Merck has no choice other than to be a good citizen. This reality is both moral obligation and strategic necessity.

REFERENCES

1. Friedman, M. (1970). The social responsibility of business is to increase its profits. *New York Times Magazine*, September 13, 32-33, 122, 124, 126.
2. Nunan, R. (1988). The libertarian conception of corporate property: A critique of Milton Friedman's views on the social responsibility of business. *Journal of Business Ethics*, 7, 891–906.
3. Godfrey, P. C. (2005). The relationship between corporate philanthropy and shareholder wealth: A risk management perspective. *Academy of Management Review*, 30, 777–798.
4. Bright, D. (2006). Virtuousness is necessary for genuineness in corporate philanthropy. *Academy of Management Review*, 31, 752–754.
5. Margolis, J. D., & Walsh, J. P. (2003). Misery loves companies: Rethinking social initiatives by business. *Administrative Science Quarterly*, 48, 268–305.
6. Margolis & Walsh. (2001). *People and profits? The search for a link between a company's social and financial performance.* Mahwah, NJ: Erlbaum.
7. Margolis, J., Walsh, J., & Krehmeyer, D. (2006). Building the Business Case for Ethics. Business Roundtable Institute for Corporate Ethics. This report is accompanied by a commentary by Kenneth I. Chenault, Chairman and Chief Executive Officer, American Express Company. A PDF version can be found on the Institute Web site at: http://www.corporate-ethics.org/pdf/business_case.pdf
8. A small number of studies addressed both questions, so that the overall count is 95.
9. Margolis, Walsh, & Krehmeyer, op. cit., report 70 measures of financial performance (p. 8) and 27 different data sources for and 11 forms of corporate social performance (p. 6).
10. Orlitzky, M., Schmidt, F. L., & Rynes, S. L. (2003). Corporate social and financial performance: A meta-analysis. *Organization Studies*, 24(3), May–June, 403–441. A meta-analysis takes methodological advantage of the 33,878 observations in the 52 studies. The meta-analysis statistically aggregates results across the various studies and corrects for sampling error and measurement error. The authors argue that there is then a positive relationship (i.e., correlation) between social responsibility, and to a lesser extent environmental responsibility, and financial performance. The relationship seems stronger for accounting-based measures than for market-based measures of financial performance. Corporate social performance reputation is the set of indicators most highly correlated with financial performance.
11. Doane, D. (2005). The myth of CSR: The problem with assuming that companies can do well while also doing good is that markets don't really work that way. *Stanford Social Innovation Review*, 3, 23–29.
12. Vogel, D. (2005). *The market for virtue: The potential and limits of corporate social responsibility.* Washington, DC: The Brookings Institution.
13. Margolis, Walsh, & Krehmeyer, op. cit., p. 9.
14. Chenault, in Margolis, Walsh, & Krehmeyer, ibid., p. 10.
15. Chenault, ibid., p. 11.

16.   http://www.globalcompact.org/AboutTheGC/TheTenPrinciples/index.html.

17.   Under labor standards, Principle 3 upholds freedom of association and right to collective bargaining; Principle 4 prohibits forced and compulsory labor; Principle 5 prohibits child labor; and Principle 6 eliminates employment and occupational discrimination. Labor standards rest on The International Labour Organization's Declaration on Fundamental Principles and Rights at Work. Under environmental protection, Principle 7 advocates a precautionary approach; Principle 8 advocates greater environmental responsibility; and Principle 9 encourages environmentally friendly technologies. Environmental standards rest on The Rio Declaration on Environment and Development.

18.   Acconci, P. (2007). International human rights breaches connected to the activities of multinational enterprises, *notizie di Politeia*, *23*(85/86), 428–438.

19.   Bales, K. (1999). *Disposable people: New slavery in the global economy.* Berkeley and Los Angeles: University of California Press.

20.   Prahalad, C. K. (2006). *The fortune at the bottom of the pyramid: Eradicating poverty through profits.* Upper Saddle River, NJ: Wharton School Publishing.

21.   Rangan, V. K. (1993). The Aravind Eye Hospital, Madurai, India: In Service for Sight. Harvard Business School case 9-593-098 (revised May 23, 1994). Kumar, N., & Rogers, B. (2003). Aravind Eye Hospital: 2000—Still in Service for Sight. IMD098 (02/21/2003). See http://www.aravind.org for latest information.

22.   Mwabu, G. (2007). Health Economics for Low-Income Countries. Yale University Economic Growth Center Discussion Paper No. 955. http://ssrn.com/abstract=988379

23.   Cutler, D. M., Fung, W., Kremer, M., & Singhal, M. (2007). Mosquitoes: The Long-term Effects of Malaria Eradication in India. Kennedy School of Government (KSG) Working Paper No. RWP07-051. http://ssrn.com/abstract=1019022.

24.   Hanley, C. J. (2006). A change for the worse? Kenyan, international researchers blame rising temperatures for spread of malaria into highlands. *Houston Chronicle*, *106* (66), Monday 8 December, A12.

25.   Otis, J. (2007). "Forgotten epidemic" afflicts thousands in Peru: Resurgence of illness now "part of the culture." *Houston Chronicle*, *106*(359), Sunday 7 October, A1, A15.

26.   Surge in dengue fever forecast. (2007). *Houston Chronicle*, *106*(169), Saturday 31 March, A26. In March 2008, Brazil announced sending hundreds of health personnel to Rio de Janeiro state, where a dengue epidemic erupted. By the time of the report, there had been more than 32,000 cases and 49 dead confirmed. ERs overwhelmed by dengue fever. (2008). *Houston Chronicle*, *107* (164), Tuesday 25 March, A12. Similarly Rift Valley Fever, spread by animals or mosquitoes, is typically mild with a 1% fatality rate. The hemorrhagic form has a 50% fatality rate. There is no treatment. In November 2007, WHO reported an outbreak in Sudan. 164 killed by fever in Sudan. (2007). *Houston Chronicle*, *107*(41), Friday 23 November, A26.

27. Lin, R.-G. (2007). Parasite poses new risk in U.S.: Latin American Chagas is turning up in blood supply and organ donors. *Houston Chronicle*, *106*(154), Friday 16 March, A14.

28. Fast-moving killer: Drug-resistant tuberculosis is a global threat. Houston has a large stake in seeing that it is stopped. *Houston Chronicle*, *106*(154), Friday 16 March, B10 (City & State).

29. U.S. Representatives Gene Green & Eliot L. Engel. (2007). We'll get nowhere on TB till we tackle it everywhere: Threat is nothing to sneeze at, as events have shown. *Houston Chronicle*, *106*(238), Friday 8 June, B9 (City & State).

30. Kristoff, N. (2007). A basic human right to be free of this suffering: Rid the world of plagues such as the Guinea worm. *Houston Chronicle*, *106*(136), Monday 26 February, B7 (City & State).

31. See http://www.smiletrain.org

32. Doughton, S. (2006). Nonprofit takes on Third World water: Long-range goal is a self-sustaining treatment industry. *Houston Chronicle*, *106*(72), Tuesday 26 December, B2 (City & State).

33. Advertisement published in *National Geographic*, *212* (2), August 2007.

34. Attaran, A., & Sachs, J. (2001). Defining and redefining international donor support for combating the AIDS pandemic. *Lancet*, *357*, 57-61. UN AIDS scientists have recently acknowledged that they long overestimated the size and progress of the epidemic. (The methodology involved is difficult.) It now appears that the peak of the epidemic may have been reached a decade ago. The latest estimates suggest 2.5 million new infections annually (a figure 40% lower than the previous year's information) and 33 million total worldwide (versus 40 million in the previous year's information). Timberg, C. (2007). U.N. lowers estimate of global AIDS crisis. *Houston Chronicle*, 107 (38), Tuesday 20 November, A1, A6.

35. Dunn, A., & Orr, F. (2006). India now tops world in AIDS: With 5.7 million sufferers, nation passes S. Africa. *Houston Chronicle*, *106*(71), Saturday 23 December, A26.

36. Baylor and the Bristol-Myers Squibb Foundation fund the project. Hopper, L. (2007). AIDS Corps' African work quickly grows: With new sites and more doctors, Baylor project in first year helping 12,000 children. *Houston Chronicle*, *106* (150), Monday 12 March, B1, B6 (City & State).

37. Maugh, T. H. (2007). Malaria vaccine promising in testing: 65% of infants in study protected after 3 injections. *Houston Chronicle*, *107*(5), Thursday 18 October, A10.

38. Daum, M. (2007). Death by the numbers in age of 24-hour news cycle: It's the math of fear and denial that transfixes us. *Houston Chronicle*, *106*(313), Wednesday 22 August, B9 (City & State). The daily average death rate world-wide from all causes is about 148,000 people (or 54 million annually by computation).

39. Finkel, M. (2007). Bedlam in the blood: Malaria. *National Geographic*, *212* (1), July, 32-67, at p. 35.

40. Ibid., p. 41.

41. Ibid., p. 41.

42. Ibid., p. 41.

43. Ibid., p. 39.

44. Ibid., p. 63.

45. Study suggests attacking malaria to halt AIDS. *Houston Chronicle*, *106*(56), Friday 9 December, A27.

46. Ebola victims. (2006). *Houston Chronicle*, *106* (66), Monday 18 December, A16. Walsh, P. D., et al. (2003). Catastrophic ape decline in Western equatorial Africa. *Nature*, *422*, 10 April, 611–614 (Letters to Nature).

47. Commission of the European Communities. (2006). Communication from the Commission to the European Parliament, the Council and the European Economic and Social Committee—Implementing the Partnership for Growth and Jobs: Making Europe a Pole of Excellence on Corporate Social Responsibility (p. 2). Brussels, Belgium: March 22.

48. Ibid., p. 4. The EC began this process in a 2001 Green Paper. European Commission Directorate-General for Employment and Social Affairs. (2001, July). Promoting a European framework for corporate social responsibility. This Green Paper stated the CSR concept continued forward into the 2006 Communication. There followed a 2002 White Paper. Commission of the European Communities (2002, July). Communication from the Commission concerning Corporate Social Responsibility: A business contribution to Sustainable Development. The EC initiated a voluntary European Multistakeholder Forum on CSR, which made its final report in 2004.

49. McWilliams, A., & Siegel, D. (2001). Corporate social responsibility: A theory of the firm perspective. *Academy of Management Review*, *26*, 117-127.

50. Dubee, F. (2007). Reflections on developments in corporate responsibility and the Global Compact, *notizie di Politeia*, *23* (85/86), 464-472.

51. Acconci, P. (2001). The promotion of responsible business conduct and the new text of the OECD Guidelines for Multinational Enterprises. *The Journal of World Investment*, *2*(1) March, 123–150.

52. Zaheer, S. (1995). Overcoming the liability of foreignness. *Academy of Management Journal*, *38*, 341–363.

53. Hsieh, N. (2006). Voluntary codes of conduct for multinational corporations: Duties of rescue and justice. *Business Ethics Quarterly*, *16*, 119–135.

54. Dunfee, T. W. (2006). Do firms with unique competencies for rescuing victims of human catastrophes have special obligations? *Business Ethics Quarterly*, *16*, 185–210.

55. "The Resource Curse": Why Africa's Oil Riches Don't Trickle Down to Africans. (2007, 31 October). Knowledge@Wharton, http://www.knowledge.wharton.upenn.edu/article_cfm?articleid=1830

56. Scherer, A. G., & Smid, M. (2000). The downward spiral and the US Model Business Principles—Why MNEs should take responsibility for the improvement of world-wide social and environmental conditions. *Management International Review*, *40*(4), 4th Quarter, 351–371.

57. Frynas, J. G. (2005). The false development promise of Corporate Social Responsibility: Evidence from multinational oil companies. *International*

Affairs, 81, 581–598. Frynas's findings are based on a twelve-month research project on the Gulf of Guinea region.

58. Ethical Investment Research Services (EIRIS) Ltd. (2007). The State of Responsible Business: Global Corporate Response to Environmental, Social and Governance (ESG) Challenges. September.

59. Dentchev, N. A. (2004). Corporate social performance as a business strategy. *Journal of Business Ethics, 55,* 395–410.

60. Misery Loves Companies: Rethink Social Initiatives by Business (June 15, 2004), http://www.wdi.umich.edu/files/old/hrn/recent_hr _publications/download_files/2004/misery_loves_companies.pdf

61. A set of Harvard Business School cases covers the river blindness decision and implementation. Hanson, K. O., & Weiss, S. (1991). Merck & Co., Inc.: Addressing Third-World Needs (A), (B), (C), (D), 991-021, 022, 023, 024. Similar distribution issues arise in the U.S. when demand outstrips supply. Eaton, M. L., Roy, M., & Curavic, M. (2004). Merck's U.S. Managed Distribution Program for the HIV Drug Crixivan, BME9. A related HIV distribution case concerns Botswana. Austin, J. E., Barrett, D., & Weber, J. B. (2001). Merck Global Health Initiatives (B): Botswana, 301–089.

62. Vagelos was head of the research labs (1975–85) prior to becoming CEO. He retired from Merck on November 1, 1994. Nichols, N. A. (1994). Medicine, management, and mergers: An interview with Merck's P. Roy Vagelos. *Harvard Business Review, 72*(6), November/December, 104–114. Vagelos, R., & Galambos, L. (2004). *Medicine, science, and Merck.* New York: Cambridge University Press. 2004. Ciulla, J. B. (1999). The importance of leadership in shaping business values. *Long Range Planning, 32*(2), April, 166–172.

63. Merck Expands Its Commitment to Eliminate River Blindness. http://www.merck.com/about/feature_story/05192004_mectizan.mhtml

64. Merck & Co., Committed to Making a Difference: Corporate Responsibility 2004–2005 Report (p. 1). Whitehouse Station, NJ.

65. Vogel, D. (2002). Recycling corporate responsibility. *Wall Street Journal,* August 20, B2 (Eastern Edition).

66. Goodman, E. (2007). Merck story is a sorry tale with a moral for parents. *Houston Chronicle, 106* (142), Sunday 4 March, E3 (Outlook).

67. Competition in the global pharmaceutical industry is examined in the following case. Collis, D. J., & Smith, T. (2006). Strategy in the 21st Century Pharmaceutical Industry: Merck & Co., and Pfizer Inc. Harvard Business School 707–509 (27 November).

68. Berenson, A. (2007) Analysts See Merck Victory in Vioxx Settlement. *New York Times,* November 10. http://www.nytimes.com/2007/11/10/business/ 10merck.html?ref=todayspaper

69. Topol, E. J., M. D. (2001). Risk of cardiovascular events associated with selective COX-2 inhibitors. *Journal of the American Medical Association; 286,* 954–959.

70. Topol, E. J., M.D. (2004). Failing the public health—Rofecoxib, Merck, and the FDA. *New England Journal of Medicine, 351*(17), 1707–1709 (Octo-

ber 21). Topol, E. J., & Falk, G. W. (2004). A coxib a day won't keep the doctor away. *Lancet, 364,* 639–640.

71.   Topol, ibid.

72.   Bridges, A. (2006). Reports of liver problems lead advisers to suggest limits on drug: FDA may exclude antibiotic Ketek from treatment for some lesser infections. *Houston Chronicle, 106* (64), Saturday 16 December, A10.

73.   Donnelly, J. (2003). Pfizer to donate $500 million in anti-blindness drugs. *The Boston Globe,* 12 November, p. 1, transmitted by Knight Ridder Tribune Business News.

74.   Ivanovich, D. (2006). Oil companies tackle malaria in Africa: Life-saving social project a win-win for one nation and Marathon, Noble. *Houston Chronicle, 106* (23), Sunday 5 November, A1, A23. The information in this paragraph derives from this article.

75.   Adam Roberts in The Wonga Coup, about a failed attempt to seize power in Equatorial Guinea, called the country the "Dachau of Africa." Residents refer to the country as "Devil Island." Roberts, A. (2006). The Wonga coup: Guns, thugs and a ruthless determination to create mayhem in an oil-rich corner of Africa. London: Profile Books, LTD. New York: Public Affairs (Perseus Books Group). Roberts worked for The Economist (London) and had served a number of years as its Johannesburg (South Africa) bureau chief. In March 2004, a group of foreign mercenaries attempted unsuccessfully to overthrow the government. In 2005, Sir Mark Thatcher, son of former UK prime minister Margaret Thatcher, was fined and received a suspended sentence in connection with provision of a helicopter. A South African court dismissed charges against some defendants upon evidence that the government of South Africa either knew or approved of the coup in advance. Bloomfield, S. (2007). Mercenaries acquitted in "Wonga Coup" case. The Independent, 24 February, http://news.independent.co.uk/world/Africa/article2300373.ece

76.   Marathon entered business in Equatorial Guinea by purchasing assets of CMS Energy. There has been a U.S. investigation into whether corrupt payments from oil companies have been funneled to suspect offshore accounts and involved partnering with an entity controlled by the country's president. Ivanovich, op. cit., p. A23.

77.   Ibid., p. A23.

78.   Reinicke, W. H. (1998). *Global public policy: Governing without government?* Washington, DC: Brookings Institution Press.

79.   The world's poor: A *Harvard Magazine* Roundtable. (2000). *Harvard Magazine, 102*(2), November-December, 64–75, 116.

80.   USAID Fact Sheet: The President's Malaria Initiative (PMI). (2006, June 8). http://www.usaid.gov/press/factsheets/2006/fs060608.html

81.   Net gain: Once-malarial Houston is gathering forces to fight disease in Africa. *Houston Chronicle, 107* (30), Monday 12 November, B8 (City & State).

82.   In November 2007, the Alaska legislature approved a bill to raise the state tax on the net profits of oil companies operating within the state from 22.5% to 25%. The increase in tax means roughly an additional $1.5 bil-

lion. In October 2007, the province of Alberta, Canada, increased its oil tax yield by $1.5 billion beginning in 2009. Venezuela and Russia have now in effect forced out all Western energy companies. Quinn, S. (2007). Alaska oil-tax debate reflects a trend: Battles for larger share being played out globally. The province of Alberta, Canada, *Houston Chronicle*, *107*(36), Sunday 18 November, D2 (Business).

83. Rueda, J. (2007). Chavez says OPEC could aid poor with revenue from rich. *Houston Chronicle*, *107* (32), Wednesday 14 November, D5 (Business).

84. Hundley, T. (2007). Oil-rich Norwegians dodge "curse," stay smart, sleek: Nation doesn't let wealth corrupt services, education. *Houston Chronicle*, *107* (36), Sunday 18 November, A26.

85. Vagelos, P. R. (1991). Are prescription drug prices high? *Science*, *252*, 24 May, 1080–1084.

86. Associated Press. (2007). Brazil to sidestep AIDS drug patent. *Houston Chronicle*, *106*(204), Saturday 5 May, D1 (Business).

87. Reuters. (2007). AIDS activists call for boycott of Abbott products. Wednesday 25 April. http://www.reuters.com/article/health-SP/idUSHKG9894520070425

88. Lohr, S. (2007). Microsoft to offer software to world's poor for low price. *Houston Chronicle*, *106*(188), Thursday 19 April, D4 (Business).

89. Deaths from measles drop around the world. (2007). *Houston Chronicle*, *107* (48), Friday 30 November, A14.

90. Maugh, op. cit.

91. Berger, E. (2007). Building a better mosquito: Scientists think genetic tinkering may end malaria. *Houston Chronicle*, *106* (158), Tuesday 20 March, A1, A4.

92. Brunwasser, M., & Sciolino, E. (2007). Libyan ordeal ends after 8 years: The release of 6 medical workers may aid Gadhafi's political fortunes. *Houston Chronicle*, *106*(285), Wednesday 25 July, A1, A4.

93. Chronicle News Service. (2006). Libya again orders six to death in HIV case. *Houston Chronicle*, *106* (68), Wednesday 20 December, A1, A12.

94. Ibid., p. A12.

95. Grant, A. (2007). Baylor AIDS drive in Libya to go forward. *Houston Chronicle*, *106* (286), Thursday 26 July, B2 (City & State).

96. McNeil, D. G. (2007). Nigeria fights new outbreak of polio virus: Mutant vaccine is linked to 70 cases of the illness. *Houston Chronicle*, *106*(363), Thursday 11 October, A11.

97. Rolls-Royce rights: Oprah Winfrey rightly applies rich-country standards to victimized South African girls. (2007). *Houston Chronicle*, *107*(27), Friday 9 November, B10 (City & State).

98. Bennhold, K. (2007). Darfur charity furor may hurt peace plan: Chad could balk at accepting French peacekeepers. *Houston Chronicle*, *107*(18), Wednesday 31 October, A11.

99. Le Carré, J. (2001). *The constant gardener: A novel*. London: Hodder & Stoughton. New York: Scribner. John le Carré is the pseudonym of David John Moore Cornwell. He graduated from Oxford University and subsequently joined the British Foreign Service from which he was later

recruited into MI6 for secret service. In 1963, he published *The Spy Who Came in from the Cold*, made into a film.

100. Le Carré's 2005 afterword (Pocket Star edition) states: "By comparison with the reality, my story [is] as tame as a holiday postcard."

101. China is becoming an important clinical trial location, both because trials are cheap there and because China is a large and increasing drug market. Kinsbury, K. (2007). China's drug addiction: Beijing is bent on attracting world-class pharmaceutical R&D labs. The bait: cheap clinical trials. Time 170 (22) 26 November: 72.

102. Jack, A., & Mahtani, D. (2007). Pfizer to fight $9bn Nigerian class action on drug trials. *Financial Times*, Wednesday 6 June, 26.

103. Harsher lawsuit hits Pfizer. (2007). *Houston Chronicle*, *106*(281), Saturday 21 July, D1 (Business).

104. Bridges, op. cit.

CHAPTER 11

LEGISLATIVE EXCESS OR REGULATORY BRILLIANCE?

Corporate Governance After Sarbanes-Oxley

Gwendolyn Yvonne Alexis

Sarbanes-Oxley (SARBOX) has been both praised and cursed for the new concepts it has brought to the business/society relationship. Stakeholder theory, internal controls, corporate accountability, corporate social responsibility, triple bottom line, corporate citizenship, corporate transparency, and corporate governance are all concepts that have either been introduced or given new life by SARBOX. It is somewhat ironic that a child of vengeance—a product of the wrath of the Angry 107th Congress—has resulted in something so positive. For SARBOX has established a new paradigm for corporate governance, one that has been wholeheartedly embraced by publicly traded corporations who have began reaping the benefits of operating on the moral high ground. The author identifies the paraenetic provisions of SARBOX that have resulted in nothing short of a moral renaissance within the corporate milieu. Noting that the new preeminence of federal law in the corporate governance area is a source of great consternation, the author navigates the much traversed terrain upon which the federal right of preemption does battle with the long-established right of states to regulate the internal corporate governance standards of the artificial beings that they

Doing Well And Good: The Human Face of the New Capitalism, pp. 215–236
Copyright © 2009 by Information Age Publishing
All rights of reproduction in any form reserved.

create. And, she comes to the conclusion that SARBOX is not a case of legislative excess, but rather should be viewed as an exemplar of regulatory brilliance.

INTRODUCTION

In a volume celebrating the new face of business in the twenty-first century, it seems appropriate to give some thought to the role legislation has played in bringing about this moral renaissance. There is no doubt that business has suddenly taken the moral high road; this is most evident in the area of corporate governance where we see multinational corporations (MNCs) with mission statements that proclaim a global commitment to fair labor practices and environmental sustainability while decrying the making of "grease payments," even when operating in lands where the low-level civil servants who help corporations navigate a bureaucratic morass depend upon receiving small gratuities to supplement their meager government wages. While the proliferation of these admirable corporate creeds is most welcome, it would be naïve not to acknowledge the role external pressures have played in generating more ethical corporations.

Opportunistic corporate behavior had reigned supreme during the last quartile of the twentieth century. The globalization of markets and of production presented internationalizing businesses with untold opportunities. Indeed, corporate wealth surpassed the wealth of nations, resulting in the majority of the world's 100 largest economies being MNCs rather than nation-states.[1] This embarrassment of riches made MNCs a ready target when the backlash against globalization escalated at the 1999 World Trade Organization meeting in Seattle—a meeting that was brought to a standstill by thousands of protestors decrying the global economy and the devastation it had wrought on LDNs, the human environment, and the working class families of the Western World for whom globalization had meant a devastating loss of jobs due to outsourcing. Already beleaguered by bad press, MNCs took another blow when the corporate scandals surfaced 2 years later lending credence to a widespread suspicion that the fantastic wealth being accumulated by MNCs was as much a product of corporate greed and corruption as it was a result of opportunities presented by the global economy.

Alas, MNCs met their Waterloo with the corporate bad will and mistrust generated by Enron and progeny. Largely consisting of publicly traded corporations with brand names to protect, MNCs are especially vulnerable when the business/society relationship deteriorates to such an extent that reproof of business is a widespread societal sentiment. In this type of anti-business environment, a special venom is reserved for and aimed at large corporations. Hence, early in this century, MNCs began scrambling to visibly demonstrate that not all corporations are crooks and predators whose products and services should be boycotted. The blistering hostility towards business in general had served as a wake-up call for MNCs. As the reality sank in that a corporation whose products and services are being shunned by an outraged public faces a very dim financial future (and, consequently, has little hope of attracting investment dollars), MNCs came to attention and put their public relations machinery at full throttle.

MNCs were not alone in recognizing the abundant ill will toward corporations as a precursor of economic disaster. Globalization has resulted in a tremendous amount of interdependency among nations. Today, even the wealthiest nation-state relies upon the ability of its domestic corporations to attract foreign investment, whether through the sale of products and services or by attracting foreign investment dollars. Hence, governments around the world were justifiably concerned when it became apparent that previously set national economic objectives had been far too ambitious in light of the widespread investor malaise that set in following the surge of corporate corruption scandals at the beginning of this century. Nations as diverse as Canada and Nigeria enacted legislation to ratchet up corporate governance standards.[2] Having corporations with sound governance standards in place has a positive effect on the national economy in that these companies are able to attract investors as well as customers, which gives a shot in the arm to a waning securities market.

This article examines the Sarbanes-Oxley Act of 2002 (SARBOX),[3] one of the many legislative initiatives that surfaced during the squall of corporate rehabilitative legislation around the globe. Focusing on the changes SARBOX has made to the corporate governance paradigm for listed corporations, I examine the extent to which the widely proclaimed turnabout in corporate culture can be attributed to specific provisions of this revolutionary legislation. Since SARBOX is prototypical of the legislation aimed at corporate moral uplift, the results of this study may be generalizable to the corporate governance legislation of countries outside of the U.S. Moreover, because there are many foreign MNCs listed on U.S. stock exchanges, and thus subject to most provisions of SARBOX, the legislation has extraterritorial reach and therefore global relevance.

THE 107TH CONGRESS ENACTS SARBOX

In January 2002 when the 107th U.S. Congress convened for its second session, the U.S. economy was in a state of turmoil. Enron and progeny had wrought havoc on the U.S. securities market and the financial chaos had reverberated throughout the economy. Massive job layoffs and bankrupt pension funds left no doubt that working class Americans, as well as the investing public, had fallen victim to corporate greed. Congress held extensive hearings to determine how Enron's long-running fraud had remained undetected despite the fact that Enron had been steadfast in filing the periodic financial reports required under then existing U.S. securities laws.

Whereas existing securities laws were aimed at making corporations transparent by means of numerous reporting requirements, the 107th Congress concluded that corporate transparency is not measured by the number of financial reports filed with the U.S. Securities and Exchange Commission (SEC), but by the truthfulness of the disclosures contained in those reports. What was needed was a law that would make the consequences of not being truthful in financial reports as dire as the consequences of failure to file the required financial reports. The 107th Congress accomplished this goal with SARBOX, which enhances the criminal penalties that can be imposed for making false or misleading statements in corporate financial reports and also expands the number of corporate insiders—officers, directors, lawyers, and accountants—that can be held accountable when a corporation files misleading and/or fraudulent financial statements.

However, the real groundbreaking feature of SARBOX is that it seeks to affect a moral renaissance from within the very bowels of the publicly traded corporation. And, there are signs that this is beginning to happen as firms adopt corporate mission statements and ethics codes that commit their employees to even higher ethical standards than those called for under SARBOX, or under the regulatory scheme put in place to implement the statute.[4] Nonetheless, SARBOX has attracted a great deal of criticism as a federal law that intrudes upon internal corporate governance matters, an area traditionally governed by state law.

THE INTRUSION OF FEDERAL LAW INTO THE CORPORATE GOVERNANCE AREA

SARBOX weaves a matrix of interlocking edicts and executory propositions that make adoption of corporate ethics codes and professional conduct codes for corporate insiders synonymous with "good corporate governance"; and, if nothing else, the post-Enron, post-SARBOX corporation strives to become a model of good corporate governance. Indeed, with respect to listed companies, it can be said that SARBOX has established a new corporate governance paradigm. One extremely important change that has been brought about is that there is no longer the all-too-cozy relationship between the corporate board and management that existed in the past. Rather than serving as a rubber stamp for management initiatives, today's board oversees management's operational activities and often second-guesses its initiatives.[5] Increasingly, there are signs that boards are settling into the role that SARBOX has assigned them of fiduciary vis-à-vis shareholders. Autonomy and independence have become the watchwords of the post-SARBOX board.[6]

The fact that a federal statute has made such inroads into an area traditionally governed by state law is a cause for great consternation among legal scholars. Since all U.S. corporations, publicly traded or not, are products of their states of incorporation, it has long been black letter law that their internal governance systems are governed by state law. State corporations law encompasses matters such as the allocation of power between the board of directors and the shareholders; qualifications for board membership; appointment and removal of directors; board election procedures and the proxy process; whether the board is deemed to be in a fiduciary relationship with the shareholders; whether or not a board is *even* required; the procedure that must be followed to amend the bylaws; how often meetings of the shareholders and the board must take place; the notice requirements for meetings; actions permissible without meetings; and required corporate officers.

Historically, it has been common for those forming major corporations to do some situs shopping before deciding on the state in which to incorporate, since there is a good deal of variance among the laws governing corporations in the various states. Some states have lenient corporations laws that allow the incorporators a good deal of leeway in adopting bylaws to set up non-traditional corporate governance systems; and some states offer the advantage of laws that make it easy to amend bylaws—for example by requiring only a simple majority of the shareholders to vote in favor of a bylaws amendment. Because it allows corporations a great deal of flexibility in constructing their corporate governance systems, Delaware has become a favorite state of incorporation for multinational corporations having no particular connection to the state:

> After a century of academic thinking that states compete for corporate chartering revenues, a revisionist perspective has emerged in which states do not compete for chartering revenues, leaving Delaware all alone in the interstate charter market. Firms either stay incorporated in their home state or reincorporate in Delaware, but rarely go elsewhere. What's more, other states don't even try to provide the services Delaware provides. Delaware has a monopoly, one that goes unchallenged.[7]

However, SARBOX has ended the advantages that listed corporations can obtain by "shopping around" for lenient corporations laws since they can no longer benefit from being incorporated in a state that will allow them to adopt bylaws establishing a corporate governance system that is inconsistent with the dictates of SARBOX. To illustrate, SARBOX, either directly or by dictating listing requirements for the stock exchanges, (1) requires each board to appoint an audit committee; (2) prohibits inside directors from serving on board audit committees; (3) designates the board as governing authority, thereby preempting any state law that provides for shareholder governance; and (4) straps the board with a fiduciary role vis-à-vis the shareholders without regard to whether or not state law vests a board with such fiduciary responsibilities.

In short, SARBOX preempts many of the corporate governance alternatives offered in the various states. Moreover, because SARBOX has extra-territorial effect in that it applies to foreign MNCs that are listed on U.S. stock exchanges, it may even preempt the laws of other countries. The overriding preeminence of SARBOX in the corporate governance area has led many legal scholars to describe the enactment of SARBOX by the 107th Congress as legislative excess. They view Congress as having exploited an unquestioned authority to regulate the national securities markets to make an unjustified incursion into an area long accepted as the domain of state law.

Nevertheless, the 107th Congress enacted SARBOX under authority of the Commerce Clause which reserves for the federal government sole authority to act in areas involving interstate commerce, such as interstate transactions in securities listed on a *national* stock exchange.[8] While the various states also have securities laws, state securities laws (known as Blue Sky laws) may not conflict with federal securities laws. And, to the extent that they do, they are preempted by the federal law. This is because the Supremacy Clause of the U.S. Constitution provides that federal law is the supreme law of the land.[9]

Hence, viewed from the standpoint of constitutionality, SARBOX is on solid ground in preempting state law with a federal statute that establishes uniform corporate governance standards for all listed corporations. However, whether or not SARBOX constitutes legislative excess is not simply a legal query, rather it is an inquiry that has political, economic, social and normative consequences. Therefore, it is important to keep firmly in mind the main objective to be achieved by this exercise of the federal preemptive power. Focusing on the end goal of the legislation makes it possible to critically assess the merits of the path being taken to achieve this goal. Here the purpose of the statute is to protect investors by improving the reliability of corporate financial statements. The modus operandi for accomplishing this objective is to improve the overall moral tone in listed companies by infusing these organizations with standardized ethical guidelines. While few would argue that increasing the ethical standards in a corporation will have no effect on the reliability of its financial statements, many question whether these standards need to be uniform and/or established at the federal level.

Of course, legislation to affect moral uplift is not new at the federal level; "Charitable Choice" and the flood of faith-based initiatives launched as part of welfare reform are recent examples of the U.S. Congress using its lawmaking powers to affect moral regeneration.[10] However, because this remains a controversial use of the federal lawmaking power, it merits looking beyond issues of jurisdictional turf. Satisfaction of constitutional hurdles that speak only to the division of labor between the central government and the states does not eliminate the need to confront the underlying substantive issue, which can be stated in the form of two questions:

1. Is the present status quo (corporations operating on the moral high ground) attributable to SARBOX-established ethical guidelines?

2. If so, can the status quo be maintained even if the SEC backs off and allows the internal corporate governance standards of listed corporations to be governed by state law?

Of course, Question 2 only needs to be answered if Question 1 is answered in the affirmative. The first step in assessing whether SARBOX-established ethical guideposts are to be credited for the moral renaissance that has taken place in the business world—and which is particularly evident among MNCs—is to undertake a detailed analysis of SARBOX's "paraenetic provisions"; namely, the provisions aimed at improving the ethical culture (or moral climate) within the corporate milieu. Only then will it be possible to determine to what extent discernable improvements in corporate governance can be linked to specific paraenetic provisions of the statute. In instances where these links do exist, consideration can be given to whether the exalted corporate governance standards can be maintained by state regulation of the internal corporate governance standards in lieu of continued federal quarterbacking of the corporate governance area.

PART A. THE PARAENETIC PROVISIONS OF SARBOX

No one should have been surprised in the aftermath of the savings and loan crisis to learn that lawyers and accountants had averted their eyes from the fraud being perpetrated by some in the banking industry during the 1980s.

—Congressional Testimony of Law Professor Susan P. Koniak[11]

Professor Koniak made the above observation while testifying during the 2002 Congressional Hearings on Enron. Her point is well-taken. Just as lawyers and accountants were the facilitators of the long undetected savings and loan deception of the 1980s, they were the brains behind the long-running Enron "house of cards." The Enron subterfuge would not have been possible without lawyers finding the gray areas of the law and accountants preparing the obfuscatory paperwork that fit into those legal loopholes, all for the purpose of keeping the con game going. Needless to say, it was not difficult to convince "the Angry 107th Congress," most of whom were lawyers themselves, that the elaborate ruse that deprived so many of their constituents—working-class Americans—of their pensions would not have been possible without the aid of lawyers and accountants.[12]

It is, therefore, not surprising that accountants and lawyers emerged as prime targets for the paraenetic provisions of SARBOX. Section 101 of SARBOX created the Public Company Accounting Oversight Board to establish, among other things, ethics and independence standards for accountants involved in any manner in the preparation or issuance of audit reports for listed companies. Section 307 of SARBOX directed the S.E.C. to establish minimum standards of professional conduct for attorneys involved in any way in the representation of listed companies. But, accountants and lawyers were not the only corporate denizens targeted for moral rehabilitation. Several sections of SARBOX are devoted to improving the moral tone at the top of the organization by getting corporations to adopt organizational ethics codes and to establish whistleblowing systems. Moreover, SARBOX raises the bar in terms of who is deemed qualified and thus eligible to serve as an officer or director of a listed corporation. Finally, SARBOX enhances the penalties and sanctions that can be imposed for violation of the securities laws by making the willful violation of certain securities laws a criminal offense.

Since SARBOX is replete with paraenetic provisions, it is not possible in an article of this size to delve into them all. Therefore, a sampling of the different approaches SARBOX takes to affecting a moral refurbishing of the corporate milieu will have to suffice. The following discussion will examine provisions that (1) provide ethical guidelines for corporate gatekeepers, (2) improve the tone at the top of the corporate hierarchy, and (3) provide incentives for whistleblowing.

I. ETHICAL GUIDELINES FOR CORPORATE GATEKEEPERS

A. Mandatory Whistleblowing for Attorneys

Proposed Part 205 responds to this directive [SARBOX §307] and is intended to protect investors and increase their confidence in public companies by ensuring that attorneys who work for those companies respond appropriately to evidence of material misconduct.[13]

Specifically aimed at attorneys, Section 307 of SARBOX directs the S.E.C. to, "issue rules, in the public interest and for the protection of investors, setting forth *minimum standards of professional conduct* for attorneys appearing and practicing before the Commission in any way in the representation of issuers."[14] Additionally, Section 307 mandates that a rule be adopted which states that an attorney who becomes aware of wrongdoing by a corporate employer (through the actions of any of its employees or agents) and does not blow the whistle has *failed* to meet the *minimum standards of professional conduct for attorneys*. Thus, for attorneys, whistleblowing is mandatory. Either the attorney comes forward and reports evidence of material misconduct of which she becomes aware, or she risks the SEC taking disciplinary action against her for violation of one of its Rules of Practice. Such a disciplinary hearing could result in the attorney losing the privilege of practicing before the SEC. Additionally, depending on the severity of the misconduct which the attorney failed to report, the attorney risks further sanctioning as an aider and abettor of a violation of the securities laws.

Moreover, blowing the whistle is not a one-shot deal under Rule 205; a great deal of tenacity is required on the part of attorneys in terms of trying to halt any misconduct of which they become aware. After reporting evidence of wrongdoing to a company's chief legal officer, the attorney must continue to monitor the situation. If remedial action is not taken, then the attorney is obliged to continue making up-the-ladder reports until such time as appropriate corrective action has been taken, even to the extent of reporting the violation to an outside regulatory authority such as the SEC if the audit committee of the board (the top rung on the internal whistleblowing ladder) does not take corrective action.

An intriguing quandary is presented by subsection 205.3 of the Rule, which takes the position that it is the corporation (and its shareholders) that the attorney is representing and not the employees and agents of the company. This interpretation of the attorney's role (whether an in-house attorney or outside counsel) is meant to allay fears that a whistleblowing attorney might be violating the attorney/client privilege by reporting evidencing of material misconduct of which she becomes aware. However, state law generally establishes the extent of the attorney/client privilege and other such privileges (spousal, doctor/patient, clergy/penitent, etc.). Moreover, the right to waive the privilege belongs to the client, not to the attorney. Hence, it is possible that under state law as well as under bar association rules of professional conduct, the attorney will be deemed to also have an attorney/client relationship with the employees and agents of the company who seek the attorney's advice about questionable corporate practices. In fact, it is possible that state law might not depend upon the existence of an attorney/client relationship, but upon the fact that the attorney is vested with a fiduciary role vis-à-vis laypersons who consult her and, thus, the layperson will be allowed to assert a Fifth Amendment right against self-incrimination to keep the attorney quiet in any criminal action brought against the layperson.

B. Moral Bellwether for Senior Officers

Section 406 of SARBOX directs the SEC to adopt a rule requiring a listed company to disclose (as part of its periodic reporting under the Exchange Act) whether it has adopted a code of ethics for senior financial officers; and if not, the reason why such a code has not been adopted. Of course, the number of listed companies with codes of ethics for senior financial officers rose exponentially as a result of the inclusion of this disclosure requirement in SARBOX.[15] Rare is the company that can conceive of an explanation for not needing a code of ethics to guide the activities of its senior financial officers, especially since this would have to be disclosed in financial statements prepared under the aegis of the very same financial officers revealed to be free of organizationally imposed ethical restraints!

Therefore, Section 406 is a de facto requirement that listed corporations have a code of ethics for senior financial officers. Notably, senior financial officers are likely to be licensed public accountants (CPAs) and therefore subject to ethics rules enforced by state licensing boards as well as being bound by the codes of conduct of various professional societies for accountants. Nevertheless, in the corporate setting, these licensed professionals are employees who are answerable to a corporate employer. Thus, it is the employer—not the employee-professional—that establishes the guidelines and implements the procedures that govern the actions of the professionals in its employ. Often, the profit-maximization goal of a particular business enterprise pits the answerability of professionals as employees against their sworn duty to adhere to specific codes of professional conduct. (This is as true for in-house attorneys as it is for in-house accounting personnel.)

In light of this quandary, it makes good legislative sense to impose ethical guidelines within the corporate setting that will allow an accountant to follow generally accepted accounting principles (GAAP) even where this will mean that the company financial statements will give a less glowing financial picture and consequently result in diminished (or nonexistent) bonuses for the corporate executives. Therefore, Section 406 is an effective means of accomplishing the Congressional objective of improved corporate transparency.

C. U.S. Sentencing Commission Safe Harbor

The requirements set forth in this guideline are intended to achieve reasonable prevention and detection of criminal conduct for which the organization would be vicariously liable. The prior diligence of an organization in seeking to prevent and detect criminal conduct has a direct bearing on the appropriate penalties and probation terms for the organization if it is convicted and sentenced for a criminal offense.

—U. S. Sentencing Guidelines, Background Commentary to §8B2.1

SARBOX Section 805(a)(5) is couched in terms of a suggestion to the United States Sentencing Commission to review its guidelines to federal judges charged with the task of imposing sentences on corporations found guilty of criminal wrongdoing, the idea being that the guidelines would be amended as necessary to serve as a more effective deterrent to organizational wrongdoing. In response to this circuitous directive, the United States Sentencing Commission added §8B2.1 titled, "Effective Compliance and Ethics Program" to the U.S. Sentencing Guidelines. As can be seen in the above cited portion of the commentary to §8B2.1, the Section creates a safe harbor for the corporation that diligently implements a compliance and ethics program in accordance with its requirements. Therefore, it would be foolish for a corporate board not to adopt a compliance and ethics program that meets the requirements of §8B2.1. Not securing this safe harbor for the corporation would constitute negligence on the part of the board and expose it to a derivative lawsuit by the shareholders should the corporation at any time in the future be at risk for fines and even for delisting because of securities fraud committed by its employees.

The Guideline contains extensive instructions for establishing an ethics program that is designed to ward off criminal wrongdoing within the corporate setting. Integral to the program is the establishment of a whistleblowing system that will serve as an additional check on the upper echelon executives with the authority (and the motivation) to implement dubious accounting practices that paint the rosy financial pictures necessary to earn them year-end bonuses. To encourage lower level employees to blow the whistle, §8B2.1 recommends that the established whistleblowing system be widely publicized and that it allow for anonymous reporting so that the low-level corporate employee or agent need not fear retaliation. Additionally, the model compliance and ethics code set forth in §8B2.1 anticipates that there will be a Compliance and Ethics Officer in charge of administering the program and that this person will be a high-level employee with access to sufficient resources to administer an effective program.

There is no doubt that the responsibility for adopting a compliance and ethics program falls squarely on the corporate board because where a board of directors exists, it is definitively identified in the Guideline as the corporation's *governing authority*.[16] Therefore the onus is upon the board to make certain that a program is implemented that will detect and prevent criminal conduct within the corporation:

> *(2) (A) The organization's governing authority shall be knowledgeable about the content and operation of the compliance and ethics program and shall exercise reasonable oversight with respect to the implementation and effectiveness of the compliance and ethics program (§8B2.1[b][1], U.S. Sentencing Guidelines).*

Moving beyond these gatekeeper provisions, SARBOX also attempts to improve the tone at the top, which is discussed next.

II. IMPROVING THE TONE AT THE TOP

Four sections of SARBOX are devoted to improving the tone at the top of a listed corporation. Section 301 mandates the creation of an audit committee of the board of directors consisting solely of independent directors. This means that regardless of the leniency of corporations law in the state of incorporation, each listed corporation must have a board of directors and the board must appoint an audit committee consisting of entirely independent directors. Further, Section 301 directs that the audit committee, not management, be "directly responsible for the appointment, compensation, and oversight of the work of any registered public accounting firm" employed to audit the listed company's books.[17]

Finally, Section 301 prohibits the listing of a corporation if its audit committee has not established procedures for "the confidential, anonymous submission by employees of the issuer of concerns regarding questionable accounting or auditing matters."[18] In other words, the board audit committee of a listed company must put a whistleblowing system in place. The apparent reason for having the board audit committee, rather than the plenary board, establish the system is because the audit committee is at the top of the whistleblowing ladder for attorneys who are subjected to an up-the-ladder whistleblowing mandate under Section 307 of SARBOX.

Section 305 of SARBOX raises the qualifying standards for officers and directors.[19] Whereas it was previously necessary for the S.E.C. to establish "substantial unfitness" to prohibit persons from acting as an officer or director of a listed company, as a result of the Section 305 directive, only "unfitness" need be proven to disqualify such persons from holding the positions of officer or director of a listed company.

Section 1105 of SARBOX gives the S.E.C. authority to prohibit persons who have been the subject of cease-and-desist proceedings on the basis of an alleged violation of the securities laws from acting as an officer or director of a listed company where such conduct demonstrates an *unfitness* to serve as an officer or director.[20] Note that both Sections 305 and 1105 represent federal incursions into the domain of state law. Traditionally the law of the state of incorporation governs who may serve as an officer or director of a corporation.

Finally, Section 1107 of SARBOX amends the United States Code to make it a crime punishable by a fine and imprisonment of up to ten years, or both, to retaliate against whistleblowers. One type of retaliation that is specifically mentioned in Section 1107 is "interference with the lawful employment or livelihood" of the whistleblower.

III. SARBOX WHISTLEBLOWING INCENTIVES

Mr. Rajappa emphasized the role internal auditors would play, in achieving that earnings target, and the monetary reward they would receive, if Fannie Mae met "Frank's goals":

"We must do this with fiery determination, not on some days, not on most days, but day in and day out, give it your best, not 50%, not 75%, not 100%, but 150%. Remember, Frank has given us an opportunity to earn not just our salaries, benefits, raises, ESPP [Employee Stock Purchase Program] but substantially over that if we make $6.46. So it is our moral obligation to give well above our 100% and if we do this, we would have made tangible contributions to Frank's goals."

—OFHEO Report on Investigation of Fannie Mae's Accounting Practices[21]

Section 806 of SARBOX has as its purpose encouraging whistleblowing by those corporate employees whose day-to-day involvement in the nuts and bolts operation of an enterprise most likely gives them a heads-up on corporate shenanigans long before the inhabitants of the corporate boardroom catch wind of possible corporate misconduct. The extensive whistleblower protections contained in Section 806 provide shelter to any employee of a publicly traded company who reports evidence of fraud upon the stockholders of the company to the proper authorities. Like Section 1107, which is discussed directly above, Section 806 makes it costly for a company to attempt to retaliate against employees who blow the whistle, while making it financially worthwhile for employees to take their information to the proper authorities. It mandates reinstatement of a wrongfully terminated whistle-blowing employee and provides for the employee to receive compensatory damages, including litigation fees. Moreover, the employee retains the right to bring a civil action under federal or state law or under any collective bargaining agreement. Of course the ability to bring a civil action opens up the possibility of the successful employee-plaintiff receiving damages for any mental anguish and distress suffered because of her employee's retaliatory actions.

Certainly, the 107th Congress had in mind the importance of giving the low-level bookkeeper or accountant the courage to refuse to go along with requests from higher ups to use "aggressive accounting" techniques in order to be a "team player." This is the type of pitch that was made by Mr. Rajappa, former head of the internal auditing office at FANNIE MAE, who is quoted at the outset of this section. In this vein, it should be noted that although whistleblowing is not mandatory for non-managerial employees under Section 806, if a non-managerial employee is a licensed accountant, then he is subject to mandatory whistleblowing just like attorneys. An accountant who discovers evidence that "an illegal act (whether or not perceived to have a material effect on the financial statements of the issuer) has or may have occurred" has a duty to (a) report the illegalities to the Board of Directors, (b) resign, and (c) notify the SEC if the Board does not furnish the accountant with proof that it has notified the SEC.[22]

PART B. ASSESSING THE PARAENETIC PROVISIONS OF SARBOX

Turning now to the two questions set forth earlier as an anchor for assessing whether continued federal regulation is a vital factor in keeping listed corporations operating on the moral high ground. For organizational purposes, this analysis will be discussed under three main headings, to-wit: (1) Federal Establishment of Ethical Guidelines for Gatekeepers; (2) Federal Role in Improving Tone at the Top; and (3) Federal Whistleblower Initiative.

I. FEDERAL ESTABLISHMENT OF
ETHICAL GUIDELINES FOR GATEKEEPERS

A. Section 307

There is no doubt that Section 307 is crucial in terms of achieving the SARBOX objective of increasing the reliability of corporate financial statements. Aside from accountants (who, as noted above, are also subject to mandatory whistleblowing), corporate attorneys are the professionals most likely to have the expertise necessary to detect financial irregularities and to unravel complex securities schemes. Thus, it makes good sense to conscript these professionals as in-house watchdogs and this can only be accomplished by legislation at the federal level. Although attorneys are already bound by professional codes of ethics and subject to discipline by the state licensing boards and censure by the bar associations in the states where they are admitted to practice, neither of these state-level authorities would subject attorneys to a mandatory whistleblowing obligation. Moreover, it is highly unlikely that the corporations laws of any state address the subject of attorney whistleblowing. What state law there is on this subject would most likely be found in a state's laws dealing with the attorney/client privilege and thus the likely place is a state constitution or a state criminal law code.

Given that protection of civil rights is the primary concern of state constitutions and criminal codes, it can be anticipated that in most states the governing law would err on the side of protecting a wide range of "clients" (in addition to the shareholders) in the corporate setting, especially where the individuals in question have been named as defendants in criminal actions. Thus, only SARBOX can be relied upon to strap the attorney who is practicing before the Commission with an obligation to blow the whistle on wrongdoing corporate employees, officers, and directors. State law tends towards protection of the civil rights of the accused and contains a presumption that the accused has not waived the right to assert a privilege against self-incrimination. And, this position is diametrically opposed to waiver by legislative or regulatory fiat—what Section 307 of SARBOX (via Rule 205.3) achieves by taking the position that an attorney is representing only the corporation (and its shareholders), not its employees or agents.

B. Section 406

Beyond a doubt, the widespread adoption of corporate ethics codes has improved the ethical climate within corporations. And, this has, in turn, enhanced the reliability of the financial reports generated by these corporations. Would it be detrimental to the status quo if a listed corporation is no longer required to reveal whether or not it has adopted an ethics code for its senior financial officers? Since the SEC is the federal agency charged with adopting rules specifying what must be disclosed in the financial reports filed by listed corporations, no state-level authority could mandate disclosure in order to coerce corporations into adopting ethics codes.

Hence, without the federally dictated rule implementing Section 406 of SARBOX, corporations would be left to their own volition in determining whether to disclose the existence of an ethics code to govern the conduct of its chief financial officer. However, this might not be so catastrophic in that ethics codes specifically aimed at senior corporate officers have now become the norm. Therefore, the fear of generating negative public relations would force most corporations to think twice before allowing their senior corporate officers to perform their functions free of any organizational ethics guidelines. Also significant is the fact that even if the disclosure incentive for having codes of ethics specifically aimed at senior corporate officers disappeared, there would still be the incentive of the safe harbor created by Section 805. This ensures that corporations would continue to have in place a Compliance and Ethics Program that complies with the model set forth in §8B2.1 of the U.S. Sentencing Guidelines.

C. Section 805 and U.S. Sentencing Guidelines

Section 805 has resulted in corporations regulating themselves and establishing corporate creeds, mission statements, and codes of ethics that far exceed the model set forth in §8B2.1 of the U.S. Sentencing Guidelines. Moreover, §8B2.1 has made adoption of a compliance and ethics program a prerequisite for good corporate governance. The Web site of every listed corporation prominently displays a "Corporate Governance" link on its homepage that will lead inquiring minds to the panorama of sub-links granting direct access to the corporation's code of ethics, conflict of interest policy, whistleblowing system, mission statement, board of directors, audit committee as well as other standing board committees, and the contact information for the Compliance and Ethics Officer.

Indeed, one criticism that might be leveled at Section 805 is that it has resulted in a degree of Proceduralism in terms of how companies demonstrate compliance with good corporate governance standards—so much so that a large institutional shareholder group awards Corporate Governance Quotient ("CGQ") ratings based on a standardized list of corporate variables.[23] Of course, corporations earning high CGQ ratings proudly display them on their Web sites. An unexpected consequence of Congress using SARBOX for moral uplift is the increasing number of MNCs that are moving beyond the limited compliance criteria embodied in §8B2.1 to establish comprehensive corporate moral codes that govern all aspects of their business operations at home and abroad. These overriding moral codes are being adopted despite the fact that many of the corporate activities being circumscribed are acceptable from a compliance standpoint;

and, indeed, discounting the fact that their stricter standards of self-regulation often prioritize the interests of non-economic stakeholders over the interests of the company's shareholders (members of the investing public that SARBOX was enacted to protect). Prominent among the corporate moral codes that move beyond the intramural §8B2.1 concern with deterring criminal misconduct, are codes taking global positions on the environment. An example of this is Toyota's global commitment to environmental sustainability:

> At Toyota we're constantly working to reduce our impact on the environment. Our Global Earth Charter promotes environmental responsibility across the entire organization. Not just in our products and operations but also through our partnerships with organizations in the communities in which we live and work. The way we see it, the more effort we put in, the less waste we'll use.[24]

It is clear that the Section 805 intrusion into the corporate governance area accomplishes the statutory objective in a way that cannot be duplicated or replaced by state law. In fact, state corporations law undermines the most powerful weapon in the §8B2.1 arsenal; namely, the designation of the board of directors as the governing authority of the corporation. Indeed, the fact that the buck stops in the board room has caused many a board to "clean up" its corporate house. By contrast, some state laws do not even require that there be a board of directors (New Jersey is one). Under other state laws, it is possible for the corporate bylaws to delegate authority to govern the corporation to the shareholders.

II. FEDERAL ROLE IN IMPROVING THE TONE AT THE TOP

Since internal governance of corporations has long been the bailiwick of state corporations law, the SARBOX sections directed at improving the tone at the top are the most meddlesome and troublesome. SARBOX uses the circuitous route of listing requirements on the national exchanges to require a board audit committee and to specify who is qualified to serve on the committee once constituted; for many, this smacks of federal paternalism. Even the positive end of keeping the corporate inner sanctum free of officers and directors who allegedly have violated the securities laws must be questioned given that investors in these corporations can be protected by merely forcing the companies to disclose in their financial statement and proxy statements the fact that convicted securities violators are sitting on the board or holding important offices in the company. Notably, compliance with the securities laws does not require one to repent; one need merely disclose the fact that one is a sinner! Once this is done, it has traditionally been deemed to be a responsibility of the investor to weigh this information when considering the risks of investing in a particular company.

States, too, have securities laws; and state courts hear civil actions for fraud and negligence. Moreover, most criminal law is state law. And, states have insurance commissions, utility boards, and many other regulatory bodies that are lacking at the federal level. This means that they are able to coordinate the various state laws that deal not only with the securities of various corporations, but also with other aspects of corporate business operations that reflect the industries in which they operate (e.g., the utilities or pharmaceutical industries). Moreover, states are better able to protect their citizens as investors and as consumers than is the federal government. States are traditionally concerned with matters that profoundly affect the quality of everyday life, such as plain-language laws restricting the use of legalese in documents that citizens need to understand (leases, sales contracts, mortgages, car loan agreements), the creation of new causes of action, and the establishment of liberal statutes of limitations that allow a state's citizens ample time to pursue legal action if this is necessary for them to vindicate wrongs and receive justice. Citizens turn first to local courts at the municipal and state levels to right their wrongs, only pursuing federal remedies when forced to do so because diversity of citizenship strips the state of jurisdiction.

All of the foregoing makes it imperative to stop and take heed before letting federal law encroach upon state law by asserting an overriding federal interest in the internal workings and power alignment of state-franchised corporations, all for the purpose of creating one type of board of directors with standardized committees and one type of internal power structure, which will be the same for Hershey's of Pennsylvania and Poland Springs of Maine. It is worth considering that even the most hard-nosed advocate of corporate democracy bemoaned the recent sale of the *Wall Street Journal* to Rupert Murdoch even though it signaled the end of a century of dominating control by the Bancroft family; and this was because of an underlying fear that the paper would lose its uniqueness and independence as it folded into the standard corporate mold.

In summary, to the extent that Sections 301, 305, and 1105 attempt to "arrange the furniture" inside of the listed corporation, they represent legislative excess. Moreover, there is no evidence that federal dictates as to the internal governance structures of listed corporations has contributed to moral uplift within the corporate milieu. On the other hand, the subsection of Section 301 that prohibits listing of a corporation that does not have an anonymous whistleblowing system in place is a nice complement to Section 805 of SARBOX since both provide strong incentives for a corporation to adopt a whistleblowing system. Section 1107 complements both Sections 301 and 805 by providing protection for whistleblowers. As will be discussed in the next section, whistleblowing is central to the intent of the 107th Congress to increase corporate transparency and accountability. Therefore, federal abandonment of the area to state law is ill-advised, even in the unlikely event that all states adopt whistleblowing statutes to protect whistleblowers.

III. FEDERAL WHISTLEBLOWING INITIATIVE

More than any other provisions of SARBOX, the whistleblowing provisions symbolize regulatory brilliance. With the SARBOX whistleblowing incentives and directives, Congress has instituted a system of checks and balances within the corporate environment that improves the corporate moral climate while lightening the regulatory burden on the SEC Like most federal agencies, the SEC must carry out both administrative and regulatory functions while staying within tight budgetary constraints and operating with limited manpower. The Enforcement staff can only investigate a small fraction of the securities fraud cases that occur during any given year; and these investigations are long and drawn out due to the immense complexity of these types of cases, especially in this age of sophisticated communications technology.

It is therefore imperative that the SEC be able to conscript those inside the corporation to supplement its efforts to detect wrongdoing. Mandatory whistleblowing for attorneys and accountants is an essential tool in the regulatory arsenal. The SEC enforcement effort would be greatly hampered if these professionals were allowed to remain mum even after their special expertise allows them to detect irregularities in the accounting practices of a company months, and very often years before the SEC could uncover these irregularities by monitoring the corporate filings of the companies. Likewise, Section 806—which encourages the low-level non-managerial employee to come forward—is critical to the enforcement effort. It is generally low-level employees who are coerced into straying from generally accepted accounting principles by supervisors who stand to gain from having the corporate financial picture presented in the most favorable light. Clearly, these non-managerial employees offer the best chance of stopping a corporate scheme to defraud during the early stages.

State corporations law cannot be relied upon as an adequate substitute for a federal-level statute that encourages whistleblowers to come forward (Sections 307 and 806), protects employees who do blow the whistle from retaliation (Section 1107) and creates coercive incentives for corporations to put whistleblowing systems in place (Sections 301 and 805). The federal interest is so overwhelming when it comes to whistleblowing that preemption is not really an issue; indeed, the federal action is the only game in town.

CONCLUSION

SARBOX has been both praised and cursed for the new concepts it has brought to the business/society relationship. Stakeholder theory, internal controls, corporate accountability, corporate social responsibility, triple bottom line, corporate citizenship, transparency, and corporate governance are all concepts that have either been introduced or given new life by SARBOX. It is somewhat ironic that a child of vengeance—a product of the wrath of the Angry 107th Congress—has resulted in something so positive; namely, the emergence of a new paradigm for corporate governance. I have argued that there is a moral thread that links all of these changes; that what has taken place is a moral renaissance. It may have started with vengeful legislators intent on accomplishing a complete overhaul of corporate culture; but somewhere along the way, the corporations started mapping out routes and destinations of their own. This is good; regulatory agencies like the SEC with their limited budgets and shortage of manpower are better at closing off pathways than charting them.

Therefore, it would be shortsighted to allow the area of corporate governance to be preempted by federal law and the SEC based upon the interstate commerce logic. Corporations sell more than securities; they manufacture products and offer services. Their operations are too broad to be regulated solely by securities laws, and federal securities laws at that. This is where state law and state regulation can lend a hand. In many ways the state is more capable of viewing the corporate entity as a whole, as more than an entity in which people invest money and nothing else. The state's citizens form these corporations, work for them, purchase their products and services. Therefore, states should have a say in what guardrails are erected and which ones are taken down. Hence, there must be a check on federalization of the corporate governance area.

Has SARBOX already gone too far in terms of regulating corporate governance? Yes, to a certain extent it has, which means that there will be no deleterious effect to the current status quo if the federal government backs off and allows states to regulate internal corporate governance matters as they have traditionally done. There is no reason to fear an end to federal-level steering of the SARBOX moral rehabilitation project. The seeds of moral growth have already been sown and there are visible signs that corporations can take it from here:

> *BP rules on facilitation payments** BP policy does not permit so-called "facilitation" or "grease" payments to be made to government officials, even if such payments are nominal in amount. (* "Facilitation payments" are payments made to secure or speed up routine legal government actions, such as issuing permits or releasing goods held in customs.)[25]

NOTES

1. Archie B. Carroll and Ann K. Buchholtz, *Business & Society: Ethics and Stakeholder Management*, 6th Edition (Mason, OH: Thomson/South-Western Publishers, 2006), 296.

2. Governance World Watch, Issue 46 (December 2002) Online. (Brazil); "PNP Group Welcomes Passage of Anti-Corruption Legislation" (Jamaica); "New Legislation Enhances Access to Justice, Modernizes Outdated Laws" (Canada: "The international community and Ontario investors expect high standards in the wake of the Enron scandal," said Young. "This legislation is another step taken by the Eves government to ensure that Ontario remains a world leader when it comes to public accounting standards."); "Brazil CBD Engages In Board Changes To Lift Transparency"; "Banker Cautions on Adoption of Corporate Governance Pattern" (Nigeria: "Nations and establishments have been enjoined to fashion out their pattern of corporate governance in a bid to ensure vibrancy and efficiency, as copying from others would only serve to defeat such objectives.") Available at (Accessed 9 Jan 2008): http://unpan1.un.org/intradoc/groups/public/documents/UN/UNPAN014269.htm#PPGAM10

3. Sarbanes-Oxley Act of 2002, Pub. L. 107-204, 116 Stat. 745 (hereafter "SARBOX").

4. An example of this is the Toyota global commitment statement with regard to environmental sustainability that is presented later in this paper.

5. Gwendolyn Yvonne Alexis, "SECOND-GUESSING MANAGEMENT: The Board Autonomy Budget," *New Jersey Lawyer Magazine* (No. 248; October 2007), 67-75.

6. Gwendolyn Yvonne Alexis, "FROM LAPDOG TO WATCHDOG: The Post-SARBOX Corporate Board," *New York State Bar Association Journal*, 79:3 (March/April 2007) 22-25. Available at (Accessed 21 Dec 2007): http://www.nysba.org/Content/NavigationMenu/Publications19Bar_Journal/Bar

7. Mark J. Roe, Abstract of "Does Delaware Compete?", 23rd Annual Francis G. Pileggi Distinguished Lecture in Law, 28 Sep 07 at Widener University School of Law. Available at (Accessed 2 Jan 2008): http://www.delawarelitigation.com/PileggiLecture07Roe.pdf

8. Commerce Clause, U.S. Const. art. I, sec. 8, cl. 3.

9. Supremacy Clause, U.S. Const. art. VI, cl. 2.

10. Congress allocated $1 billion for performance bonuses to be awarded to states for moving welfare recipients off welfare and into jobs; and another $100 million annually was appropriated for bonuses to states that promote marriage and reduce the number of out-of-wedlock births and abortions in their states. ACF Press Room, "Administration for Children and Families," 24 Feb 2000. 08 Jan 2008. U.S. Dept. of Health and Human Services. http://www.oig.hhs.gov/oas/reading/acf2098.html

11. Senate Judiciary Committee Hearings, 107th Congress, 6 Feb 2002. 30 May 2006. Available at http://judiciary.senate.gov/print_testimony.cfm?id=149&wit_id=135 (Hereafter, "Koniak testimony").

12. That the 107th Congress was especially irate over the fact that ordinary working class Americans lost their pensions as a result of the collapse of Enron is evident from the fact that it included Section 904 in SARBOX, substantially increasing the criminal penalties for violation of the Employee Retirement Income Security Act of 1974. H.R. 3763, 107th Cong., 2nd Session (2002).

13. "Proposed Rule: Implementation of Standards of Professional Conduct for Attorneys," Securities and Exchange Commission, Release Nos. 33-8150; 34-46868; IC-25829; File No. S7-45-02 (November 21, 2002); 1.

14. Emphasis Added. Section 307, SARBOX.

15. "The relevant concept here is so-called 'therapeutic disclosure.' In other words, the Act uses disclosure requirements to effect changes in substantive behavior. For example, the corporation must disclose whether it has adopted a code of ethics for its financial officers." Stephen M. Bainbridge, "The Creeping Federalization of Corporate Law," *Regulation* (Spring 2003) 26–31; 29.

16. U.S. Sentencing Guideline §8B2.1, added by SARBOX, provides that the "governing authority" of a corporation is "(A) the Board of Directors; or (B) if the organization does not have a Board of Directors, the highest-level governing body of the organization." U.S. Sentencing Guidelines Manual §8B2.1 (Commentary) (2004).

17. Section 10A (m)(2)of the Exchange Act as amended by SARBOX Section 301.

18. Section 10A (m)(4)(B) of the Exchange Act as amended by SARBOX Section 301.

19. Section 21(d)(2) of the Exchange Act and Section 20(e) of the Securities Act of 1933 (15 U.S.C. 77t[e]).

20. Section 21C of the Exchange Act and Section 8A of the Securities Act of 1933 (15 U.S.C. 77h-1).

21. Statement by Sampath Rajappa in OFHEO, Report of the Special Examination of Fannie Mae (May 2006). Accessed 16 June 2006, from http://online.wsj.com/public/resources/documents/ofheo20060523.pdf

22. Exchange Act 10A(b)(3), 15 U.S.C. 78j-1(b)(3).

23. Institutional Shareholders Services (ISS) bases the CGQ rating on: (1) board structure and composition, (2) audit issues, (3) charter and bylaw provisions, (4) laws of the state of incorporation, (5) executive and director compensation, (6) qualitative factors (7) director and officer stock ownership, and (8) director education. More information available at: http://www.isscgq.com/abouttheratings.htm. Accessed 7 Jan 2008.

24. Toyota Homepage, "Environment" Link. Online. Accessed 17 November 2007, http://www.toyota.com/about/whynot/index.html?gclid=CK7T2Jjs448CFQ1ZHgod30j4YQ

25. BP, "Governments and communities," Online. Accessed 30 Nov 2007, from http://www.bp.com/liveassets/bp_internet/globalbp/STAGING/global_assets/downloads/C/coc_en_gov_comm.pdf

ABOUT THE AUTHORS

Gwendolyn Yvonne Alexis is the lead instructor for Business Ethics at Monmouth University, W. Long Branch, NJ. A Harvard Law School Graduate and a member of the New Jersey, New York, and Florida Bars, she has taught Securities Regulation at Suffolk University Law School and worked in the Enforcement Division of the U.S. Securities and Exchange Commission. She is a member of the Supreme Court of New Jersey Ethics Committee (District X-B), a trustee of the New Jersey State Bar Foundation, and a member of the New Jersey Corporate and Business Law Study Commission. She holds an M.A. in Ethics from the Yale Divinity School and a Ph.D. in Sociology and Historical Studies from the New School for Social Research.

Denis Collins is Professor of Business at Edgewood College in Madison, Wisconsin, where he teaches classes in management and business ethics and is a Sam M. Walton Free Enterprise Fellow. He holds a PhD in Business Administration from the University of Pittsburgh. He has published numerous books and articles including *Essentials in Business Ethics: Creating an Organization of High Integrity and Superior Performance* (2009: John Wiley & Sons).

Julian Friedland is Visiting Professor of Business Ethics at Fordham University's Gabelli School of Business. He has taught philosophy and business ethics for over a decade, primarily at the University of Colorado at Boulder. He is half French, obtaining his PhD in philosophy at the University of Paris 1-Pantheon Sorbonne, where he studied the nature of meaning and value from a Wittgensteinian perspective. Since then, he has

237

specialized in ethics, primarily as applied to business. His current research involves restoring the ethical a priori to the field of management. He has published widely in ethics and philosophy and maintains a business ethics blog: www.businessethicsmemo.blogspot.com.

Eugene Heath is Associate Professor of Philosophy at the State University of New York at New Paltz. He specializes in eighteenth-century British moral philosophy and business ethics, and is the author of essays on Bernard Mandeville, Adam Smith, and Adam Ferguson. He edited *Adam Ferguson: Selected Philosophical Writings* (Imprint Academic, 2007) and is the co-editor, with Vincenzo Merolle, of two volumes of scholarly essays on Ferguson, *Adam Ferguson: History, Progress and Human Nature* and *Adam Ferguson: Philosophy, Politics and Society* (Pickering & Chatto, 2008 and 2009). His work in business ethics includes, *The Morality of the Market: Ethics and Virtue in the Conduct of Business* (McGraw-Hill, 2002), as well as essays on the ethics of genetic commerce and the relation between responsibility and pensions. He holds a PhD from Yale University.

Larry W. Howard passed away in March of 2009. He was an associate professor at Middle Tennessee State University. His research interests included ethics, social justice, and development of students' critical thinking skills. He published numerous articles particularly on justice and fairness in organizational behavior. He was recently awarded a grant by the Tennessee Board of Regents to study critical thinking skills. He held a PhD from the University of Missouri.

Steve May is Associate Professor of Communication Studies at the University of North Carolina at Chapel Hill. His research focuses on the relationship between work and identity, as it relates to the boundaries of public/private, work/family, and labor/leisure. Most recently, he has studied the challenges and opportunities for organizational ethics and corporate social responsibility, with particular attention to ethical practices of dialogic communication, transparency, participation, courage, and accountability. He has published numerous articles and books including *Case Studies in Organizational Communication: Ethical Perspectives and Practices* (Sage, 2006). He holds a PhD from the University of Utah.

Michael Pirson is an Assistant Professor of Management at Fordham School of Business, New York and a Lecturer at Harvard Extension School. His research focuses on the conditions of stakeholder trust in organizational contexts. He is also examining the impact of organizational design on stakeholder well being and looks at social enterprises as humanistic alternatives to traditional business design. He has started several social enterprises in the area of economic development, serves on the board of three social enterprises based in the United States, and cofounded the Humanistic Management Network: www.humanetwork.org. He holds a PhD from the University of St. Gallen, Switzerland.

William H. Shaw is professor of philosophy at San Jose State University, where he was chair of the philosophy department for 11 years. He has been a Fulbright Lecturer and a von Humboldt Fellow, and recently served for 2 years as the resident director of the California State University student exchange program at the University of Zimbabwe. He has published numerous articles and books including *Contemporary Ethics: Taking Account of Utilitarianism* (Blackwell 1999), *Business Ethics* (Wadsworth, 6th ed. 2008), and (with Vincent Barry) *Moral Issues in Business* (Wadsworth, 11th ed. 2009). He holds a PhD from the London School of Economics.

Mark S. Schwartz is Associate Professor of Governance, Law and Ethics at the School of Administrative Studies, York University (Toronto, Canada). He has published numerous articles and co-authored Business Ethics: Readings and Cases in Corporate Morality (McGraw Hill, 2000). His research interests include: codes of ethics, corporate ethics programs, corporate governance, corporate social responsibility, ethical leadership, and ethical investment. He holds an LLB and a PhD from York University.

Tony Simons is an associate professor of organizational behavior at Cornell University's School of Hotel Administration. He has published numerous articles and authored *The Integrity Dividend: Leading by the Power of Your Word* (Jossey Bass, 2008). He has spoken and trained executives in negotiation skills and in leadership at Northwestern University's Kellogg School of Management (where he obtained his PhD), Cornell University, and in seminars around the United States and Europe. He maintains a consulting Web site: http://integritydividend.com.

Max Torres is an assistant professor at the Ohio University Pettit College of Law and a visiting professor at IESE Business School, University of Navarra in Barcelona, Spain. His academic career is international in scope. He has published widely in business ethics in several languages, namely, in English, Spanish, and German. His research centers on the interrelation between business, ethics, and law as it influences human decision making and affects social life. For nearly a decade prior to joining academe, he worked in the brokerage industry at various firms including Merrill Lynch and ultimately as an independent financial consultant. He holds a JD from Harvard University and a PhD From IESE Business School, University of Navarra. He a lifelong fan of the San Francisco Giants and 49ers.

Duane Windsor is Lynette S. Autrey Professor of Management in the Jones Graduate School of Management at Rice University, where he has been on the faculty since 1977. He is editor of the journal *Business & Society* and co-authored *The Rules of the Game in the Global Economy: Policy Regimes for International Business* (Springer, 2007). His recent research has focused on corporate social responsibility, the stakeholder theory of the firm, and the role of business and society and business ethics in business school curricula. He holds a PhD from Harvard University.

CPSIA information can be obtained
at www.ICGtesting.com
Printed in the USA
FFOW01n1916140916
27627FF